WHAT YOUR THIRD GRADER NEEDS TO KNOW

THE
CORE KNOWLEDGE
SERIES

RESOURCE BOOKS FOR
GRADES ONE THROUGH SIX
BOOK III

DOUBLEDAY

New York   London   Toronto   Sydney   Auckland

THE·CORE·KNOWLEDGE·SERIES

WHAT YOUR THIRD GRADER NEEDS TO KNOW

FUNDAMENTALS OF A GOOD THIRD-GRADE EDUCATION

Edited by

E. D. HIRSCH, JR.

PUBLISHED BY DOUBLEDAY

a division of Bantam Doubleday Dell Publishing Group, Inc.
1540 Broadway, New York, New York 10036

DOUBLEDAY and the portrayal of an anchor with a dolphin are trademarks of Doubleday, a division of
Bantam Doubleday Dell Publishing Group, Inc.

Arrangement for "She'll Be Comin' Round the Mountain" from *Best Loved Songs of the American People*
by Denes Agay, © 1975. Reprinted by permission of Doubleday, a division of Bantam Doubleday Dell
Publishing Group, Inc.

Library of Congress Cataloging-in-Publication Data

What your third grader needs to know: fundamentals of a good third-
   grade education / edited by E. D. Hirsch, Jr.— 1st ed.
      p.   cm. — (The Core knowledge series; bk. 3)
   Includes index.
   1. Third grade (Education)—United States—Curricula.
2. Curriculum planning—United States.   I. Hirsch, E. D. (Eric
Donald), 1928–   .   II. Series.
LB1571 3rd.W47   1992
372.19—dc20   91-40971
                                                   CIP

ISBN 0-385-41117-0

This Book is Dedicated to
Leah A. Hirsch
Staunch Supporter and Benefactor of Core Knowledge
A Third Grader in 1909
Still and Ever Young at Heart

Acknowledgments

This series has depended upon the help, advice, and encouragement of some two thousand people. Some of those singled out here know already the depth of my gratitude; others may be surprised to find themselves thanked publicly for help they gave quietly and freely for the sake of the enterprise alone. To helpers named and unnamed I am deeply grateful.

Project Manager: Tricia Emlet

Editors: Tricia Emlet (Text), Rae Grant (Art)

Artists and Writers: Nancy Bryson (Physical Science), Leslie Evans (Artwork), Jonathan Fuqua (Artwork), Julie C. Grant (Artwork), Marie Hawthorne (Science Biographies), John Hirsch (Mathematics), Pamela C. Johnson (History & Geography), Blair Logwood Jones (Literature), Phillip Jones (Artwork), Gail McIntosh (Artwork), Elaine Moran (Visual Arts), A. Brooke Russell (Life Science), Peter Ryan (Music & Mythology), Lindley Shutz (Language and Literature), Helen Storey (Sayings)

Art and Photo Research: Rae Grant

Research Assistants: Martha Clay (Permissions), Beth Juren (Text), Bethanne H. Kelly (Text), Elaine Moran (Text), Kimberly A. C. Wilson (Text), Carl A. Young, Jr. (Art)

Advisers on Multiculturalism: Minerva Allen, Frank de Varona, Mick Fedullo, Dorothy Fields, Elizabeth Fox-Genovese, Marcia Galli, Dan Garner, Henry Louis Gates, Cheryl Kulas, Joseph C. Miller, Gerry Raining Bird, Dorothy Small, Sharon Stewart-Peregoy, Sterling Stuckey, Marlene Walking Bear, Lucille Watahomigie, Ramona Wilson

Advisers on Elementary Education: Joseph Adelson, Isobel Beck, Paul Bell, Carl Bereiter, David Bjorklund, Constance Jones, Elizabeth LaFuze, J. P. Lutz, Jean Osborne, Sandra Scarr, Nancy Stein, Phyllis Wilkin

Advisers on Technical Subject Matters: Richard Anderson, Holly DeSantis, Andrew Gleason, Eric Karell, Joseph Kett, Michael Lynch, Joseph E. Miller, Margaret Redd, Mark Rush, Ralph Smith, Nancy Summers, James Trefil, Nancy Wayne

Conferees, March 1990: Nola Bacci, Joan Baratz-Snowden, Thomasyne Beverley, Thomas Blackton, Angela Burkhalter, Monty Caldwell, Thomas M. Carroll, Laura Chapman, Carol Anne Collins, Lou Corsaro, Anne Coughlin,

Henry Cotton, Arletta Dimberg, Debra P. Douglas, Patricia Edwards, Janet Elenbogen, Mick Fedullo, Michele Fomalont, Nancy Gercke, Mamon Gibson, Jean Haines, Barbara Hayes, Stephen Herzog, Helen Kelley, Brenda King, John King, Elizabeth LaFuze, Diana Lam, Nancy Lambert, Doris Langaster, Richard LaPointe, Lloyd Leverton, Madeleine Long, Allen Luster, Joseph McGeehan, Janet McLin, Gloria McPhee, Marcia Mallard, Judith Matz, William J. Moloney, John Morabito, Robert Morrill, Roberta Morse, Karen Nathan, Dawn Nichols, Valeta Paige, Mary Perrin, Joseph Piazza, Jeanne Price, Marilyn Rauth, Judith Raybern, Mary Reese, Richard Rice, Wallace Saval, John Saxon, Jan Schwab, Ted Sharp, Diana Smith, Richard Smith, Trevanian Smith, Carol Stevens, Nancy Summers, Michael Terry, Robert Todd, Elois Veltman, Sharon Walker, Mary Ann Ward, Penny Williams, Charles Wootten, Clarke Worthington, Jane York

The Three Oaks Elementary School: Constance Jones, Principal; Cecelia Cook, Assistant Principal

Teachers: Joanne Anderson, Linda Anderson, Nancy Annichiarico, Deborah Backes, Katherine Ann Bedingfield, Barbara Bittner, Michael Blue, Coral Boudin, Nancy Bulgerin, Jodene Cebak, Cheryl Chastain, Paula Clark, Betty Cook, Laura DeProfio, Holly DeSantis, Cindy Donmoyer, Lisa Eastridge, Amy Germer, Elizabeth Graves, Jennifer Gunder, Eileen Hafer, Helen Hallman, Donna Hernandez, Kathleen Holzborn, Robert Horner, Jenni Jones, Zoe Ann Klusacek, Annette Lopez, Barbara Lyon, Cindy Miller, Lelar Miller, Laura Morse, Karen Naylor, Joanne O'Neill, Jill Pearson, Linda Peck, Rebecca Poppe, Janet Posch, Judy Quest, Angie Richards, Angie Ryan, April Santarelli, Patricia Scott, Patricia Stapleton, Pamela Stewart, Jeanne Storm, Phillip Storm, Katherine Twomey, Karen Ward

Special Thanks: Mary Ann Kohl for a recipe from *Mudworks: Creative Clay, Dough, and Modeling Experiences,* Bright Ring Publishing, 1989.

Benefactors: the Brown Foundation, the Dade County School District, the Exxon Education Foundation, the Lee County School District, the National Endowment for the Humanities, the Shutz Foundation

Morale Boosters: Polly Hirsch, Robert Payton, Rafe Sagalyn, Nancy Brown Wellin

Our grateful acknowledgment to these persons does not imply that we have taken their (sometimes conflicting) advice in every case, or that each of them endorses all aspects of this project. Responsibility for final decisions must rest with the editor alone. Suggestions for improvements are very welcome, and I wish to thank in advance those who send advice for revising and improving this series.

Contents

II. GEOGRAPHY, WORLD CIVILIZATION, AND AMERICAN CIVILIZATION

III. FINE ARTS

V. NATURAL SCIENCES

WHAT YOUR THIRD GRADER NEEDS TO KNOW

General Introduction

I. *The Critical Early Grades*

In 1987 I published a book, *Cultural Literacy,* that described the decline of American education over the past four decades, and offered suggestions for reversing that decline. Though sprinkled with scholarly footnotes and descriptions of research, the book, to everyone's surprise, became a best-seller. Hundreds of supporting letters from parents and teachers inspired me to set up a foundation devoted to the educational improvements that *Cultural Literacy* advocated. For the past three years, that organization, now called the Core Knowledge Foundation, has sought and gained the help of some two thousand teachers and scholars in focusing on a single education reform: imparting a core of shared knowledge to all elementary school students from first through sixth grade. The present series is the first fruit of that cooperative, nationwide effort.

After a long process of consultation and consensus building (which I shall describe in a moment), agreement was reached on a specific sequence of core knowledge that young Americans should, at a minimum, learn. That is the knowledge sequence upon which this series of books is based. The sequence itself is available to publishers and educators through the Core Knowledge Foundation. Our hope is that this sequence, duly revised over time, will gradually come to be accepted, and that publishers, schools, parents, and educators will join in the cause of promoting shared knowledge in the elementary school years.

This core sequence is not meant to be the whole of the school curriculum, nor is the information imparted in this series meant to be constantly stressed above other forms of knowledge and skill. Teaching a common core of knowledge can coexist with a great diversity of instructional methods, emphases, and additional subject matters. In fact, confidence that a core of essential knowledge has been imparted to children allows parents and teachers a freer rein to encourage variety, imagination, and inventiveness in education, as well as to cultivate the specific character of the child, the home, the school, or community. In this period of our national life, to ensure that all young children possess a core of shared knowledge is a fundamental reform that, while not sufficient by itself to achieve excellence and fairness in schooling, is nonetheless a *necessary* step in developing a first-rate educational system in the United States.

The weakest link in the chain of our public education is elementary school—grades one through six. Although the usual evidence that we are "a nation at risk" comes from achievement tests taken in grades seven and twelve, the poor performance of American students in those grades can be traced directly to shortcomings inherited from elementary schools that have not systematically imparted the knowledge students need for further learning. Poor early preparation hinders many unfortunate students from learning what is *in* the seven-through-twelve curriculum, while fortunate ones are enabled to learn only by having gained needed background knowledge outside school. The inequitable result, surprising for a nation built upon ideals of equality, is that our public educational system is the least *fair* system in the developed world. Because knowledge builds upon knowledge, the differences between our academic haves and have-nots increase dramatically as our students advance through the elementary grades. By the time of junior high school, many knowledge-deprived students of high native ability are put into special "low ability tracks" where the deprivation is further compounded. Small wonder that the comparative performance of American public education, poor by all standards, is worst by the standard of fairness.

II. Why Core Knowledge Is Needed

A core of shared knowledge in elementary grades is necessary to promote excellence and fairness in schooling. Before I outline the reasons for making this blunt assertion, I shall briefly mention a striking piece of evidence which supports it. All of the best, i.e., the highest-achieving and most egalitarian elementary school systems in the world such as Sweden, France, and Japan, teach their children a specific core of knowledge in each of the first six grades, thus enabling all children to enter each new grade with a secure foundation for further learning. By contrast, those educational systems that have recently declined in educational achievement, such as England, Australia, and the United States, do *not* give children a specific core of shared knowledge in early grades. Research could have predicted that result for several reasons. Here they are, briefly.

(1) **Shared background knowledge makes schooling more effective.** The one-on-one tutorial is the most effective form of schooling, in part because a parent or teacher is able to provide tailor-made instruction for each individual child. The tutor is aware of what the child already knows, and can build upon that already-acquired knowledge to teach something new. In a non-tutorial situation, say, in a classroom of twenty-five students, the instructor cannot effectively impart new knowledge to all the students unless each one shares the background knowledge that is being built upon. When all the students in a class *do* share that relevant background knowledge, a classroom can begin to approach the effectiveness of a tutorial.

(2) **Shared background knowledge makes schooling more fair and democratic.** When all the children who enter a grade can be assumed to share some of the same building blocks of knowledge, and when the teacher knows exactly what those building blocks are, then all the students are empowered to learn. Even when some children in a class don't have elements of the core knowledge they were supposed to acquire in previous grades, the possibility of identifying the knowledge gaps enables the teacher or parent to make up for lost time, giving all students a chance to fulfill their potentials in later grades. By the same token, under a core knowledge system students who have to move from school to school are treated more fairly. When they enter a new school, they are on a more equal footing with their classmates, who have attained the same level of core knowledge. For these reasons, school systems that use core standards have proved to be more democratic and fair than systems like ours which do not.

(3) **Defining a specific core of knowledge for each grade motivates teachers and students through definite, attainable standards.** This is not the place to discuss the great political issue of

making schools accountable for the achievement of their students by defining more concretely the goals that are to be achieved. On the other hand, accountability in education is important and can be motivational for children themselves. Children who are made aware of clearly defined, achievable learning goals can monitor and take pleasure in their progress. Attainment of those defined goals should be expected, demanded, and when achieved, praised. The self-esteem of children, so important for building confidence and ambition, must be *earned*; it cannot arise from praise that is automatically handed out on a regular basis regardless of accomplishment.

(4) **Shared background knowledge helps create cooperation and solidarity in schools and in the nation.** The shared background knowledge that makes for communication and learning in academic work also encourages cooperation and toleration among students within the classroom community. In our diverse nation, classrooms are usually made up of students from a variety of cultural backgrounds, and those different cultures should be honored and understood by all students as part of the common core. Education should create a *school-based culture* that is common and welcoming to all because it includes knowledge of many cultures. Such shared, multicultural knowledge gives all students, no matter what their background, a common foundation for understanding cultural diversity.

The schools of a modern nation are the institutions through which children become members of the wider national community. These children grow into adults who will live cooperatively and sustain one another only if they feel that they truly *belong* to the larger society. Such universal belonging has always been the hope and promise of the United States. As the great American writer Herman Melville said in 1849: "We are not a narrow tribe.—No: our blood is as the flood of the Amazon, made up of a thousand noble currents all pouring into one. We are not a nation so much as a world." Shared, school-based knowledge, which alone can lead to educational and social fairness, should be encouraged as part of our best traditions.

The evidence of educational decline and widening social unfairness has become ever more obvious and undeniable since my book *Cultural Literacy* was published in 1987. Verbal aptitude scores have continued to drop. Declines are commonly explained by the claim that they arise from our democratic progress in bringing minorities into the school system. Alas, it is not true; the greatest decline has been in the numbers of students who make *high* scores. Worst of all, our educational decline seems even steeper when we compare our current situation with the educational advances made by other developed countries. They have moved forward as we have retreated. In 1970, American elementary students ranked seventh in science achievement among the seventeen countries measured. By 1980, we ranked fifteenth—third from the bottom, just above the Philippines. This decline can be reversed. But no modern nation has achieved both excellence and fairness in education without defining core knowledge for the elementary school. It is reasonable to predict that we will fail to reverse our educational decline unless we do the same.

III. The Core Knowledge Sequence: How Consensus Was Achieved

The first question that many Americans ask of those who advocate a core sequence in elementary schools is: "*Who decides* what the core will be?" That difficult question, so admirable and so American in its suspicion of central authority, has caused many to conclude that the subject of core standards is best left alone. In democracies like Sweden, Japan, and France, the question, "Who decides?" has the following answer: "A central ministry of education that is accountable to the national legislature." But American traditions go strongly against such an arrangement, even though historians have shown that a common elementary school core was achieved informally in earlier periods of our history, through an unspoken agreement among a small group of educational publishers in New York and New England. In the past forty years, that unspoken agreement has vanished.

Sensing the need for a common sequence, the National Council of Teachers of Mathematics, the American Association for the Advancement of Science, and other professional organizations as well as state departments of education have begun to recommend general outcomes for elementary and secondary education. The recent reports that these organizations have produced are useful as general guides, but are not specific enough to induce the teaching of a common core of knowledge in a common sequence. My colleagues and I have therefore used their recommendations as starting points, and have further amplified them in order to reach consensus on a definite sequence.

First, we analyzed the knowledge and skills that the reports recommended. We also tabulated the knowledge and skills through grade six that were defined in the successful educational systems of several other countries, including France, Japan, Sweden, and West Germany. In addition, we formed an advisory board on multiculturalism that evaluated the core knowledge of diverse cultural traditions that American children should share as part of their school-based common culture. We sent all these materials to three independent groups of teachers, scholars, and scientists around the country, asking them to create a master list of the core knowledge children should have by the end of grade six. About 150 teachers (including college professors, scientists, and administrators) were involved in this initial step.

These items were amalgamated into a master list, and further groups of teachers and specialists were asked to agree on a grade-by-grade sequence of the list. That sequence was sent in turn to some one hundred educators and specialists who participated in a national conference called to hammer out a definite agreement. This important meeting took place in March 1990. The conferees were elementary school teachers, curriculum specialists, scientists, science writers, officers of national organizations, representatives of ethnic groups, district superintendents, and school principals from every region of the country. A total of twenty-four working groups decided on revisions in the sequence, and these revisions were presented to plenary sessions, where they were accepted or rejected by majority vote. The sequence that ultimately came out of the conference was fine-tuned during the 1990–91 academic year at the Three Oaks Elementary School in Lee County, Florida.

Thus was the sequence agreed upon that forms the basis for this series. In the United States, each school and district decides its own curriculum. But there is a growing recognition that students will greatly benefit if *part* of that curriculum includes a sequence of core knowledge goals that are pursued throughout the nation. Whether the core sequence that is finally agreed upon will be based on the one presented here is not known; perhaps some other group will bring forward a sequence that is a more attractive candidate for public acceptance. But whatever sequence is chosen, we can be sure that the answer to the question, "Who decides?" will ultimately be, as always in a democracy, "The people decide."

IV. The Nature of This Series

The Core Knowledge Series is a grade-by-grade presentation of the knowledge young people should acquire in early grades. The books have been sequenced to help children make secure progress in learning; each book presents knowledge upon which later books will build. Our writers have drawn on their experience and common sense to make the materials interesting, clear, and challenging. We have *not* used discredited grade-level formulas regarding vocabulary and sentence length. Instead, we have gone to the toughest critics of all; drafts of the materials have been revised on the basis of teachers' actual experiences with children at the Three Oaks Elementary School.

Although we have made these books as accessible and useful as we can, parents and teachers should understand that they are not the only means by which the core knowledge sequence can be imparted. The books represent a first step in the core knowledge reform effort—a single version of the possibilities inherent in the core knowledge sequence. We hope that publishers will be stimulated to offer educational videos, computer programs, games, alternative books, and other imaginative vehicles based on the core knowledge sequence.

The books are designed to be useful tools for parents and teachers, both at home and in school. They are called "resources" to signal that they neither replace the regular local school curriculum, nor provide everything parents should impart to their children. The books are strategic instruments designed to help children gain some of the knowledge they will need to make progress in school and be effective in society.

Each book is divided into five main sections: language arts, social studies, fine arts, mathematics, and science. The main sections are further divided into subsections. It is a good idea for parents or teachers to read from two different main sections whenever they read aloud, in order to provide variety and help children make connections between disciplines. There is no one right way to combine the readings; indeed, there are many good ways.

During the school year, children go to classes in the United States an average of one hundred and eighty days. In that time, using just twenty minutes a day, a parent or teacher could read aloud and discuss everything in a book of the series three times over. Excluding the math section of these books, which takes special practice, every child who is not learning-disabled could be on familiar terms with everything in each book by being read aloud to for just a few minutes each school day.

If it's so easy for children to become familiar with core knowledge, and if children *like* to be informed about the world, why do our children tend to know so little about the sorts of things narrated in these books? Part of the answer is that the "basal readers" that our children are given to develop their reading skills tend to be content-poor, conveying little that is of value for later learning. American children spend so much time in early grades nourishing their reading skills upon thin gruel that they haven't much time left in which to gain significant knowledge.

Observing this, some experienced teachers have asked, "Why not teach reading *and* systematically impart knowledge at the same time?" To give parents and teachers that option is one purpose of this series. What young children learn should not be limited to what they can read for themselves. Much of what they learn should come from what they hear and observe when they are *not* focusing their minds on sounding out letters and words.

The act of listening to someone read is an important part of early learning. It makes the world of books familiar to children, and it increases their knowledge of words and things. In almost all children who reach the end of seventh grade, the ability to read and the ability to listen have reached exactly the same level. Thus, if a child in early grades knows a lot and can listen well, that same child will normally be reading well in later grades. And the opposite is true. If a child in early grades does not know very much and cannot listen with much understanding, he or she will tend to be a poor reader later on. In the end, it is a child's knowledge and his consequent aural comprehension of books that determine how skillfull he will become at reading and learning.

Teachers and parents who use these books should remember that nothing can take the place of good teaching and parenting. The need for interactive, hands-on activities and patient practice are obvious in the sections on mathematics, the fine arts, and the natural sciences. The language of books must be supplemented for young children, to whom these books will serve mainly as sources of interesting stories and pictures. For parents and teachers, they will serve primarily as helps and guides. The books modestly announce themselves to be resources. We hope that they will serve their function well.

V. What You Can Do

The processes of education are so complex that almost any good educational idea, pursued single-mindedly or exclusively, will likely lead to failure. Unfortunately, one single point of view has dominated American elementary education over the past forty years, and a principal reason for the failure of our schools has been the elevation of a single set of insights to the level of universal truths. "Education should shun rote learning and encourage understanding." "Students should not be stuffed with mere facts, which are constantly changing, but should learn *how* to learn." "The child, not the academic subject, is the true focus of education." "Do not impose knowledge on children before they are developmentally ready to receive it." "Do not bog children down in mere facts, but rather, inculcate critical-thinking skills."

Who has not heard these sentiments, so admirable and humane, and—up to a point—so true? But these positive sentiments in favor of developing a child's understanding are also expressed as negative sentiments *against* such practices as "rote learning" and concern for "mere facts." By taking this strong negative stand against imparting "mere" information, even carefully selected information, American elementary education has become fatally one-sided. Those who have entered the teaching profession over the past forty years have been taught to scorn the rote imparting of information to children.

Thus it came about that many educators, armed with partially true slogans, seemingly took leave of common sense. Seeing their enemy as a cruel and joyless method of schooling, they persuaded themselves that the endless memorization of facts was a very real dragon that had to be slain. Even today, after forty years of antifact slogans, the dragon of "rote learning" is still perceived to guard the elementary school door, despite current failures which suggest that the new dispensations are in danger of turning into dragons themselves. Hard as it is to achieve a balanced view, we owe it to our children to do so. The first step for parents and teachers who are committed to reform is to refuse to be bullied by oversimplified slogans like "learning to learn" which have not worked.

Many parents and teachers have come to the conclusion that elementary education must strike a better balance between the development of the whole child and the narrower but fundamental duty of the school to ensure that all children master a core of information that is essential to their competence as learners in later grades. A great majority of parents and at least half the teachers I have spoken to have reached this conclusion through their own firsthand observations. But they cannot act on their convictions without access to an agreed-upon core sequence of concrete materials. Our main motivation in producing this series has been to give parents and teachers something concrete to work with.

Parents and teachers are urged to join in a grass-roots effort to restore balance to schooling by instituting core knowledge standards in elementary school. The place to start is in your own school and district. You are also invited to become a member of the Core Knowledge Network by writing The Core Knowledge Foundation, 2012-B Morton Drive, Charlottesville, VA 22901.

Good luck to our children!

E. D. Hirsch, Jr.
Charlottesville, Virginia
September 1991

How to Use This Book

The book you are holding in your hands is an unusual one. It is a collection made for children, but it is not limited to the usual treasury of best-loved stories and poems. It offers, in addition, engaging accounts of language, literature, history, geography, science, fine arts, and math—the core academic subjects that our children need in this new age of global information. It also contains knowledge that may help them become fulfilled and productive people. But it is not a textbook or a workbook filled with exercises. It offers the academic core—the sort of core knowledge that the best educational systems provide to children all over the world—written in a lively and absorbing manner that includes tips for making those knowledge domains come alive. But such a book must also leave much to you and to your child in the way of additional conversation and practice.

Each book in *The Core Knowledge Series* builds upon knowledge presented in previous books. We know from learning theory that we learn best by building upon what we already know. Hence, this third-grade book refers back to previous books. Moreover, the sections of the third-grade book also refer you to other sections of the same book. Because subjects and interests cut across disciplines, we encourage you to help your child see connections between art and math, history and literature, physical sciences and language just as we have tried to do. And you should also feel free, using the tables of contents or the indexes, to make your own connections among the books of the series.

We have tried to make this book attractive and interesting by using an interactive, storybook format. We address the child directly as reader, asking questions and suggesting projects that he or she might do. Advice to parents and teachers about teaching specific subject matter is provided in the introduction to each section. You can help your child read more actively both by conversing while you are reading and by bringing the subjects up at a later time when connections occur to you. You and your child can read the sections of this book in any order. You need not begin at the beginning and work your way through to the end. In fact, we suggest that you skip from section to section, and that you reread as much as your child likes.

To help your child use this book, you might think of it as a guidebook that tries to be as informative and suggestive as possible in a concise format. We encourage you to help your child find ways to explore further what she or he reads about here. If possible, take your child to plays, museums, and concerts; help your child find related books (some are suggested here). In short, this guidebook recommends places to visit, and describes what is important in those places, but only you and your child can make the actual visit, travel the streets, and climb the steps.

Bon voyage!

I.

LANGUAGE ARTS

Introduction to Stories and Speeches

FOR PARENTS AND TEACHERS

In Book Three under Stories, we have included *Alice in Wonderland, Pollyanna,* and tales from *The Arabian Nights* as well as stories from African-American, Hispanic, Native American, and Asian traditions. In this book we also begin including great speeches from our tradition, in the belief that these belong to our cultural heritage as fully as stories do.

Good stories help instill ethical values. In many cultures, the act of story-telling is a kind of ceremony, and stories are revered as gifts of wisdom. They convey history, tradition, and the ethical and social values that bind together a community and a nation. Next to actual living people who exemplify patience, courage, tolerance, and civility, the heroes and heroines of good literature are among the best sustainers of ethical and social values. Many of those values are universal, and are found in stories from all cultures. The tale from Asia about "The White Bone Demon" teaches that appearances sometimes deceive, which is also one of the main lessons of the Hispanic tale "Three Words of Wisdom." Courage is exemplified both in the American-Indian tale, "The Quillwork Girl and Her Seven Brothers," and in the Swiss tale "William Tell."

Children recognize the power of stories every time they tell a story of their own. Encouraging them to tell their own stories carries many benefits, including, of course, practicing their language skills. You can combine story-reading with writing and drawing by encouraging children to write and illustrate their own stories.

You can help draw children into a story and practice their language skills if you sometimes ask questions about the stories you are reading together. You might ask, "What is going to happen next?" "Why did one of the characters act as he did?" "What might have happened if . . . ?"

After reading one of the stories in this book, you might ask your child to retell it. Don't be bothered when children change events or characters, thus making the story their own. That is in the best tradition of story-telling, and explains why we have so many different versions of traditional stories.

Stories and Speeches

Aladdin and the Wonderful Lamp
(a tale from *The Arabian Nights*)

An evil magician in faraway China learned through his secret arts of a magic lamp. Since the lamp was hidden in a dangerous place, the magician decided to find someone to fetch it for him. He happened upon an innocent boy named Aladdin, who was the son of a poor widow. Pretending to be the boy's long-lost uncle, he invited Aladdin to walk with him outside the city.

After passing through many beautiful gardens, they came at last to a faraway hill. The magician built a fire and threw some magic powder upon the flames. There was a great burst of smoke, then suddenly a door appeared in the ground. Aladdin shrank back, but the magician cuffed his ears and ordered him in a rough voice to open the door. A flight of narrow steps was revealed, winding into the darkness. Giving him a ring, the magician said, "Put this on your finger and descend the steps, being careful not to touch the walls with your garments, for if you do, you will die. There is an old lamp in the cave which I want you to fetch for me. Now go quickly!" Aladdin obeyed, walking carefully until he had made his way safely to the bottom. Here

The evil magician pretends to be Aladdin's uncle.

he saw trees shining with colorful fruits, which he picked and stuffed into his pockets. Then, spying the lamp in a niche, he snatched it up and hurried back.

As Aladdin was climbing the steps, the magician reached down for the lamp. Suspecting that the magician would close him in the cave, the boy said, "You shall have the lamp when I have climbed out." The magician grew furious and slammed shut the heavy door, leaving Aladdin trapped in darkness, afraid to move lest he should touch the deadly

Aladdin finds the lamp.

walls. As he wrung his hands in despair, Aladdin happened to rub the magician's ring. A spirit appeared! "I am the genie of the ring," said the spirit. "Command and I obey." "I wish to escape!" cried Aladdin. Instantly, he was outside the cave.

Aladdin told his mother all that had happened and showed her the lamp. "Perhaps we can sell this if we polish it a bit first," she said. So Aladdin set to work rubbing the lamp and, behold! Another spirit appeared. "I am the genie of the lamp," he said. "Command and I obey." Delighted, Aladdin asked the genie for some food, and immediately a great feast appeared before them. Now Aladdin began to dream of accomplishing wondrous things with the help of the genie. He told his mother that he wished to marry the princess. "Marry the princess!" she cried. "But the King will be insulted if a poor woman like me should ask such a thing for her son." By this time, Aladdin had begun unloading his pockets. To his delight, he discovered that the fruits were actually precious gems of all kinds. "Mother," said Aladdin, "do not fear the King's displeasure, for look at the gifts you can take him!"

Indeed, the King was so impressed with the jewels that he allowed Aladdin to court his daughter. The two fell in love and soon began to plan their wedding. "But first, I must build a castle for us," said Aladdin. The princess and her father protested. That could take years! "I shall do it in one day," said Aladdin. He went home and rubbed the lamp. When the genie appeared, Aladdin told him to build a fine castle next to the King's own. "Command and I obey," said the genie.

The next morning the King and all of the court were amazed to see a magnificent new palace standing nearby. Aladdin married the princess that very day and took her to their new home, and in the days that followed, he made many friends at court.

Then one day, the evil magician heard of the King's impressive new son-in-law, who had built his palace overnight. Immediately he suspected the truth. Disguised as a peddler, he waited outside the palace gate until he saw Aladdin ride away. Then he approached the palace calling, "New lamps for old, new lamps for old." One of the palace maids, hoping to please her mistress, grabbed up Aladdin's tarnished old lamp and traded it to the disguised magician for a shiny new one. No sooner had the peddler obtained the old lamp, than he rubbed it and commanded the genie to transport the whole palace, with the princess inside, to a remote desert.

When Aladdin returned, he guessed what had happened and summoned the genie of the ring. "Restore my princess and my palace!" he cried. But the genie of the ring could not undo the magic of the lamp. "Then take me to them!" said Aladdin. Instantly he found himself at the side of his wife, who was overjoyed to see him. Aladdin gave her a small vial containing a powder. "When the magician joins you at dinner tonight," said Aladdin, "pour this into his wine." The princess did as he said, and after drinking his wine the magician immediately fell to the floor, senseless. Then Aladdin snatched up the lamp, rubbed it, and commanded the genie to take them all home. Instantly the palace was returned to its rightful place. The magician was sent to a faraway land, and Aladdin and his princess lived together in happiness and prosperity for the rest of their days.

Ali Baba and the Forty Thieves
(a tale from *The Arabian Nights*)

A poor man named Ali Baba was leading his donkey through the forest, gathering firewood, when he heard a band of robbers approaching. Fearing that they might harm him, Ali Baba and his donkey hid in the bushes and watched as the robbers carried their bags of stolen gold toward a large, flat rock in the mountainside. The captain of the robbers said, "Open Sesame!" To Ali Baba's astonishment, the rock opened, revealing a cave. The robbers carried their booty inside, and reemerged, empty-handed. "Close Sesame!" said the captain. The rock closed, hiding the cave once more, and the robbers departed.

As soon as they had left, Ali Baba stepped to the rock, spoke the magic words, "Open Sesame," and went inside. He filled his saddlebags with the robbers' gold, then closed the cave with the words, "Close Sesame," and hurried home.

The robbers were furious to find that they had themselves been robbed. Determined to get back their lost gold, the captain went to the village to discover who had taken it. Since everyone was talking about Ali Baba's new wealth, the captain soon guessed where his gold had gone.

The next day the captain appeared at Ali Baba's door disguised as an oil merchant with a cartful of large jars. He needed a place to stay for the night, he said, and a place to store his forty large jars of oil. He removed the lid from the first jar so that Ali Baba might see his wares. Ali Baba kindly invited him in and offered his shed for storage.

Later that evening, Ali Baba's slave Morgiana discovered that her lamp was out of oil. Thinking that it would do no harm to borrow a small quantity from the merchant's large store, she ran to the shed and lifted the lid from the first jar. She nearly dropped the lid in surprise when she heard a voice whisper from inside the next jar, "Is it time yet?" Now Morgiana was clever

and she knew the story of how her master, Ali Baba, had found the cave of the forty thieves. In an instant she realized that all the jars after the first one contained not oil, but robbers plotting murder, and that the grimmest robber of all was dining under her master's own roof! She whispered back, "Wait a bit." Quickly, she heated a large kettle full of oil to the boiling point, then poured just enough into each of the jars to scald the robbers to death.

Then she returned to the house to deal with the captain.

Morgiana dressed herself as a dancing girl. With bracelets glittering and scarves flowing, she entered the dining room. Ali Baba and the false oil merchant watched with delight as she swirled before them, shaking her tambourine. Closer and closer she moved toward the robber captain. Suddenly, she threw her tambourine aside and thrust a dagger into the robber's heart.

Ali Baba seized her. "What have you done!" he cried. But Morgiana pointed to the dead robber's outstretched hand, which held another dagger. "He would have killed you, master," she said. "Come and see what is in the shed."

When Ali Baba saw the thirty-nine robbers, dead in the jars where they had hidden, he understood that Morgiana had saved his life. He was so grateful that he granted her freedom and gave her his own son for a husband. For the rest of his long and prosperous life, he loved her as his own daughter.

Alice in Wonderland
(retold and excerpted from Lewis Carroll's original)

Alice was tired of sitting on the bank watching her sister read a book with no pictures in it. Suddenly a White Rabbit in waistcoat ran by. "Oh, dear! I shall be late!" said the rabbit, looking anxiously at his watch. Alice ran after the rabbit and followed it right down a large rabbit hole.

Alice fell down the hole for a long time, until at last she landed with a thump. Here was a garden door, too tiny for her to pass through, and a little table with a bottle labeled, "DRINK ME." Alice drank the delicious mixture and soon began to feel like a telescope opening out. "Good-bye, feet!" she cried, growing taller and taller. When she stopped growing, she was nine feet high and had to lie down on her side to look into the garden,

"Oh, dear! I shall be late!"

where she longed to go. She began to cry; her tears fell by the gallons, until a pool had formed around her feet. Then suddenly, she grew smaller and smaller, until she was swimming in the pool. The door disappeared, and she washed up upon a riverbank.

As she was shaking off the water, along came the White Rabbit mumbling, "Oh, my fur and whiskers! Where can I have put them?" He said to her angrily, "Mary Ann! Run home this minute and fetch me a pair

of gloves and a fan!" "He has mistaken me for his housemaid," Alice said to herself. But off she ran until she came to his house. Upstairs she found a tiny pair of gloves and a fan, along with a corked bottle. Curious, she drank the bottle's contents and soon felt herself growing as before. In a moment her head had crashed against the ceiling, her arm was sticking out the window, and one foot was going up the chimney. Outside, the rabbit and a lizard named Bill pelted Alice with pebbles. As the pebbles hit her, they became little cakes. Alice swallowed one and shrank until she was small enough to fit through the door.

Alice wandered until she came upon a caterpillar, who sat upon a mushroom, smoking a kind of pipe called a hookah. "Who are you?" he said.

Alice replied, "I—I hardly know, sir—at least I knew who I was when I got up this morning, but I have changed since."

"Explain yourself!" said the caterpillar sternly.

"I can't," said Alice, "because I'm not myself, you see."

"I don't see," said the caterpillar.

"Well, I should like to be a little larger," said Alice. "Three inches is such a wretched height to be."

"It is a very good height indeed!" said the caterpillar angrily (for the caterpillar was exactly three inches high). It shook itself, got down, and crawled away into the grass, remarking,

"One side will make you grow taller, and the other side will make you grow shorter."

"The other side of what?" thought Alice to herself.

"Of the mushroom," said the cater-pillar as it disappeared, just as if she had
spoken out loud. Alice stretched her arms around the mushroom and broke off a bit of the edge with each hand. Very carefully, she nibbled first at one and then at the other, growing sometimes taller, and sometimes shorter, until she brought herself back to her usual height.

Next Alice came upon a cat, sitting in a tree and grinning from ear to ear. "I never saw a cat grin before," she said.

"I am a Cheshire cat," explained the cat.

"Would you tell me," she said, "which way I ought to go?"

"That depends on where you want to get to," said the cat. "In that direction," the cat said, waving its right paw, "lives a Hatter, and in that direction," waving the left, "lives a March Hare. Visit whichever you like: they're both mad."

"But I don't want to go among mad people," Alice remarked.

"Oh, you can't help that," said the cat, "we're all mad here." Then it vanished slowly, beginning with the tail and ending with the grin, which lingered after the rest was gone.

Alice soon came upon a large table set out under a tree, where the March Hare, the Mad Hatter, and a dormouse were crowded together at one corner, having tea. "No room! No room!" they cried out when they saw Alice coming.

"But there is plenty of room!" she said. They made a place for her, but whenever she began to pour her tea, they all moved down one chair and Alice found a used empty cup in front of her. She listened to their nonsense for some time, and at last marched away, thinking that it was the stupidest tea party she had ever attended. Suddenly, in front of her she saw the little door leading into the beautiful garden. She nibbled at the bit of mushroom in her left hand until she was small enough. Then in she went.

Inside she saw three men who looked exactly like playing cards, busily slapping red paint onto a white rosebush. "The Queen wanted red, you see," said the number-two card to Alice. "But we planted white by mistake. She'll be furious if she finds out!" There was a flourish of trumpets and Alice saw a parade of card people coming her way, led by the Queen of Hearts. "Who's painting the roses red?" the Queen screamed. "Off with their heads!" Immediately the three cards were seized and carried off. Then the Queen invited Alice to play croquet.

The croquet game proved to be rather difficult, as the players used flamingos turned upside down for mallets and hedgehogs for balls. Throughout the game, the Queen lost her temper at one player after another until all of them but Alice had lost their heads. Finding the game tedious, Alice nibbled a bit of the mushroom and instantly grew very tall.

"I decree that no one over nine feet high shall remain in the kingdom!" the Queen screamed furiously. "Off with her head!"

"Off with her head!"

"Who cares for you?" said Alice. "You're nothing but a pack of cards!" At this the whole pack rose up into the air, and came flying down upon her; she gave a little scream and tried to beat them off, and found herself lying on the bank, with her head in her sister's lap. "Oh, I've had such a curious dream!" said Alice. And she told her sister all the strange adventures you have just been reading about.

Frankenstein

(retold with excerpts from the novel by Mary Shelley)

My name is Victor Frankenstein. Perhaps my story will sound to you like madness, but I pray that you will believe me and learn from my suffering and misfortune not to do as I have done.

I was raised by loving parents in a wonderful home, with my beloved friend Elizabeth and my little brother William as playmates. Yet blessed as I was, I chose to leave my family and friends to shut myself away from the world. In my laboratory I worked night and day to discover the secret of life.

For I wished to do what no man had ever done: I wanted to create the perfect human being.

It was on a dreary night in November that I first looked upon the creature I had made. How can I describe the wretch whom I had taken such pains to form? I had meant for him to be beautiful. Beautiful! Great God! His yellow skin scarcely covered his muscles and veins. His flowing black hair and white teeth made a horrid contrast with his watery eyes, shriveled complexion, and black lips. As he reached out to touch me, his wrinkled cheeks formed what seemed the most horrible of grins. I escaped and ran from the house. When I returned, the monster I had created was gone. Yet so wild were my thoughts that I seemed to see him everywhere. Raving madly, I fell into a fever and did not recover for many months.

With the coming of spring my strength returned, yet my suffering had only just begun. I received a letter from my father, telling me the sorrowful news that my brother William was dead. An unknown murderer had strangled him. I was overcome with grief and with a mysterious fear which soon proved well founded. For as I rushed home to my family, I saw moving in the darkness near their home an unmistakable shape. I then knew that William's killer was the horrible fiend I had created!

As the days went by I was torn with anguish, yet I could tell no one my thoughts. One day, to ease my mind, I climbed a mountain. When at last I reached the top and sat upon the rocks, wishing I could end my sorrow, I suddenly beheld a tall figure moving toward me at great speed. It was the wretch whom I had created. "Devil," I exclaimed, "do you dare approach me? Begone! Or stay, that I may trample you to dust."

"Be calm," he warned. "Remember, you have made me bigger and more powerful than you. Have I not suffered enough, that you wish to harm me further? Oh, Frankenstein, be kind to me as you should. Remember that I am your creature. I ought to be your son, but you rejected me for no reason. I was once good and kind, but everywhere I went, people hated and feared me because of my hideous appearance. Misery has made me evil. Make me happy, and I shall again be good."

The wretch told me that if I would create a female companion for him, he would flee with her far away and never trouble me further. Reluctantly, I agreed to do as he demanded, and began collecting materials for my disgusting task. In a lonely laboratory on a remote island in Scotland, I worked to finish my second horrible creature. One night as I worked, I looked up and saw by the light of the moon the demon at the window. A ghastly grin wrinkled his lip as he gazed on me. Suddenly my promise to create another such monster seemed sheer madness. Trembling, I tore to pieces the thing on which I worked. When the wretch saw me destroy the creature on which his future happiness depended, he went away, howling in despair, and vowing revenge. "Beware!" he said. "I will be with you on your wedding night."

I had always expected to marry my dear childhood friend, Elizabeth, just as she had always expected to marry me. Now the day approached for our wedding, but I was filled with fear and dread. I could not forget the fiend's words, "I will be with you on your wedding night." Elizabeth saw that I was worried, but I could not tell her the reason for my gloominess. She tried to cheer me, insisting that our marriage would bring us the happiness we had long deserved.

But on our wedding night, I could not rest. As Elizabeth lay in bed, I wandered about the house carrying my pistol, ready to face my monstrous creation. Suddenly I heard Elizabeth scream. I rushed into the bedroom and found her lifeless and still, thrown across the bed, her head hanging down and her face half-covered by her hair. I saw at the window the hideous face of the fiend, grinning and pointing at Elizabeth's dead body. I fired my gun, but the wretch escaped.

Since that day, I have roamed the world seeking the creature to which I gave life, that I may put an end to him once and for all. Always he stays one step ahead of me, luring me on and laughing at my failure. But someday I shall find him, and all his words shall not convince me to spare him. Calling on the names of William and Elizabeth, I shall thrust my sword into his evil heart.

The People Could Fly

There are many versions of the following story, because for a long time it wasn't written down. African-American slaves told and retold this story to each other as they worked in the fields.

They say that these people could fly. Long ago in Africa, some of them would shout a few magic words and lift themselves into the air like crows, flapping their black wings. They say that when these people were put on the ships as slaves, they had to leave their wings behind. There was no room for flying on those cramped ships. And they say that when these people were put to work in the fields, they lost the freedom to spread their wings and they could not imagine flying.

But not all of them forgot the magic words.

One afternoon, the sun was so hot it seemed to singe the hair on their

*The overseer raised his whip
in warning.*

heads. They had been picking cotton since sunup without a rest, and the whole sky seemed to boil over with heat. One young woman, Sarah, was carrying her child on her back and was wearier than she had ever been. She fainted.

"Back to work," the overseer snarled.

"This isn't the time for rest!" He raised his whip in warning.

All of the other slaves stopped to watch him. Sarah staggered to her feet, put her child on her back, and began to pick again. An old man worked his way toward her. Before he could reach her, she fell again. Snapping his whip, the overseer roared, "Up!" and Sarah rose a second time.

When the old man reached Sarah's side, he whispered quietly in her ear. Sarah began to pass the message on. The whispering spread from slave to slave as swiftly as a breeze, and the overseer never noticed. The slaves kept working.

But Sarah's baby was too young to withstand the heat. Suddenly, he began to cry, and Sarah had to stop to comfort him. The overseer rode toward her, his whip whistling in the air. Just as the lash was about to hit her back, the old man shouted the magic words. Sarah began to rise. Her arms lifted and fell like wings and she rose above the overseer's whip like an eagle.

Wheeling his horse around, the overseer bellowed, "Who was that shouting those words? What did he say?" but the slaves were quiet and busy with work. Sarah had flown to freedom.

The sun was unbearable, and soon others began to fall. The overseer cracked his whip at one man. But before it could make contact, a shout rang out and the weary slave rose into the air. Then the overseer aimed for a woman crumpled over nearby. But again the magic words raised the woman away from the whip.

In fury and confusion, the overseer watched as each slave he tried to whip rose into the air. Then, as he snapped his whip at yet another collapsed slave, he saw the old man open his mouth to shout.

They flew above the field, beyond the fences and the whip of the overseer.

"Seize the old man," he cried. "Seize the old man!" And bearing down upon him, he raised his whip.

"Now," the old man shouted. The people joined hands in a ring, and chanting the magic words, they slowly rose with the notes of their song. They flew above the field, beyond the fences and the whip of the overseer.

They say those slaves flew back to Africa. We don't really know. But we remember, and their story is still whispered by those who try, in their hearts and minds, to lift their wings and fly.

Pollyanna
(retold from the book by Eleanor H. Porter)

Pollyanna knew she ought to be glad that Aunt Polly had sent for her, yet as she sat upon her bed in the plain, stuffy little attic room without carpet or pictures, she found it hard to play the game her father had taught her. Pollyanna called it the "just being glad game," and she played it by thinking of things to be glad about, even when she was unhappy. Since she had come to live with her aunt after her father's death, Pollyanna had sometimes found it hard to be glad. If only Aunt Polly didn't have so many rules!

The next day Pollyanna astounded her proper, serious aunt by telling her how glad she was that her room had no mirror and no pictures. "For now I needn't see my freckles that I've never liked," said Pollyanna, "and instead of looking at my walls, I'll look out my window at the lovely trees and hills, for they're ever so much prettier than a picture could be!"

Aunt Polly listened to her with astonishment, murmuring to herself, "What an extraordinary child!" There was something about Pollyanna's bright smile and happy chatter, something about the way she always found something to be "glad" about, that made Aunt Polly feel as if she had lost her bearings. Pollyanna was able to turn every disappointment into a reason to be glad. That very afternoon, Aunt Polly moved Pollyanna into a bright airy room downstairs, with carpets, drapes, and pictures.

Aunt Polly hadn't always been so serious. Everyone in town knew that she had once been in love with Dr. Chilton. Because of a silly quarrel, Aunt Polly had banished him from her house and had vowed that if she ever invited him there again, it would mean that she was sorry for their quarrel and had agreed to marry him. For many years the two had not spoken, yet neither of them had ever wished to marry anyone else.

Pollyanna loved to walk in the town and in the woods, for wherever she went she made new friends. She taught them all the game of how to find something always to be glad about, and her presence made their lives happier.

One day, Pollyanna happened upon grouchy Mr. Pendleton, who lay by the roadside with a broken leg. He sent her to fetch Dr. Chilton, who came at once. In the days that followed, Pollyanna often visited the recovering Mr. Pendleton, who seemed to change into a different man when he was with her. His housekeepers were amazed to see the grim-faced miser showing Pollyanna how the prisms on his lamp made rainbows dance upon the wall. She even taught him how to play her game, and he became glad that he had broken his leg, for otherwise, he might never have met Pollyanna. Dr. Chilton said that Pollyanna was better than any medicine.

Then one day as Pollyanna was crossing the street, she was hit by a speeding car. Aunt Polly turned

white with fear when the child was brought home, unconscious. In the days that followed, her aunt sat beside the bed anxiously, trying to comfort the little girl when she asked why she was unable to move her legs. Special doctors came to see her, and she overheard them tell her aunt that she would never walk again.

Heartbroken, Pollyanna tried to play the game, but she could think of nothing to be glad for. How could she ever be glad again, knowing that she would always be confined to her bed? Soon the news had spread all over town that Pollyanna would never walk again and that, worse still, she was no longer glad. Her many friends began coming to the house to visit, and each had a story to tell of how Pollyanna's happy outlook had forever changed their lives for the better. Each story made Pollyanna's sadness more bearable, and at last she said, "I am at least glad that I had my legs, so that they could take me into so many homes."

Meanwhile, Dr. Chilton was beside himself. He believed that he could help Pollyanna, if only her aunt would allow him to examine the child. Aunt Polly had repeatedly refused to call him in as a consultant because of their old quarrel and the vow she had made. But at last, filled with love for Pollyanna, her heart grew kinder toward Dr. Chilton. Thanks to Pollyanna she could finally admit into her home the man she had loved but denied for so long.

The day that Dr. Chilton came to call was a happy one indeed for him, for Pollyanna, and for Aunt Polly. Not only could Dr. Chilton help Pollyanna to walk again, he was also going to become her new uncle! And so Pollyanna was taken to a special hospital where, after many months of hard work, she learned to use her legs once more. And Aunt Polly and Dr. Chilton were married in a ceremony performed right at Pollyanna's bedside.

The Quillwork Girl and Her Seven Brothers
(a Cheyenne tale)

In the grasslands of America, before the Europeans came, great herds of buffalo roamed the prairie, and the Indians hunted them for food. Sometimes, when thousands of buffalo began to run in the same direction in a stampede, their hooves sounded like thunder. Any creature that stood in their way was sure to die.

In those days, when Indians needed only a few buffalo for their food, humans and buffalos usually lived in peace. At night it was quiet and safe in the grasslands. If you looked up in the sky, you could see the North Star and the pattern of seven stars we call the Big Dipper. The Cheyenne Indians told a tale about how the buffalos caused the North Star and the Big Dipper to appear in the sky.

There was once a Cheyenne girl who dyed quills from porcupines to decorate the buffalo hides that people wore. With the bright quills she made pictures of stars and animals.

One day her mother noticed that she was making a quillwork shirt that showed buffalo running across the sleeves. On the front were seven stars. "Who are you making this for?" asked her mother.

The girl told her, "I am making seven of these shirts. At night when I close my eyes, I have a vision of my seven brothers living in the north. The youngest one calls to me, and tells me to come join them when I have finished making my shirts."

When the girl finished making the seventh shirt, she and her mother walked north with their dogs until they came to a great river.

"Now is the time for you to turn back," the girl said to her mother. "When I find my seven brothers, I'll send the dogs home to you again so that you'll know that I am safe."

The girl walked on alone, until one morning she woke to discover a bright tepee before her, shining like the sun. In front of it was her younger brother, who had dreamed of her coming. "My brothers are hunting," he explained. "So we will surprise them on their return." With that, the girl sent the dogs home to her mother.

The boy looked at the quill shirts and said that he had seen them in the night sky. He put one on, and it fit him perfectly.

For many days the girl and her brother waited for the six brothers. One day the two of them discovered a huge herd of buffalo. When the largest buffalo saw the girl, he decided that she was the most beautiful creature he had ever seen.

That night, the six older brothers returned, tired, and without any buffalo meat. They gladly greeted their sister, and put on the beautiful quillwork shirts she had made for them.

The next morning they saw a buffalo calf waiting outside. "I have been sent by my big brother, the most powerful buffalo living," the calf said. "He told me to find the girl who gathers quills. We want her for our sister. If she won't come with me, he will return for her."

Later that day, the girl was startled by the sound of thunder. The earth began to shake and the tepee trembled. The brothers knew that it was buffalo.

From across the plain, a nation of buffalo came running toward them. Leading them was the largest buffalo they had ever seen. The girl told her brothers that they must dress in their quillwork shirts for safety. Taking the youngest boy in her arms, she led them to the tallest tree on the prairie. Swiftly, they climbed to the highest branches.

The largest buffalo began to charge. When he struck the trunk of the tree, the branches shook wildly, and the girl and her seven brothers were nearly flung to the ground below. They knew that the tree could not withstand the charges for long.

The buffalo charged again. This time, the girl and her brothers knew there was no hope. The youngest aimed his bow and arrow toward the sun, and let the arrow fly. Just as the tree was splitting in two, the girl and her seven brothers flew after the arrow. Glistening in their quillwork shirts, they floated right up to the sky, never to fall back down among the buffalo.

There you can still see them on a clear night in the northern sky. The girl became the North Star. Around her turn the seven stars we call the Big Dipper. We see them there just as the Cheyenne Indians saw them long, long ago.

Three Words of Wisdom
(a tale from Mexico)

There were once three poor farmers who lived in the country. Their crops failed year after year, and their families were starving. They decided to find jobs in the city.

Just a few miles from town, they met an old man who offered to travel awhile with them. They asked him if he knew of any work. He replied:

"You may have either my golden coins or my golden wisdom."

"In my lifetime, I have gathered heaps of gold and much wisdom. I am willing to share them with you. But you must make a choice. You may have either my golden coins or my golden wisdom."

Two of the farmers had large families, but one had a smaller family with only his wife and a son who was studying to be a priest.

"We'll take the money," said the two men with large families.

"I'll take the wisdom," said the man with the wife and the son who was studying to be a priest.

The old man divided his gold coins between the two men, and to the third he said:

"Here are my three pieces of wisdom: Don't take shortcuts. Don't ask about what does not concern you. Don't jump to conclusions."

When the old man walked on, the two men scolded their friend for his stupidity. "You can't feed your family with wisdom." And they set off for home with their gold.

As the two men left the main road to take a shortcut through the forest, the third man said, "Remember what the old man said. Don't take any shortcuts."

But the two men ignored him and plunged into the woods. There, they were attacked by bandits, and they lost their money and their lives.

Unaware of what had happened to his friends, the third man traveled on toward the city. As night fell, he reached the main house of a huge ranch. The owner was starved for good company, and asked the traveler to stay for dinner and the night.

And what a feast the man served! Our traveler had never tasted more delicious meat. The fruit was piled in silver bowls, and the candles glistened overhead in gold chandeliers. Washing down the last mouthful, our traveler wanted to ask: "How did you make the money for all these things? I'd like to live like this." But then he remembered the words of wisdom: "Don't ask about what does not concern you."

Just then, the rancher lifted the cover from the last platter. There was the cut-off head of a man! "You are very wise not to ask me how I gained my riches, for this is what happened to the last man who asked me that. All of my life, I have waited for someone simply to accept me as I am, to share in my gifts without asking how they could make them too. Now that I have found you and seen your wisdom, I will share my riches with you!"

Taking our traveler's arm, the rancher led him to the window. "This land and all that lives and grows here are yours to use, whenever you are in need."

The next morning when our traveler woke, he found a cart and donkey loaded down with more food and money than he could ever ask for. He was eager to get home.

He came to his house quietly because he wanted to surprise his wife and son with his good fortune. But no one came out to greet him. He peeked into the window. What he saw nearly choked him with rage! His wife was hugging another man—a priest!

He was very angry to see his wife hugging another man. But then he remembered the old man's words of wisdom: "Don't jump to conclusions."

He pounded on the door to let them know he was coming. When his wife saw how angry he was, she turned to the priest, and said, "What ever has gotten into your father?" The son had become a priest during his father's absence! Our traveler greeted his family as a wise man would, with love and joy, and the three lived happily ever after.

Tom Thumb

Once there was a boy who was no bigger than his father's thumb, and so he was called Tom Thumb. Though he never grew an inch, he was brave and clever, and his parents adored him.

One day when Tom was going with his father to cut wood, he begged to be allowed to drive the horse and cart. His father laughed and said, "However could you manage it, son?"

"Just put me in the horse's ear, and I shall tell him when to go or turn or stop," said Tom. So his father placed Tom in the horse's ear, and the horse did just as the boy told him.

One day when Tom was playing outside, two men happened to see him, and they could hardly believe their eyes. "What a remarkable child!" they said to one another. "If he were ours, we could put him on display and charge people a lot of money to see him." So they asked Tom's father if he would sell the boy to them.

Tom's father refused, for the boy meant all the world to him. But Tom whispered, "Father, take their money and give me to them. I shall escape and come back in a twinkling." So Tom's father sold him to the men, and off they went, with Tom riding on the brim of one man's hat.

After a while Tom asked to be let down, but the man told him to wait. "But it's urgent!" said Tom. "I can't wait!"

"Well, all right, but make it snappy," said the man. No sooner had he lowered the boy to the ground than Tom ran down a mouse hole where, try as they might, the men could not reach him. At last they went away and Tom cautiously crept out.

"What a remarkable child!"

Tom began the long walk home, stopping that night to sleep in a barn. Unfortunately, a hungry cow happened to gobble up Tom with a mouthful of hay. Suddenly the boy awoke to find himself in the darkness, with more and more hay coming in upon him by the second. "No more hay!" he cried.

When the maid who was milking the cow heard these words coming from its stomach, she fled in terror, crying that the cow was bewitched. The poor cow was killed, and its stomach thrown upon the trash heap, where a hungry wolf found it and swallowed it in one gulp. Now Tom called out from inside, "Oh, wolf! I know where you can get a better meal—all the bacon and sausage you can eat."

"Where?" asked the wolf. The voice in his stomach directed him to Tom's very own house. The wolf hurried there and squeezed through a crack into the pantry. When he had stuffed himself until he was too fat to get out again, Tom called out to his parents. "Help! Get me out of here! I'm in the wolf!"

Tom's father killed the wolf and his mother used her sewing scissors to cut Tom out. They were all overjoyed to see one another, and Tom's father vowed never to sell his son again.

The White Bone Demon

This story, about a famous character named Monkey, is retold from a sixteenth-century Chinese tale by Wu Cheng-en.

Monkey was a lovable creature who had the powers of a god, but when he was young, he played naughty tricks. To keep Monkey out of mischief, Buddha hid him away for five hundred years under the Mountain of Five Elements. Then he set Monkey free, and Monkey became a follower of the holy monk Hsuan-tsang.

Our story begins when Hsuan-tsang was on his way to the west to find the Buddhist scriptures. He was escorted by Monkey and two other disciples, Sandy and Pigsy. Monkey was leading the way.

As they hiked through the mountains, Monkey became suspicious. The mountains seemed to grow taller and more dangerous with each step they took, and the clouds overhead grew darker. Monkey warned, "Beware, brothers, I think there are demons around. This is the land of the White Bone Demon."

Pigsy chuckled, "Oh, Monkey," he said, "you are too suspicious."

But Monkey insisted. Drawing a magic circle around them, he said, "Stay here, and I'll have a look around."

No sooner had he gone than a young maiden appeared. Whispering Buddhist scripture, she made her way toward the travelers. Pigsy could not sit still, for the young girl carried a basket overflowing with the aroma of hot sweet cakes.

"Hello," Pigsy said. The girl giggled and ran a few feet away. Forgetting Monkey's warning, Pigsy slipped from the circle, pulling Hsuan-tsang with him. Suddenly, Monkey appeared overhead.

"You are an evil demon," he said, and down he flew, striking the girl dead. As she crumpled to the ground, the White Bone Demon escaped from the body in a wisp of smoke. No one else saw this, so Monkey took chase.

"Oh, foolish Monkey," the monk cried, "what have you done!"

As the monk was worrying about the girl, an old woman appeared. "Monk," the old woman moaned. "What have you done to my sweet daughter?"

Sorrowfully, Hsuan-tsang explained that Monkey had killed her. The old woman scolded, saying Buddha would never forgive them. "At the least," she said, "you should help me find a coffin to bury my child in." Hsuan-tsang went willingly.

Suddenly Monkey swooped down from the clouds overhead and struck the old woman down. Again, the White Bone Demon slipped away in a wisp of smoke, and Monkey gave chase.

"Are you crazy?" Hsuan-tsang cried after him. "First you kill a young girl, and now you kill her mother!"

An old man appeared. "Excuse me, kind monk," he said. "I am looking for my daughter and wife. I'm afraid that they have lost their way." Now the monk was sure that they had been human. Begging for the old man's forgiveness, he explained what Monkey had done.

Weeping, the old man fell to his knees. "Oh, my poor wife," he cried. "Something must be done to that Monkey."

No sooner said than Monkey appeared and struck the old man dead. But the White Bone Demon slipped from the old man's body in a wisp of smoke. Again, neither Sandy nor Pigsy nor Hsuan-tsang saw it. Monkey was about to give chase when a yellow scroll of paper floated to the ground. The monk read, "Buddha is compassionate and will never tolerate killing any creature. If you keep Monkey with you, you'll never find the scriptures you are looking for."

Despite Pigsy's and Sandy's pleas, Hsuan-tsang sent Monkey home to the Mountain of Fruit and Flowers. Monkey flew off toward home, and the three continued alone. Soon, they saw a temple rising up through the trees. Grateful for a place to rest, they entered and kneeled before the Buddha. As they prayed, the Buddha opened his mouth . . . and laughed. Everywhere in the temple, statues dissolved into demons and Hsuan-tsang and Sandy were captured. Only Pigsy escaped, and he flew home to the mountain to find Monkey. Monkey sent him back with this message: "Don't worry. Master's kindheartedness will persuade the demons to set him free."

When Hsuan-tsang received Monkey's message, he was worried, for he knew White Bone Demon planned to serve them all in a feast. He didn't know that Monkey had a plan.

In the temple, the White Bone Demon greeted her mother and her demon friends, bragging about the feast she had captured for them. The mother smiled and said, "Tell me, daughter, how you captured this trusting monk."

As the monk watched, the White Bone Demon turned herself into the girl, the old woman, her husband, and the yellow scroll. "And he never saw through my disguises!" she said. "Now, to feast! Let's kill these foolish creatures!"

The monk said, "I have been fooled."

Suddenly, he heard Monkey's voice. "Don't worry, master, I am here," and before their eyes all the demons disappeared. In their place stood Monkey and all his monkey helpers. "You can't take pity on a demon!" he cried.

That was how Monkey killed the White Bone Demon and all of her followers. When she died, the temple went up in a wisp of smoke, and Monkey, Hsuan-tsang, Sandy, and Pigsy found themselves on the path again in search of the scriptures, with Monkey once more in the lead.

William Tell

Many years ago, the proud people of Switzerland were forced to pay taxes to the powerful Emperor of Austria. Among the Swiss was one especially fearless man named William Tell. He made no secret of his disrespect for the Emperor and of his anger about the huge taxes his people were forced to pay. His boldness gave others courage to speak out against Austria, and so the Emperor's soldiers feared and mistrusted William Tell. But the people of his village looked up to him, and no one admired him more than his own little son, Walter.

One day the soldiers placed a hat upon a stick high in the air. "This hat shall stand for the Emperor," they declared. "Anyone who passes through the town square without bowing to the hat will be arrested as a traitor." The people were so disgusted by this silly requirement that they decided to avoid the hat altogether by going a roundabout way. So the town square stayed deserted.

One night William Tell strode through the square without giving the hat so much as a glance. Immediately the soldiers were upon him. The Emperor's chief representative, the governor, presented William Tell with a cruel choice. "I hear you are an expert marksman," he said. "You may go free if you can shoot an apple off the top of your boy's head."

"I would never put him in such danger, even to save my life," said Tell defiantly.

"Then you shall both be executed!" said the governor. "Make your choice."

Seeing that there was no other way to save his son, William Tell gently told the boy to have courage. But Walter was not afraid. "I will stand very still, Father. Have no fear." Then the boy took his place, standing with his back against a sturdy tree to brace himself. His father's heart pounded as he watched the grim-faced governor place an apple on Walter's head. Then William Tell lifted his bow, inserted the string in the arrow's niche, and pulled it back until the bow trembled. The townspeople who had come to watch scarcely breathed as Tell hesitated, taking aim more carefully than he had ever done before in his life. At last he let go, and the arrow zinged through the air. It pierced the apple's core, pinning it to the tree with a "twack!"

The townspeople cheered. Walter triumphantly pulled the arrow from the tree, holding the apple high. "Now you must let my father go!" he told the governor.

"Not yet," said the governor. "First, Tell, I want to know why you placed two arrows in your belt. One yet remains."

"Because," said William Tell angrily, "had my first arrow missed and harmed my boy, the second would have gone straight to your heart!"

"Give Me Liberty or Give Me Death!"

The colonist Patrick Henry was still a very young man when he spoke out against British laws. He was a new member of the assembly in Virginia, but he rose to speak against the Stamp Act, a British law that forced Americans to pay taxes on newspapers, licenses and legal papers. (You can read more about the Stamp Act and other events leading to the American Revolution in the American Civilization section of this book.) Standing in the crowded assembly hall, Patrick Henry dared his peers to take action with this fiery proposal.

Henry shouted: "Caesar had his Brutus, Charles the First his Cromwell, and George the Third—"

"Treason!" cried the speaker of the House.

"—may profit by their example. If this be treason, make the most of it!"

His words were electrifying; Brutus and Cromwell were men who, in earlier times, rose up against their leader. Henry meant that, like Brutus and Cromwell, the colonies should rebel against their King. Patrick Henry's speech convinced others, and Virginia refused to pay the tax.

Over the next ten years, Patrick Henry became a leading rebel against the British. In 1775, on the eve of the American Revolution, Henry stood up in a small church and made a speech that became famous in American history. He knew that the British were preparing for war, so Henry argued that Americans too must arm themselves:

Patrick Henry gives his famous speech. How do you think his listeners feel? What makes this picture so dramatic?

"Mr. President . . . This is no time for ceremony. The question before the House is one of awful moment to this country. For my own part, I consider it as nothing less than a question of freedom or slavery . . .

"There is no longer any room for hope. If we wish to be free . . . we must fight!

". . . They tell us, sir, that we are weak; unable to cope with so formidable an adversary. But when shall we be stronger? Will it be next week, or the next year? Will it be when we are totally disarmed, and when a British guard is stationed in every house? . . . The battle, sir, is not to the strong alone; it is to the vigilant, the active, the brave. There is no retreat but in submission and slavery! Our chains are forged! Their clanking may be heard on the plains of Boston! The war is inevitable—and let it come! I repeat it, sir, let it come!

". . . Gentlemen may cry, 'Peace, Peace'—but there is no peace. The war is actually begun! The next gale that sweeps from the north will bring to our ears the clash of resounding arms! Our brethren are already in the field! Why stand we here idle? What is it that gentlemen wish? What would they have? Is life so dear or peace so sweet to be purchased at the price of chains and slavery? Forbid it, Almighty God! I know not what course others may take; but as for me, give me liberty or give me death!"

Norse Mythology

In Scandinavia, Germany, and Iceland, lived the Norsemen. They created stories about the gods that many people of Europe came to believe. Today we call these stories Norse myths. Everybody in the United States uses parts of the Norse myths, because the names for some of our days of the week came from Norse mythology.

How the Days of the Week Got Their Names

Wednesday, which is short for Woden's day, is named after Woden, the most powerful god in Norse mythology. His usual name was Odin. Odin and his brothers made the world by slaying a tremendous giant. They made the earth out of the giant's body, the oceans out of his blood, the mountains out of his bones, and the trees out of his hair. They made the sky out of the top of his head, and the clouds from his brains. The grassy earth where men live was made from the giant's eyebrows.

Odin is often pictured with the wolves Greedy and Gobbler and the ravens Thought and Memory. The two birds bring him tasty scraps of news from their travels around the world.

Here are some of the other Norse gods, and the days of the week that are named after them:

Thor was Odin's oldest son. He was the god of thunder, which he made with a mighty hammer. Can you think of a day that sounds like Thor's day?

Tyr was the god of war. What day is Tyr's day? If you said Tuesday, you were right.

Thor rides a chariot driven by the goats Toothgnasher and Toothgrinder.

Tyr has only one hand. He lost the other hand trying to keep a monstrous wolf cub from destroying the gods.

Freya was the goddess of love and beauty. Is there a Freya day? Yes, it's Friday.

If you are wondering where the other names of the days came from, here are the answers. Monday is named after the moon. Sunday is named after the sun. And Saturday is named after the Roman god Saturn, who also gave his name to the planet Saturn.

Another Norse name that people still use is the name of the underworld where people went who were not killed in battle. It was called Hel, after the Norse goddess of death.

Early Norsemen honored the cat. Freya's chariot is even drawn by cats.

How the Norse Gods Lived

The gods' home, Asgard, stretches into the heavens.

The Norse gods lived in a heavenly place called Asgard. It was ruled by Odin. Odin was waited on by maidens called the Valkyrie. The Valkyrie hovered around the battlefields of men, and carried the heroes who died to a great hall in Asgard called Valhalla. To go to Valhalla, the fierce Norsemen believed, was the greatest honor a person could achieve.

Odin was very wise, and always sought out more wisdom. Once he went to the Well of Wisdom, but he was told he would have to trade one of his eyes if he wished to drink. He sacrificed one of his eyes, so he might become wiser! This is how precious wisdom was to him. Because he gave up his eye for wisdom, Odin is often shown in pictures with only one eye.

The Enemies of the Gods

The enemies of the gods were evil giants. Although the gods had defeated the giants at the beginning of the world, the Norsemen believed there was going to be a second battle. The giants would win this terrible battle and the entire world would be destroyed.

Loki was the only one in Asgard who liked the giants. Loki was actually the son of a giant and a god. He was very, very bad. He tried to cause

Even though the parents of many Norse gods were giants, the gods and giants were enemies.

mischief among the gods whenever he could. Because he was very clever, to get his way he outsmarted others. But for some reason, Odin liked Loki, and allowed him to come and go in Asgard and sit at the great feasts of the gods. Perhaps one reason he did so is that Loki helped the gods build Asgard in the first place. Here's how.

How the Gods' Home, Asgard, Was Built

The gods had finished building the earth, and were going to build their home. They wanted a place that was so strong and high that they would always be safe from the giants there. A builder came along and offered to build them a towering fortress. In return, the builder wanted the gods to give him the sun, the moon, and Freya, the goddess of beauty. Of course the gods didn't want to give up the sun or the moon, and especially not Freya. So they said they would pay the builder only if he could finish the fortress in one winter, without anyone's help. The builder said that the only help he needed was that of his horse. Following Loki's advice, the gods agreed.

But when the builder began to build, he had his mighty horse work all night, pulling tremendous stones to the fortress. The horse was doing most of the builder's work! As the winter came to a close, the fortress was almost done. All that had to be built was the great gateway, and the builder had three days left, in which he could easily build it.

The gods called a great meeting. Soon they would have to plunge the earth into darkness by giving away the sun and the moon. And they would lose Freya, too. They realized that Loki had tricked them into letting the builder use his horse. So they seized Loki and threatened to put him to a cruel death unless he helped them. Loki promised that the builder would not complete the gateway, and the gods would not have to pay him.

The next night, when the builder's workhorse was pulling stones for the great gateway, a beautiful white horse appeared in the moonlight. She whinnied to the great workhorse to come and play. The workhorse dropped the stones he was pulling and ran into the forest after the white horse. (The white horse was really Loki, who could magically change his shape.)

By the time the builder had captured his workhorse again, he was too far behind in his work. He could see he wouldn't complete the fortress in time, and he wouldn't get his reward. So he quit working and took off his disguise:

he was really an evil giant! When Thor saw it was an evil giant, he crushed him with his mighty hammer and finished the gateway himself. And that is how the gods paid the giant, and how their great home Asgard was built.

Balder and Loki

Balder was the god that everyone loved the most. He was always sunny and pleasant and had a kind word to say to everyone. All the gods felt happy when Balder came into the hall. All the gods but one: Loki!

Loki was jealous of Balder because everyone liked him so much. Balder could tell, and one night he had a dream that he was going to be hurt. So Frigga, Odin's wife, went to everyone and everything she could find in the whole world, and made them promise not to hurt Balder. The gods were happy that Balder was safe, and played a game to prove it. They would throw stones and spears at Balder, and none of them would hurt him. This made them laugh aloud.

But Loki was very clever. He found out that Frigga had overlooked a small plant called mistletoe. Loki gave the plant to a blind god and helped him throw it at Balder as part of the game. The mistletoe pierced Balder's heart and he died. The gods were overcome with grief. At the funeral, Balder's wife was so sad, her heart broke and she died beside him. The gods wanted to punish Loki so they caught him and bound him up in a dark cave beneath the earth where he remains for all eternity. Over his head they hung a serpent, whose mouth drips poison that causes Loki terrible pain. Loki's wife stands beside him with a cup to catch the poison. But when she takes the cup away to empty it, the venom falls on Loki, who trembles with pain and causes the earth to shake. This, the Norsemen thought, is why there are earthquakes!

Loki's wife, Siguna, is the only being who feels sorry for him.

Why the Universe Doesn't Fall Down

The Norse believed the whole universe was held up by a giant tree called Yggdrasill. It had three roots: one root stretched to the land of ice, one root reached to Asgard, the land of the gods, and one root reached to the land of the giants. Three sisters lived beside the tree and controlled everyone's past, present, and future. A giant serpent continually chewed at the tree's roots to make it fall and bring the world down with it. At the end of the world, according to Norse mythology, Loki would escape his prison and lead the giants in battle against the gods. In the battle, everything would be destroyed—but the world would begin anew, and be perfect this time.

The great World Tree, Yggdrasill, holds the earth in its branches.

Other Magical Creatures

Many Northern European people believed in other magical creatures besides the gods, such as elves and dwarfs. Elves are sunny spirits that love people, though they sometimes play tricks on them. Of course you've heard about how elves help Santa Claus with his task of bringing presents to everyone. Dwarfs are night elves that live in dark caves, because if they're ever caught in the light, they turn into stones! Dwarfs look old and ugly, but they're very clever and make wonderful treasures out of gold and silver and other things. Some say Santa's presents come from the dwarfs. Even today, some people believe in elves and dwarfs to explain mysterious things that happen around them.

Introduction to Language and Literature

FOR PARENTS AND TEACHERS

In grade three, children should continue to identify and talk about the parts of speech, including adjectives, articles, pronouns, proper nouns, and conjunctions. They should understand helping verbs, the idea of grammatical agreement, and the parts of a sentence.

Experts say that our children already know more about the grammar of language than we can ever teach them. But standard written language does have special characteristics that need to be talked about with children. As with other parts of this book, the account of language conventions for third grade is a summary account. It needs to be worked out by giving your child opportunities to read and write and to discuss reading and writing in connection with grammar and spelling. Any child needs lots of discussion and practice in addition to the examples we give here. To make the information really interesting, your child needs you. Such activities as asking questions, seeking new examples together, praising right answers, and playing guessing games will liven up the proceedings.

Grammar is only part of an integrated language arts program, and should be connected with spelling and composition. We also advise parents and teachers not to restrict composition to stories and essays, but to include poetry, biography and autobiography, and discussions of science.

Children love language. Teaching about language can be deadly dull, or it can be a fascinating game. We have tried to give life to the subject but only a parent or teacher can truly make the subject come alive.

Learning About Language

Grammar Isn't Hard

Suppose your friend said to you, "I am went to your house." What did she mean? Is she going to go to your house, or did she already go?

When we talk to each other, we have to use words in ways that the other person understands. That's not hard when we talk inside our families. At home we know how to understand each other. But when we write or talk to people outside our homes, we need to be sure that everyone is using the same rules for speaking and writing. We study grammar to learn these rules.

Writing and reading are for everybody, so writing and reading make it necessary for everyone to use the same rules. When you write a letter to the local newspaper or the President of the United States, you have to use the grammar rules for written language. The people who wrote this book had to use the grammar rules for written language. In fact, the word "grammar" comes from a Greek word for writing. Correct grammar is so important for writing and reading that the first grades of school are sometimes called "grammar school"!

Grammar really isn't hard, because you already know much of it. Maybe you aren't aware that you are already using grammar, but, really, you *have* to use some grammar every time you speak. Spoken grammar isn't always exactly the same as the grammar that people use in writing, but it's mostly the same. You already know about nouns and verbs. It's time to learn the names for other kinds of words.

Names for Words: The Parts of Speech

To say anything more than "Wow" or "Bang" you have to put words together. When you do that you have a sentence. Try saying something that makes sense, like "Let's see." That's a sentence. You can't do without sentences. A written sentence begins with a capital letter (this one started with capital A), and it usually ends with a period (.). A sentence isn't a part of speech: it's the thing that contains the parts of speech.

There are eight parts of speech. Their names are nouns, verbs, adjectives, adverbs, pronouns, conjunctions, prepositions, and interjections. (Some people also identify a ninth part of speech, articles, which you will read about below.) You don't have to remember all these right now. You already know the two most important parts of speech—nouns and verbs. (If you want to review nouns and verbs, you can read about them in Book Two of this series.) You can make a whole sentence with just a noun and a verb, without using any other parts of speech. "John runs" is a sentence with one noun (John) and one verb (runs).

Like the parts of a car, each part of speech does a particular job that helps a sentence express what you mean. You can recognize the parts of speech by asking, "What does this word *do* in this sentence?" In the following pages you can read about what the parts of speech we call adjectives, pronouns, proper nouns, conjunctions, and articles do.

Adjectives—Words That Describe

Slippery fish.

Slippery. Slimy. Pretty. Brave. These words are adjectives. Adjectives are the words we use to describe nouns. Nouns, remember, name the things we are describing, such as "you" or "sky" or "school" or "bird." Adjectives are the words we use to describe *how* something looks or feels or tastes or sounds, such as the *green* trees, or the *stormy* sky, or the *loud* singing or how much or how many of them there are, such as the *five* birds.

Pretty bird.

If we need to use more than one adjective, we can just line them up next to each other and put a comma in between each one. For example, you might say, "I made a model airplane with *thin, gray wings.*"

Adjectives are easy to find because they almost always go right next to the thing or person they are describing. If the adjective isn't right next to the noun, you can find it by asking yourself if there are words anywhere in the sentence that describe the noun.

What adjectives can you pick for this toad?

We use adjectives to help us pick things out of a crowd. For instance, if you were picking a puppy out of a litter, you might say, "Can I hold the *small, cuddly* one?" "Which one?" the owner might ask. "*That* one," you would say. And "which," "small," "cuddly," and "that" would all be adjectives because they all limit the number of things we could be talking about to show the one we mean.

Pronouns Stand for Nouns

Pronouns take the place of nouns. They save time and energy. "When Ramona heard Ramona had won a prize, Ramona jumped with joy." Compare that with, "When Ramona heard she had won a prize, she jumped with joy." Putting in "she" for "Ramona" saves time.

Pronouns are words such as *it, he, she* and *they*. They refer back to the noun and save us from having to hear or say the noun again and again. We will have more to say about pronouns later on.

Names Are Proper Nouns

You already know about nouns. When something has its own name, the name is called a proper noun. Proper nouns include your name, nicknames, any

name you give your pet, the name of your school, and
the names of the town and state where you live.

We use proper nouns to pick out something definite.
Your school isn't just any school—it has its own name.
That's why proper names start with a capital letter.
Look at which nouns are capitalized in the following
sentence and which aren't: "Sandra asked her father
to take her to the circus because she wanted to see Jasmine, the elephant."
Capital letters say, "This noun is special and different from any other."

Conjunctions Join Things

Conjunctions are the words we use to connect words together. *And* adds
things together, as in "I like baseball *and* soccer *and* football." *Or* also joins
words together, but it makes you choose one: "Which game do you like best,
baseball *or* soccer *or* football?"

and or

You can use *and* and *or* to connect two sentences, and make them into
one. Here's an example:

Sentence One	*Sentence Two*
I am going to play.	I am going to study.

Using *and* to join the sentences:
I am going to play, and I am going to study.

Using *or* to join the sentences:
I am going to play, or I am going to study.

When we use a conjunction to connect two sentences, we usually put a
comma before the conjunction. The comma and conjunction say: these two
thoughts could be two sentences, but they are so closely tied I put them in
one. There are many conjunctions that do this, but these are some we use
most often: *so, and, because,* and *but.*

No one came to save him, *so* he began to explore the island.

He grew up on the plains, *and* he wants to stay there.

Alice smiled, *because* the rabbit looked as if he were about to speak.

Rosa Parks could have given in, *but* she refused to give up her place on the bus.

Articles: A, An, and The

Whenever you see the articles *a, an,* and *the,* you can be sure that a noun will follow. Sometimes, you will come to an adjective along the way (as in "an electric eel"), but a noun will always follow. *A* goes before nouns that start with a consonant, such as "a cactus."

An goes before nouns that begin with a vowel, such as "an army." The "n" gives your tongue something to do between the two vowels so that they don't blend together and get lost. Try saying "a odor" or "a octopus." Not easy is it?

We call *a* and *an* indefinite articles because they don't point out any definite thing. When we say "a kangaroo" we don't mean any definite one. But when we say "the kangaroo" we mean one specific kangaroo and no other. You already knew that, didn't you? You already know plenty of grammar.

When you say, "I need a hat," you mean that you need a hat but you don't have a specific one in mind. But if you say, "I need *the* hat," you mean one hat in particular—the one on the very top of the hat rack. *The* is the definite article.

Words, Games

Be a grammar detective. *Now that you've read about all these parts of speech, you can do some sleuthing. Take a piece of paper and divide it into rows, one row for each of the parts of speech you've learned about so far: nouns, proper nouns, verbs, adjectives, articles, pronouns, conjunctions. Then take one of your favorite books and open to a page you like. As you read, enter every word you can as a specific part of speech on your list. (You haven't learned all the parts yet, so some words won't go on your list.) After you've read at least six sentences, look over your list. What do the different rows show you?*

Word play. *If you keep asking, "What does this word do?" you will eventually find that some words can act as several different parts of speech. Take, for example, the word "stop" in this sentence: "The biker didn't stop at the stop sign." The first "stop" tells the biker's action; it's a verb. The second "stop" describes the sign; it's an adjective. Now see if you can use the following words as different parts of speech, making them do different things in a sentence or sentences:* howl, frown, cut, peanut, paint, skate, model.

The Two Parts of a Sentence

Whether we are speaking or writing, sentences are the building blocks of our language. Sentences are made of two main ingredients: subjects and predicates. The subject of a sentence is the person or place or thing that the sentence is about. In these sentences the subject is italicized.

The beautiful *ballerina* leaped into the air like a deer.
The *Seminole Indians* traveled over water in dugout canoes.

The quickest way to find the subject is to read the sentence and ask, "Who or what is this sentence about?" The answer might be one word or several. If you use all of the words that name the subject, such as, "The beautiful ballerina," or, "The Seminole Indians," you are naming the complete subject. If you boil down those words to just one noun or pronoun, such as "ballerina" or "Indians," you are naming the simple subject.

The predicate of a sentence is the verb that tells us what the subject is doing. Like a battery in a flashlight, a predicate gives a sentence its life and energy.

The beautiful ballerina *leaped* into the air like a deer.
The Seminole Indians *traveled* over water in dugout canoes.

One quick way to find the predicate is to read the sentence and ask, "What is the subject doing?" If you use all of the words that name the predicate, such as, "leaped into the air like a deer," or, "traveled over water in dugout canoes," you are naming the complete predicate. If you choose just one verb such as "leaped" or "traveled," you are naming the simple predicate.

The question, "What is the subject doing?" will only help you find active verbs: verbs that express doing. The verb *to be* is a special kind of verb. It usually expresses a way of being, as in, "Tom Thumb *was* small," or, "This drink *is* too cold." To find this sort of predicate, you can ask, "What is the subject like?" Later, we'll learn some of the different forms of the *to be* verb. When you know all of them, you'll be able to find the predicate easily.

Helping Verbs

The action of a verb isn't always happening in the present time. Helping verbs, also called auxiliary verbs, tell us when things happened. They show us whether the verb is in the past, the present, or the future. The grammatical term for past, present, and future is "tense." A verb is in the present tense, the past tense, or the future tense.

There are helping verbs that help a verb show tense. The verbs *be* and *have* become auxiliary verbs when they pair up with a main verb to show tense. The present of *be* is *is* or *are*. Do you know the past tense of *be*? It's *was* or *were*. The future is *will*.

The ballerina *will* leap into the air like a deer.
The ballerina *had* leaped into the air like a deer.

The main verb expresses the action, and the auxiliary verb tells you when the action happened. Look at what happens when you pair the verb *skate* with different auxiliary verbs:

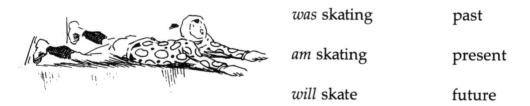

was skating	past
am skating	present
will skate	future

If a sentence is referring to the future, the verb will begin with words that refer to the future, such as *will*. If you're talking about the past, you can use verbs that refer to the past, such as *had* or *was* or *had been*, as in *was sprinting* or *had warbled*.

Getting Words to Agree

How do you know whether a subject is singular or plural? Most plural subjects end with the letter *s*, as in "two minotaur*s*" or "five rocket*s*." But verbs in sentences with *he* and *they* can seem tricky because an *s* doesn't always indicate the plural. Remember, "He *goes*," but, "They *go*."

Matching a plural verb with a plural subject is a lot like making dinner for your family: you want to have enough verb to go around. So, when you have a plural subject, such as "five boys," you'll give them a plural verb, such as "run."

If verbs have more than one part, they also have to agree in tense. If the first part of the verb is talking about the past, the second part of the verb must also be in the past tense. If the first part of the verb refers to the future, the second part of the verb must also be in the future tense. Otherwise, you'll have a time warp in the middle of your sentence.

Can you make these verbs agree?

I *will mowed* the grass tomorrow.
Mark *was sprint* when he twisted his ankle yesterday.

The Three Main Kinds of Sentences

Almost everything you say is in sentences, and sentences come in three basic kinds. These are called interrogative, declarative, and imperative. All have subjects and predicates and all end with a punctuation mark.

Declarative sentences are the most common. We use them to tell people what we think and what we see, and we punctuate them with a period. They can be as simple as, "I am cold," or as powerful as dynamite. With the brief declarative sentence, "I have a dream," Martin Luther King called up a dream that was shared by many people, and the declarative sentences he used to describe it helped to change our country.

We know an interrogative sentence by its telltale punctuation mark: the question mark (?). Interrogative sentences are questions. If you ask enough of them, you can begin to understand almost anything, such as: "Why are my eyes this color?" and, "Do stars burn out?"

To make an imperative sentence, you may need no more than one or two words. Imperative sentences are the kind of sentence we use to give orders or to make requests. "Stop!" "Please listen." If the order is urgent, we often punctuate it with an exclamation point. If an imperative is a request, it usually ends with a period, as in, "Hug me."

Where is the subject in a sentence like, "Stop!"? It's not spoken, but it's understood. It means, "You stop!" In many imperative sentences the "you" is not spoken or written, but is understood.

Learning About Literature

Biography

A biography is the true story of a person's life.

How do we find out enough about other people to write their biographies? Suppose you wanted to write the life story of someone you know. How would you find out about her? You could talk to her, and ask her questions about what happened in her life. You could find out about her from her parents, relatives, and other people who know her well. You could learn about her from her letters, if she let you look at them.

But suppose you were writing about someone who lived two hundred years ago. Suppose nobody who knew the person is still alive. How could you find out about the person's life? You would have to use mainly writings that people left behind, like old letters, and diaries, and newspaper stories.

Biographies are very interesting stories because they show the many different ways people can achieve things; maybe we can achieve such things, too. They show the mistakes people made; maybe we can avoid those mistakes. But most of all, biographies satisfy our curiosity about people, and help us understand other people as well as ourselves.

Autobiography

Some people write biographies of themselves. These are called *auto*biographies, because *auto* means *self*. An *auto*mobile is a car that goes by itself. An *auto*graph is your name written by yourself. An *auto*pilot on an airplane lets the plane fly by itself. So, it makes sense that an autobiography is the name for your own life written by yourself.

What would you write about if you wrote your autobiography? Things that happen to you can be exciting, if you write about them in an interesting way.

Most autobiographies are written in prose, but you can also write your autobiography in poetry or as a play or a song.

We read autobiographies to learn about the things people did, and the times they lived in. For example, you might read the famous autobiography of a German girl named Anne Frank. She wrote about what happened to her as a four-teen-year-old girl when she stayed in an attic with her family to hide from enemies during wartime. Or you could read about Frederick Douglass, an African-American man who escaped from slavery and wrote a book about his own life.

Fiction and Nonfiction

Fiction is the name we use for stories that are make-believe, such as fairy tales, or *Pollyanna* and *Alice in Wonderland.* But fiction isn't always different from the way things usually are. It can be so close to the truth that it seems as real as something that happened to you this morning. Or, fiction can be as fantastic as the most unbelievable fairy tale.

Not everything in a fictional story has to be made up. You could write a story in which you fly to the moon. *You*, of course, are real, and the *moon* is real, and many of the things that you could describe, such as the stars, and the wind, and the pull of gravity, would be real—but your trip through space would be fiction. It would be a trip you took in your imagination.

Nonfiction, on the other hand, is all about true things. Nothing is made up. Someone's biography is nonfiction; so is your autobiography. So are articles in your local newspaper, and school reports on science. History is nonfiction, too. Imagine writing history about the 1989 San Francisco earthquake, or a report about a high school sports team. An old proverb says, "Truth is stranger than fiction." Do you think that's true?

Introduction to Sayings

FOR PARENTS AND TEACHERS

Every culture has phrases and proverbs that make no sense when carried over literally into another culture. For many children, this section may not be needed; they will have picked up these sayings by hearing them at home and among their friends. But the category of sayings in the Core Knowledge Sequence has been the one most singled out for gratitude by teachers who work with children from home cultures that are different from the standard culture of literate American English.

Sayings and Phrases

Actions speak louder than words

This saying is used to explain that sometimes people don't mean what they say. We can often tell what they really mean, though, by observing what they do.

"Dad always says he hates cats—even JoJo!" Stewart shook his head.

"But," Tracy said, "last night, I saw Dad kiss the top of JoJo's head when he thought no one was looking!"

"Well!" Stewart said, "maybe he really loves JoJo, but keeps it a secret! They say actions speak louder than words!"

Beggars can't be choosers

People use this saying to mean that when you are needy you shouldn't be picky if someone offers help—even if it isn't exactly the ideal sort of help you would like.

"I didn't have time to eat breakfast," Janel said, "and I'm starving! But the only thing left in the cafeteria is spinach salad—yuk!"

"Beggars can't be choosers, Janel," Nikki said. "Looks like you'll have to eat something healthy for a change!"

Let bygones be bygones

People use this saying to mean that people should forget about the bad feelings they have about each other, and try to become friends again.

"I can't believe you wouldn't help me with my science project!" Tyrone banged on his desk with his fist. "Why wouldn't you help me?"

"Come on, Tyrone," Janine said. "I'll help you study now. There's no sense in staying mad. Just let bygones be bygones!"

Look before you leap

This saying applies to risks we might take in life. It means that you should be careful and think about a thing before you do it. You always look before you leap across a brook, so you know how far to jump and so you can judge how to land. If you forget to look and simply leap, you might land in deep water, or slip and fall on the rocky bank.

"Mom, Andrew asked me if I want to take over his paper route. Isn't that a great idea? Then I could save money to buy a new flute!"

"I don't know, honey," replied Mrs. Kravits. "You have music lessons almost every day after school, and you have to practice. Have you asked yourself if you really have time for lessons and a job? Better look before you leap."

One rotten apple spoils the whole barrel

People use this saying to mean that, sometimes, one bad person or thing can spoil a good group.

The kids in Mr. Small's homeroom class were known as the most well-behaved kids in the school. One day, a new boy joined the class. He was noisy and rude and encouraged the other kids to become rowdy. "I guess the days of this being a well-behaved class are over," Mr. Small said. "One rotten apple spoils the whole barrel!"

A place for everything and everything in its place

This expression means you should put things where they belong. People use this saying when they want people to be neat.

Josh always kicked his boots off in the hall when he came inside from playing. Josh's mother would tell him over and over again to put them in the closet instead of leaving them in the hall, but Josh always forgot "How many times do I have to tell you?" Josh's mother would say as she picked up his boots and returned them to the coat closet. "There's a place for everything, and everything in its place!"

The show must go on

When people say this, they mean that no matter what happens the project has to be finished. People usually say, "The show must go on," when a difficult problem has interfered with something they have been planning. We think this saying comes from the circus, where, even if dangerous acts like tightrope walking or lion taming sometimes led to tragedy, the circus, or Big Show, had to continue.

"We can't play in the championship next Saturday!" Karen said to her coach. "Lisa just sprained her ankle, Cecilia has the mumps, and Jenny has a cold—and they're the best soccer players on the team!"

"We've been practicing all season for this, Karen"—the soccer coach put her hands on her hips—"and we're not giving up now. The show must go on!"

His bark is worse than his bite

People use this saying to describe a person who seems a lot scarier or meaner than he or she really is.

"Mr. Kreckle sure is a grouch," Jason said.

"Yeah," Mickey said. "They shouldn't call him 'principal,' they should call him 'princi-paddle'!"

"You two are so silly!" Missy said. She sat down next to Jason. "You know Mr. Kreckle would never paddle anybody! He might get mad easily, but he's really a nice man. His bark is worse than his bite!"

Beat around the bush

People use this phrase to mean that someone is trying to avoid talking about something.

"So, how'd you do on your math test, Carlos?" Mr. Ramey asked.

Carlos cleared his throat. "Mom said dinner is almost ready. Maybe we should go to the table—" Carlos's father did not move from the couch. "She's making spaghetti and meatballs," Carlos said. "Isn't that your favorite?"

"Sure is," Mr. Ramey said. "Didn't you say you were getting that math test back today, Carlos?"

"Well, I did get my volcano project back today, and my spelling quiz . . ."

"Come on, Carlos, stop beating around the bush." Mr. Ramey got up and put his arm around Carlos's shoulder. "Tell me about your math test."

Clean bill of health

People use this saying when they are explaining that something is in perfect shape.

Latasha worked for an hour on her math homework. She went over every problem, and did her best to make sure every equation was done correctly. When she was finished, she showed the two pages of homework to her mother. Latasha waited quietly for her mother to correct her mistakes. But, instead, her mother looked up at her and said, "You've certainly improved, Latasha. This homework gets a clean bill of health. You did all of these equations perfectly!"

Cold shoulder

When someone ignores you, even though they know you, they could be giving you "the cold shoulder." People use this saying to describe the way someone ignores or acts unfriendly to someone else.

"Ever since I told Daryl he should lose some weight, he pretends he doesn't know me," Christina said. "I said 'hi' to him at recess, and he turned to his friend and said, 'Did you hear that, Billy? I thought I heard a chipmunk squeak'!"

"Well, if you told me I looked like a small hippopotamus, I'd give you the cold shoulder too!"

A feather in your cap

This expression is used when a person gets credit for something that he or she can be proud of.

Camille loved to play the violin and practiced every day in her bedroom. She played in the school orchestra, and dreamed of one day being first chair.

One day during rehearsal, Camille played along with the rest of the string section. They were playing a piece she had practiced by herself for days.

"Stop!" the conductor said. Everyone in the music room went silent. "Camille, let me hear that measure again."

Camille picked up her bow and played ten perfect notes.

"Beautiful!" the conductor said. "*That* is the way to play."

As Camille beamed, the violinist next to her leaned over to whisper: "What a wonderful compliment! It's a real feather in your cap."

Last straw

When a person has been pushed as far as he will go, he might say that it is "the last straw." This term comes from the saying, "The straw that broke the camel's back," in which one small straw can have a big effect if the camel is already weighed down.

"What's wrong, Paul?" Linnie asked. "Do you need any help?"

Paul was kneeling down next to his bicycle, trying to remove his front tire, which had gone flat. "Just leave me alone, Linnie!" he snapped. "First I fell off of my bike on the way to school and skinned my elbow. Then, once I got to math class, I remembered that I left my homework at home. Then Bob Banks tripped me when we were playing basketball and I bruised my knee." Paul fiddled with the air valve on his tire. "And now this—I've had it! This is the last straw!"

On its last legs

People use this phrase when they are saying that something is about to die or break down for good.

"This has been a good old truck," Mr. Johnson said to his grandson, Vincent. They drove down the bumpy dirt road and the truck sputtered and groaned. "I've had it for nearly twenty years!"

Vincent was amazed that the truck was so much older than he.

"But you hear those noises it's making, Vincent?" The old man shook his head. "I'm afraid this truck is just about on its last legs."

Rule the roost

People use this to describe what a person is doing when he or she is the head of a group of people, or bosses a group of people around.

Katey and June were watching television in their living room. When Megan came in from playing, she ran in front of her sisters and changed the channel.

"Hey!" Katey said. "We were here first."

"Too bad," Megan said. "I'm the oldest."

"You may be the oldest," June said, "but that doesn't mean you rule the roost!"

Touch and go

People use this phrase to describe a situation where things are a little tricky, and you don't know what may happen.

The tightrope walker began his trip across the Grand Canyon. He walked steadily and slowly upon the thick rope, using a long pole to help keep his balance. When he got to the middle, he looked down for a moment, then began to teeter on the rope. The crowd gasped. Then, just in time, he regained his balance and continued to walk. When he got to the other side, he told a reporter, "Everything was fine until I looked down into the canyon. From then on, it was touch and go, and I wasn't sure whether or not I'd make it across."

II.

GEOGRAPHY, WORLD CIVILIZATION, AND AMERICAN CIVILIZATION

Introduction to Geography

FOR PARENTS AND TEACHERS

The first two books in this series explained that young children can build a strong foundation for geography by learning the main features and places of the earth—continents, countries, states, major rivers, mountains, and cities. In the second book, children learned that some of our states have the odd shapes they do because they are bounded by rivers that don't flow in straight lines. Both books provided maps, information, and activities to help children enjoy map work. Even in the earliest grades, children can begin to understand the effects of land on people and people on land.

By third grade, children are ready for more numerous and subtle connections. In this book they will not only read about great Roman engineers who built roads to connect their sprawling empire, they'll also learn that those roads, built for commerce and control, allowed the spread of Rome's language and laws. They'll read about the search for gold that lured explorers across the sea in small ships and about the furs that kept Europeans interested in the "New World" even when they didn't find gold.

In this book, geography continues but goes beyond the initial, necessary learning of spatial forms. Here we broaden the field, introducing the relationships among culture, agriculture, history, economy, and the land. With clear and engaging examples from history, children can begin to learn the importance of geography in both the past and the present.

We all know that where we live gives a certain shape to our lives. But we may not think about this very much unless the freeway backs up for an hour or heavy spring rains make their way into the basement. And even then we are probably not thinking in the broadest sense of the ways the land, with its rivers, rainfall, and vegetation, its mountains and minerals, shapes the lives of the people who live on it.

The geography and history sections of this book ask children to think about land in this broad sense, connecting characteristics of the land to peoples' lives or to historical events. This transforms geography from the rote learning of lists of geographical features into the living subject it should be.

NOTE TO PARENTS AND TEACHERS: *We strongly recommend a review of Geography, World Civilization, and American Civilization in Books One and Two of* The Core Knowledge Series.

Bellerophon Books, (805) 965-7034, offers three coloring books, Ancient Greece, Ancient Rome, *and* The Thirteen Colonies, *that complement the material in this section.*

Dover Publications offers a Story of the Vikings Coloring Book *and a* Historic Sailing Ships Coloring Book, *which would be very useful in giving today's children some idea of the hardships of travel in the past. A good vacation project would be Dover's easy-to-make* Columbus Discovers America Panorama *or their* Maya Diorama. *For a free catalogue write to Dover Publications, 31 East Second Street, Mineola, NY 11501.*

World Geography

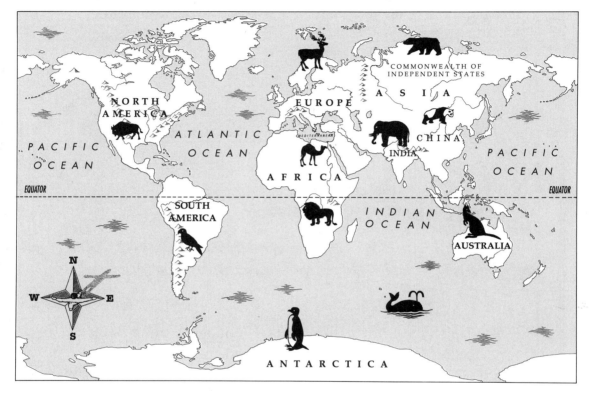

Our Watery World

O ur world is mostly water as you can see from the map of the world above. Now look at a globe, and you will easily see the largest ocean. It is the Pacific Ocean. The next largest is the Atlantic Ocean. Third in size is the Indian Ocean. Say these names aloud as you point to them on the map above.

Now we'll look for smaller bodies of water. Some of these are called seas. Can you find the Mediterranean Sea? It separates Europe from Africa. We have talked in previous books of this series about the Mediterranean, in stories about King Tut and Alexander the Great. Their countries, Egypt and Greece, border the Mediterranean Sea.

Soon we are going to learn more about civilization near the Mediterranean Sea. But first, let's make sure that we know the basic map names. Look at your world map again for the seven largest pieces of land. They are called continents. Do you remember their names? In order of size, they are Asia, Africa, North America (where our country is), South America, Antarctica, Europe (which is attached to the western side of Asia), and Australia.

Say these names aloud as you put your finger on their places on the map.

Back to the Mediterranean

Now we can go back to the Mediterranean Sea. Earlier we looked at the eastern end of this large sea (look right for east, left for west). But now we want to study the middle part. Do you see a peninsula jutting south from Europe into the middle of the Mediterranean? It looks almost exactly like a boot you could wear on your foot. This is Italy.

Halfway up the boot is a city called Rome, on the Tiber River. This is the city that came to rule all the land around the Mediterranean Sea. At that time, Rome's power was so great that the whole Mediterranean Sea was thought of as a Roman lake!

The Roman Empire: All Kinds of Lands

When Rome came to rule all the land around the Mediterranean Sea, it spread writing and laws to places in Western Europe from the countries we now call Spain, France, and Great Britain to the area east of the Rhine River at least as far as the Danube River. Can you find these places on the map of Roman lands? Spain is at the far western end of the Mediterranean. After you find Spain, look for the Strait of Gibraltar, which is the narrow water passage between the Mediterranean Sea and the Atlantic Ocean. Spain is part of the continent of Europe. North of Spain and the continent of Europe and on the eastern side of the

Atlantic Ocean, you will see two large islands that are close together. The larger island is Great Britain. Great Britain is separated from the rest of Europe by two bodies of water, the English Channel and the North Sea.

Rome came to rule many of the Mediterranean lands by winning battles. As the Roman army conquered lands, it built new roads. Cities grew up along these roads. Some cities started as army camps. Others started as farming colonies for army veterans. Veterans were men who left the Roman army when they became too old to fight. The city of Cologne in Germany, for example, was first a veterans' colony called Colony of Agrippina, named for the wife of a Roman ruler.

The Romans were great engineers.

This road, built by the Romans over two thousand years ago, is called the Appian Way.

They connected towns and cities with roads paved with stone slabs. These roads lasted for centuries. (After Britain was separated from Rome, it took the British over a thousand years to build roads as good as those the Romans had made there.) There were many hills and mountains in the lands that Rome ruled in Europe, Asia, and northern Africa. But Roman road builders were so skillful they could build bridges across the valleys using great rows of arches.

A ceremonial carriage like this one might have rolled down the Appian Way during a festival.

Rome also used these great rows of arches to bring clean, fresh water from the mountains to the cities. These were called "aqueducts," meaning channels for water. The arches held up the ducts so they could cross over valleys in a straight line, channeling water to the city. Some of these aqueducts are still standing in the countryside in Spain, France, Italy, and elsewhere. One of them still supplies water to a town in Spain, and another to a famous fountain in Rome. Think about how often you use water and you will see how important these aqueducts were. You can read more about aqueducts in the Fine Arts section of this book.

You can read more about this famous aqueduct in the Fine Arts section.

Collecting stamps is an excellent way for children to learn geography. Very inexpensive packets of canceled stamps can be purchased from stamp dealers, and notebooks to hold them are also reasonable in price. You can ask a local stamp dealer for help and information.

Geography of the Americas

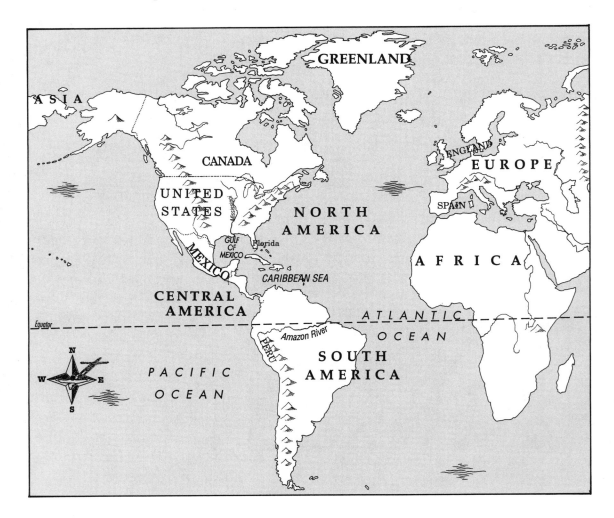

Back to North America

NOTE TO PARENTS AND TEACHERS: We recommend a brief review of Spain's conquests in the New World in Book One of this series to help place the American Indians and colonists who lived further to the north in their proper context.

Let's look at our continent, North America, on the map. Can you name the three largest countries of this continent? Are you in one of them right at this minute? Which one?

Long after the Indians came to North and South America, a European named Christopher Columbus crossed the Atlantic Ocean in 1492. Columbus wasn't trying to come here. He was looking for a shorter route to Asia.

On his first voyage Columbus explored the islands in the Caribbean Sea where he landed. (Look at the map again and find the Caribbean Sea.) On a later voyage, he crossed the Caribbean and found the North American continent. But he still thought he had reached Asia! He called the people he and his sailors met here Indians because he thought he was near the Indies, which are islands southeast of Asia. Descendants of these natives of America still call themselves American Indians or Indians, but they are also called Native Americans. You'll hear all three names in this book.

This old painting shows Christopher Columbus landing on the Caribbean island of San Salvador.

Not long after Columbus's voyage, many Spaniards came to the New World. They found a way to sail around the bottom of South America and discovered the Pacific Ocean. Cortés and Pizarro and their fighting men defeated the Aztecs in Mexico and the Incas in Peru. The cities of these Native Americans were full of gold! The Spaniards became rich. Men from other countries in Europe sailed west to make their fortunes, too.

No Gold

Spaniards ventured into North America. One explorer, named Ponce de León, went to present-day Florida. Some say he was trying to find a Fountain of Youth. This water was supposed to keep people forever young! Do you think he found it?

Other Spanish explorers were led by a man named Coronado. They rode horses through the south-western part of our country for almost three years. They went searching because of a legend, too. They had heard of the Seven Cities of Cibolá (see bow LA), which you may also hear called the "Seven Cities of Gold." There were no cities of gold. Instead they found the villages of the Zunis, a farming tribe that is part of the Pueblo Indians, and they came upon the Grand Canyon.

Francisco Coronado and his men.

Another explorer, Hernando De Soto, helped to conquer the Incas and made a fortune. Then he went to Florida. He kept going north and then west until he

Hernando De Soto.

De Soto discovering the Mississippi. How would you feel if you found a great river? How do you think De Soto and his followers feel in this picture?

found the great Mississippi River. De Soto died soon after he found the Mississippi, and was buried in its waters.

Many of these explorers thought they had failed because they could find no gold in North America. But later on, their country, Spain, laid claim to the lands they had seen. In Florida, Spain built our country's first European settlement and called it St. Augustine. Settlements were also made in our Southwest and in California. Also, horses were brought to American Indians by Spanish explorers. These animals would change the Indians' lives.

Building St. Augustine.

Spanish priests came to the New World as missionaries to bring Christianity to the Indians. They traveled as widely as the soldiers, and they set up small Christian settlements where they lived and preached. Most of these settlements, called missions, were in the Southwest and in Texas and California. You may have heard of one of them—the Alamo.

The Santa Clara Mission in California.

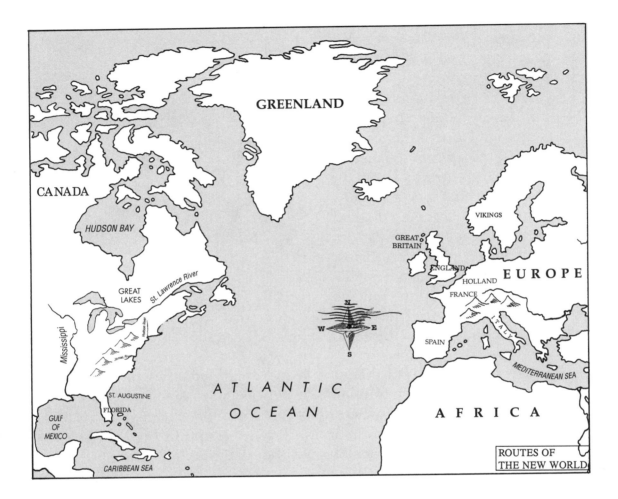

ROUTES OF
THE NEW WORLD

Before Columbus

Now let's look at the Atlantic coast of Canada. Can you find it on the map above? Almost five hundred years before Columbus sailed, men from the far north of Europe had reached that land. They were called Vikings, and their leader was Leif Ericson.

Leif's father had set up a colony on the huge island of Greenland. Can you find the island? Leif and his warrior-sailors set out westward, perhaps looking for waters rich with fish. Or a storm

Leif Ericson

might have forced them west until they landed on the shore of Canada. No one is really sure.

These journeys weren't known to Columbus, though. We know about the Vikings today from stories and because archaeologists have found traces of them in Canada.

More Exciting Journeys

After hearing reports of the New World and the treasure found there by the Spaniards, other Europeans were excited. Some hoped to find gold in the New World. Others sailed north of where Columbus landed, looking for a water passage through the New World to Asia. This fabled route was called the Northwest Passage.

John Cabot sailed from England and reached the lands near Canada that the Vikings had settled so long before. Like Columbus, Cabot was born in Italy, but he sailed as an Englishman. So, when he landed he set up flags from both places.

Another Italian sailed to the New World. His name was Verrazano, and he was sent by the King of France. He sailed up the Atlantic coast to Canada but he had no luck finding a way through to China. He went on a later voyage from which he never returned.

Then the King of France sent Cartier. Cartier found the St. Lawrence River in Canada in 1535. Can you find it on the map? He was thrilled because

Jacques Cartier in front of a map of the territory he explored.

he thought it was the Northwest Passage to China. But as he sailed up the river, he realized his mistake.

Look at a globe or the map on page 76. Do you see any way to get to Asia through the New World?

Another Bargain

It took over seventy years for the French to try again. Then Champlain sailed to the New World and into the St. Lawrence River. But he was not like the French explorers who had gone before him. He was not just looking for gold or a way to Asia. He wanted furs. He traded with native peoples who trapped beavers and other fur-bearing animals. France sold the furs for a lot of money in Europe.

Champlain claimed the land for the French King, calling it New France. And he founded the first settlement in New France, at a place the Algonquin Indians called "Quebec." Soon many French people came to live in Canada to trade with the Indians and fish the waters along the Atlantic shore. (Now, when you hear of Lake Champlain, in the state of New York, will you know where the name comes from?)

The Dutch, too, sailed for America to set up trading posts. Henry Hudson, who was English, worked for Dutch traders. He discovered a great river. Have you heard of

Henry Hudson.

the Hudson River in New York? (Find it on your map.) Hudson later claimed land in Canada for England. A large bay there is named for him.

The Dutch settled at the mouth of the Hudson River. Their leader bought the land from the Indians for twenty-four dollars in trinkets! Today that little settlement has turned into New York City.

Mother Country

But it was England, an island country in northern Europe, that really began our country. Do you remember where England is? (Hint: Look back on the Routes of the New World map. You looked for Great Britain when you read about the Roman Empire. England is the country that takes up most of the land on the island of Great Britain.)

The Englishman Sir Walter Raleigh tried to start a colony along the Atlantic coast. He sent men and women by ship to live in the New World. People who settled the New World were called colonists. But no one knows what happened to Raleigh's colony. English people who came later with supplies found that the island settlement had disappeared. (You can read about the lost colony in Book One of this series.)

English settlements were finally made along the James River in the area we now call Virginia, and on the coast of Massachusetts. Later, other colonies were started along the whole length of the Atlantic coast north of Florida. Soon, many more colonists came from England. They moved westward to the Appalachian mountains.

Sir Walter Raleigh poses for a portrait with his son.

The Land Shapes the Ways People Live

It's very important to think about how the land shaped the way people lived in the colonies. For one thing, there are many rivers. You can see them on the map below. That meant boats and ships could connect the settlements with one another. It meant that using the ocean and rivers, people could ship goods back and forth between England and settlements in the New World.

RIVERS OF THE
EASTERN UNITED STATES

Notice the mountains, too. For almost 150 years, the mountains kept the English colonists from moving further west. The settlers stayed in one area and started towns and governments. This helped them learn how to govern a new country, which would later become the United States.

There are two more things you should look at before you leave this map: the Great Lakes and the Mississippi River. From the Great Lakes and the Mississippi eastward to the Atlantic there were many huge forests. And in these forests lived the native people whom the colonists were going to meet. (As you will learn, their ways were different from the Indians farther west or down in Mexico and South America. And there weren't nearly as many of them as there were Aztecs and Incas.) These Native Americans were going to be very important to the colonists. And the colonists were going to change the Indians' lives completely. The land itself had a share in shaping everyone. It always has.

What Makes a River Great?

Why are some rivers so famous? Because of their beauty? Their length and width? The songs and stories written about them?

Some rivers are famous for all those reasons. But another, more scientific measure of a river's greatness is the size of the land the river drains. That area is called a watershed or river basin. (You might know another word for basin: sink.)

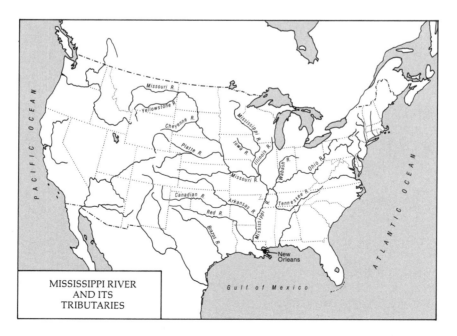

MISSISSIPPI RIVER
AND ITS
TRIBUTARIES

Not just one river but a whole system of rivers flows into a river basin. A river system is made up of a river and all its tributaries. (A tributary is a stream or river that flows into a larger river.)

Look at the map of the Mississippi and its tributaries. Put your finger where the river pours into the Gulf of Mexico (look in the state of Louisiana, around the city of New Orleans). Move your finger to the north, going up the path of the Mississippi. You'll see that the waters of many other rivers eventually flow into the Mississippi: the Arkansas, Ohio, Tennessee, Missouri, and Yellowstone, to name a few. The Mississippi River system drains about 3,250,000 square kilometers of land—that's almost half of the United States!

Around the world there are great rivers with huge watersheds. Look in an atlas to find these rivers and the lands they drain. In Asia, look for the Ob, the Huand He, the Ganges, and the Indus. In Africa, look for the Zaire (sometimes known as the Congo), the Nile, and the Niger. In South America, look for the Amazon, the Orinoco, and the Paraná. In North and Central America, look for the Mackenzie and the Yukon. In Australia, look for the Murray-Darling. In Europe, look for the Danube, the Rhine, and the Volga. Do all of these rivers drain into an ocean? Can you tell which river has the largest river basin?

Introduction to World Civilization

FOR PARENTS AND TEACHERS

In the World Civilization section of Book Three, we devote a segment to ancient Rome, followed by a segment on the rise of Islam in Asia and Africa. Amid the stories, you will find suggested activities that will help make these historical stories more vivid and memorable. These suggestions, in turn, can serve as models for other hands-on activities.

Nowadays young children all over the world are learning some of the same things about the history of human civilizations—about Egypt and other African civilizations, about Chinese history, the Babylonians, the Incas, Aztecs, and Maya, the Persians, Greeks, and Romans. Today, perhaps for the first time ever, children on all continents are learning not just the history of their ancestors, but also the broader history of all mankind.

The study of world history is particularly appropriate in the United States, where our population has come from every part of the world. To know world history is partly to know ourselves. Writing about the United States, the great American writer Herman Melville said:

> Settled by the people of all nations, all nations may claim her for their own. You cannot spill a drop of American blood without spilling the blood of the whole world . . . We are not a nation so much as a world.

The diversity of America is becoming the norm for other nations of the modern world. People from all over are to be found in almost every country. Some come to find better jobs, others to participate in international business. The modern international economy has turned the whole world into a single marketplace. The new global economy has created a new cosmopolitanism which makes it desirable that children in all countries, and especially in our own culturally diverse one, should share a basic knowledge of world history.

How reassuring it is to know that our children, by studying the larger history of mankind, will learn much the same history as children in other lands. The historical knowledge they will share will cause them to understand that people in every country have a common human heritage and a common stake in fostering a peaceful and civil world.

World Civilization

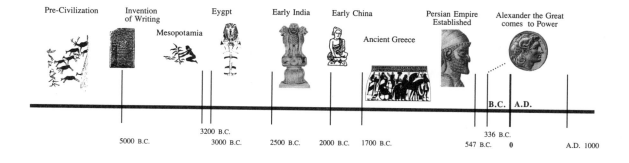

Pre-Civilization   Invention of Writing   Eygpt   Early India   Early China   Persian Empire Established   Alexander the Great comes to Power

Mesopotamia   Ancient Greece

B.C. | A.D.

3200 B.C.

5000 B.C.   3000 B.C.   2500 B.C.   2000 B.C.   1700 B.C.   336 B.C.

547 B.C.   0   A.D. 1000

What Happened So Far

In Books One and Two of this series, we said that the first cities began because people were able to grow extra food along the fertile banks of the Nile River in Egypt and the Tigris and Euphrates rivers in Babylonia. Because of the extra food, more people could settle in these places.

The same thing happened beside the rivers of ancient India and China. The land near rivers in those countries was also rich. That meant farmers could harvest food crops to feed more people than just themselves. And many people there could stop moving around to find food.

When people lived together in one place, there had to be rules and rulers. In Book One, you can read about one of these ancient rulers, King Tut.

In Book Two you can read about a people, the Persians, who conquered the cities of the eastern Mediterranean and went all the way to India. You can also read about another people, the Greeks, some of whom tried a new way of governing themselves—democracy. For a time these Greeks voted for their leaders, as we do.

But a King from northern Greece defeated all of the cities of the Greeks, and his son went on to conquer the whole Persian Empire. This young man was Alexander the Great. In Book Two we followed his army all the way from Greece to Egypt to India!

Alexander won his empire in only ten years. Then he died, still a young man, and his generals governed what he had won. This new empire mixed

Greek ideas with the ideas of other ancient civilizations. Out of these mixed ideas the Greeks created beautiful buildings and flourishing trade, and studied science and mathematics. This Greek-speaking civilization spread westward to meet a city that spoke Latin, and was not nearly as "civilized" as Alexander's empire. But the new city, Rome, was growing in strength.

What We Owe to Ancient Rome

You may have heard of the city of Rome even before you opened this book. You may have seen Rome, the capital city of Italy, on your television. Often, the pope of the Roman Catholic Church is seen on television in St. Peter's, a huge church. Or perhaps your family came to this country from Italy.

You may have heard the pope use a language you didn't understand. That language is Latin. It isn't used anymore except on special occasions, but it was once spoken by ancient Romans throughout their empire. Many languages spoken today in Europe and America grew out of the Latin language. In the Americas, the Hispanic countries, including Mexico and all of Central and South America, are called Latin America. That's because the Spanish and Portuguese languages spoken in those countries come from Latin. The French language and many words in English also have Latin roots, so even North America has a connection with ancient Rome.

But Latin wasn't the only thing that Rome spread. Many of the most important parts of our religions, governments, building design, art, and law came from Rome. Or, because Rome borrowed them, many of these things came *through* Rome from Greece and the earlier places you read about in Books One and Two. Many of today's civilizations received from Rome not only their languages but also some of their habits and ideas. Why is ancient Rome so important to so many of today's nations? Its empire was so big that it included dozens of today's nations, and it lasted so long that its habits and ideas took root in them.

We are going to find out how a tiny town of round huts grew to become the city of Rome, and how that city became the ruler of so many lands in Europe, Asia, and Africa. In a way, we will be finding out where some important ideas and customs in the United States came from.

Writing Down Dates

To understand which cities and events came first and which followed, we have to put numbers on the years of history. Let's talk about how to write dates. Have you learned to write the month and the day and the year? You certainly know what month and day your birthday is!

But you may not know that we give years their dates based on another birthday. The birthday of Jesus, whom Christians call "Christ," is the starting point. Every date "before Christ" was born is called "B.C.," and the years B.C. count down to the year zero—when Jesus was born. If we say that the city of Rome began in the year 753 B.C., we mean it started 753 years before Jesus was born. Every date after Jesus's birth is called A.D., and the years A.D. go up from zero. A.D. is an abbreviation for the Latin words "Year of Our Lord"—*Anno Domini*. If you were born in A.D. 1983, that means you were born 1,983 years after Jesus was born. Our Declaration of Independence was written in A.D. 1776, or 1,776 years after Jesus was born. If we see a date like 1776 with just numbers, it usually means A.D.

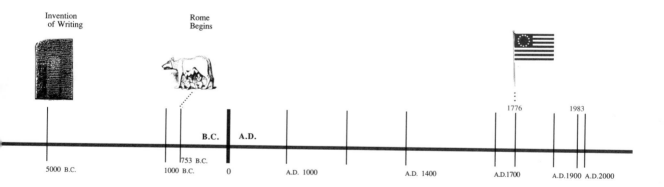

Rome Begins with Two Boys and a Wolf

We don't really know when farmers and shepherds first put up round huts on one of the seven hills where Rome now stands. But the Romans had an exciting story about it. They said that Romulus, a son of the war god, Mars, began their city.

Romulus and his twin brother, Remus, were supposed to be the descendants of Mars and a Latin princess. But they had no royal house to live in. As babies, the twins were thrown into the Tiber Tiver by a jealous uncle! But they did not drown. They were found on the river's bank by a female wolf, who gave them milk and saved them. That's why the wolf became the symbol of Rome. Later, a shepherd took care of the twins until they were young men.

When Romulus and Remus left the shepherd's home they decided to build a city on the Tiber, near the place where they had almost drowned. But they argued terribly over who would rule the city and Romulus killed Remus. Romulus built the city alone and became its first king. He ruled Rome for many years and then mysteriously disappeared during a storm. The Romans believed Romulus had been changed into a god and began to worship him. Does this story explain how Rome got its name?

This is a drawing of a famous statue of Romulus and Remus. You can look for the statue in the picture of the Forum on page 94.

Roman Gods and Goddesses

The Romans worshiped not only Romulus, but many other gods and goddesses. Each was supposed to have special powers and concerns. Some of these were very much like the Greek gods. (See Book Two for an introduction to the Greek gods and goddesses.) Jupiter, their chief god, was not very different from the Greeks' Zeus. Neptune, like the Greek god Poseidon, ruled the sea. Venus was the goddess of love and beauty, and Mercury was the

Inside a temple of Jupiter.

"messenger of the gods." (Have you noticed that the planets in our solar system have these Roman names—Jupiter, Venus, Mercury, Mars, Pluto, Neptune, Saturn, and Uranus?)

Many beautiful temples honoring these gods were later built in the city of Rome and elsewhere in the empire. In these temples you could see huge statues of the gods. People would bring gifts as offerings to the gods, and priests would perform ceremonies intended to keep the gods happy with the people.

One goddess, Vesta, was guardian of the Roman fireside. A group of young women called Vestals were supposed to keep a fire lit in her honor. Romans believed their city would fall if the flame ever went out. They also believed that spirits inhabited places and things, just as other peoples including Egyptians and many Native Americans did.

Vestals keeping the fire lit.

A coin honoring the goddess Vesta.

The Roman Republic: Something New

The story of the twins Romulus and Remus is a legend. Rome wasn't really started because the twins almost drowned there but because the land Rome occupies by the Tiber River was an especially good place for people to settle.

You can see how busy the Forum was from this drawing. What sorts of things are the people doing?

The river and the hills around it probably made it hard for enemies to approach. The people settled on the hills first; later they built places in the valley to meet and trade. Their buildings and markets were called forums.

At the forums they also met to argue and settle their differences. Often they fought there, too. But gradually they developed a new form of government called a republic. This is how it happened.

The Roman people didn't want anyone too strong to lead their country. They had been ruled by kings, but after they forced a particularly bad one to leave Rome, they didn't want anyone like him to get power over them again. So they decided to elect not one, but two leaders every year. These leaders were called consuls. Why do you think the Romans found it safer to give control over their army and money to two consuls, rather than just one?

Since the consuls changed so often, the real ruler of the Roman Republic was an assembly called the Senate, a group of about three hundred older

The Bellerophon coloring book *Ancient Rome* has drawings of temples and festivals. *Bellerophon Books (805) 965-7034.*

A consul wearing a loose garment called a toga.

This mural painted on a wall shows a famous speaker, Cicero, talking to the Senate.

men who owned land. The Senate had even more say about money than the consuls, often telling consuls where and how much to spend. The Senate also communicated with other cities and countries.

There were other assemblies of Romans, but they were controlled by the Senate and the upper class in various ways. In Rome, upper-class people were called patricians to distinguish them from ordinary people, called plebeians.

Plebeians Versus Patricians

As Rome grew larger and more wealthy, the plebeians grew more and more angry at the patricians. Many plebeians had become as wealthy as the patricians, and they wanted the government to represent their interests. Some of the wealthy plebeians thought they should be allowed to be consuls, as the patricians were. After about

Roman clothes were different from ours. This plebeian man wears a short cloak over his toga. Why do you think they wore cloaks instead of coats?

two hundred years of arguing and fighting, the plebeians gained nearly equal rights.

The main reason the patricians came to share their rights with the plebeians was that Rome needed all its people for warfare. Rome was constantly struggling with nearby towns or northern invaders for farmland. When the city was at war, the plebeians were needed to make up an army. When a victory was gained, the plebeians wanted a part of what was won.

A carving of a patrician family.

At this time Rome was still a republic run by wealthy people, and generally these people were intelligent, honest, and loyal to the city. The Romans believed that the wealthiest people made the best rulers. But later, when they became too rich, the wealthy forgot their duty and lived only for themselves.

The Proud Coriolanus

Here is a story about the Roman Republic that shows how the people struggled for power, how they viewed duty and pride, and how bravery and mercy shaped the culture of Rome. After you read it, try to describe what the story tells you about the Romans.

A proud patrician named Marcius had been fighting for the city since his youth. The plebeians admired Marcius's courage and forcefulness. But they also felt bitterly toward him, for they thought Marcius spoke and acted as though ordinary people like themselves had no rights. The plebeians were hungry and poor, and they resented Marcius's wealth, comfortable life, and proud ways.

One day, the people of Rome learned that a neighboring town, Corioli, was getting ready to attack them. In the battle, Marcius fought with so much bravery that the army gave him the name Coriolanus, after the town he defeated. He didn't want the new name. He was too proud to accept any reward for doing what he saw as his duty. But he was called Coriolanus anyway.

The plebeians were so grateful to Coriolanus for protecting them that they wanted to make him a consul. But some of their jealous leaders reminded the people that they should hate Coriolanus because he was a patrician. Many of the plebeians became angry. They admired Coriolanus and wanted his protection, but they did not know if they could trust him. Would he provide them with food? Would he give them the rights they desired? Then when Coriolanus spoke out, they had their answer. Coriolanus himself told the plebeians that they were not loyal to him and shouldn't have any rights.

The plebeians became enraged. Although many wished to take his life, they decided to put Coriolanus on trial instead. Angered by this treatment, Coriolanus's pride flared up and he spoke harshly against the plebeians. He was banished from the city, which meant that he had to leave and could not return.

Coriolanus wanted revenge. He wanted to pay back Rome for banishing him. So he returned to Corioli, the town he had once conquered, and led their army in another attack against Rome.

A Brave Mother and Wife

Rome was helpless, and her people begged for mercy. But Coriolanus was unmoved and refused them. Then an amazing thing happened. Coriolanus's proud, patrician mother and his gentle wife came forward. They told him they loved him and wanted to save him from the disgrace of destroying the city that was once his home. Suddenly these two women, members of the highest class of Roman citizens, went down on their knees in the dusty road. Looking up at the proud, angry Coriolanus, they said that he and his army would have to enter Rome over their dead bodies.

Coriolanus could not kill his mother and wife. In the

Coriolanus's mother and wife persuade him not to destroy Rome.

face of their bravery, he and the Corioli army turned around and left. Rome was saved by these two brave women.

Many other Roman stories have female heroines. Although women in Rome were not considered equal to men, they had much more freedom and wealth than women in other ancient civilizations. For instance, Greek and Eastern women were supposed to live in a separate part of the house from the men. But in Rome, women could do business, write their own wills, and, if divorced, keep their own money.

Cornelia, a Roman noblewoman, was greatly admired for her learning.

What were the names of these brave women you just read about? Coriolanus's mother and wife have names you probably haven't heard, Venturia and Volumnia. But we still use quite a few names from the Latin language. Here are just a few: Clara, Julian, Justin, Maria, Natalie, and Mark. Clara means "bright," and Mark comes from Mars, the Roman god of war.

Do you have a friend or a relative called Patricia? When you were reading about the patricians were you surprised to hear a whole group of people called by a name you've heard before? That name comes to us from the Romans, and it's not surprising to discover it means "well born."

Do you know where your name comes from and what it means? There are books in the library that can tell you.

You may want to act out the story of Coriolanus yourself. Here are some questions you might want to discuss: Why would Coriolanus, a patrician, want to keep certain rights from the plebeians? Why would the town of Corioli, once conquered by Coriolanus, side with him against Rome? Why would Coriolanus's mother and wife be willing to lose their lives to save Rome? Can you think of other ways his wife and mother could have prevented Coriolanus from attacking Rome?

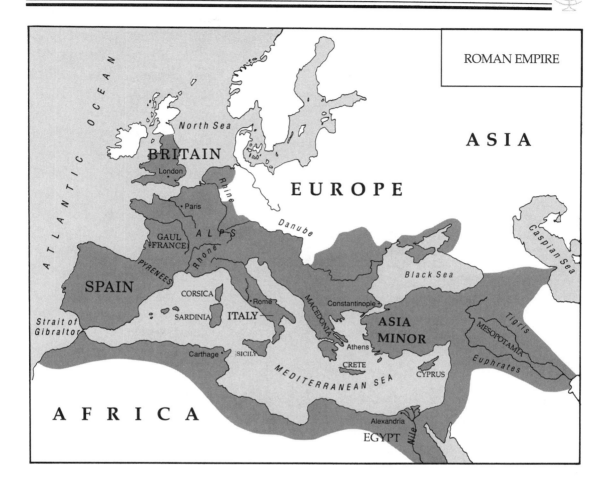

War with Africa

By 265 B.C. Rome gained power over all of Italy. The other towns and tribes of Italy were often partners of Rome. The partnerships weren't always happy ones, but most of the time the towns and tribes didn't hate Rome. And that became very important when, later on, a really big war began with a city in Africa. The city was Carthage. On the map above you can find it if you look at the coast of Africa, across the Mediterranean from Italy's "toe."

At the time Carthage controlled the island of Sicily, half of North Africa, and the south of Spain. You can look for these lands on the map. Carthage had spread even farther than Rome. In two separate, long wars, Carthage and Rome fought for rule of the Mediterranean. The Romans called these the Punic Wars.

Rome won the first Punic War and gained most of Sicily. But, during the

Hannibal and his army crossing the Alps.

second war, a very famous Carthaginian general almost conquered Rome. This general was named Hannibal. During the Punic Wars, Hannibal put together a great army in the country we now call Spain. On a map, you can trace Hannibal's journey from Spain to Italy in his attempt to conquer Rome. You can see that he had to go through France (then called Gaul), and cross the high mountains called the Alps.

He had over sixty thousand soldiers with him, not to mention forty huge beasts that, it is said, terrified many Roman soldiers who had never seen such creatures before. What were these frightening animals? Elephants!

Hannibal won many battles against the Romans, although he never captured the city of Rome itself. The Romans finally won the second Punic War because they just wouldn't give up, and also because they had a navy. They attacked Carthage from the sea. Hannibal had to go home to defend Carthage, and was finally defeated. Rome took a lot of money from Carthage to make up for the terrible damage Hannibal had done. Rome took the part of Spain ruled by Carthage too, with its silver mines. Much later, in a short war, Rome destroyed much of Carthage and made it and northern Africa part of the Roman Empire.

The Romans as Rulers

When the Romans conquered new lands, they would put a Roman governor in charge of the defeated people. The defeated people would pay a tax, in the form of money or food, which was sent back to Rome.

Sometimes the Roman governors were greedy, and the defeated people suffered. Usually, though, the Romans respected the customs and religions of the people they conquered. Although the Roman governor remained in charge, he would let the local ruling class take care of local matters.

As Rome became more used to ruling its growing empire, the Romans learned to make partners of the people they defeated by declaring the people in the lands held by Rome to be Roman citizens.

The Greeks Conquer Roman Hearts

Do you know what a century is? A century is one hundred years. That's about how long it took Rome to make her empire twice as big as before. Some of this land came from wars with kingdoms around the eastern Mediterranean. Sometimes Rome started the wars, sometimes others did, but, with its big and powerful army, Rome always ended up winning them. One king just left his land to Rome, because he wanted it to be in good hands. Much of what had been the Greek empire of Alexander in Asia now belonged to Rome.

Many enemy soldiers captured in war were made slaves. Well-educated Greeks went to Rome as slaves along with thousands and thousands of other prisoners. They became teachers and physicians to the rich, and a very large number were freed by their masters. But many remained slaves.

Then an odd thing happened. The Roman masters of the Mediterranean began to be won over by Greek culture and ideas. Romans built their temples the way the Greeks had and put Greek statues into every corner of their homes and gardens. They learned to speak the Greek language and read Greek books on how to think and behave. Later, the Romans passed the Greek civilization on to the peoples they conquered

The Temple of Fortuna in Rome blends Greek and Roman styles.

in Western Europe. And these people, more than a thousand years later, traveled to what would become our own country, the United States of America, and brought some Greek ideas and ways with them. That's why in our country today you can still see the influence of Greek architecture in buildings with tall columns. (See the Fine Arts section of Book Two of this series for more about Greek architecture.) And that's why we still believe in democracy, which comes from the Greek words *demos* (people) and *kratia* (power): the power or the rule of the people.

The Republic Ruined

The ordinary Roman saw his or her world turned upside down by all these slaves and all this newfound money. The rich were grabbing more and more land, and using thousands of slaves to farm it. Because the slaves worked without pay, the rich Romans could grow crops more cheaply than ordinary farmers could. That meant rich Roman farmers could lower their prices in order to sell more of their goods. So the ordinary farmer often couldn't sell his goods anymore, and lost his land.

Poor farm families crowded into Rome looking for help. The few upper-class Romans who tried to return lands to their original owners were stopped by the powerful and wealthy families who controlled the Senate. The old loyalty of the upper class to the city was forgotten.

For seventy years, from 100 B.C. to 30 B.C., the story of Rome was a story of fights between the rich and the rest of the people. The land conquered by Rome was ruled very badly by greedy governors. The older, nobler ideas were gone. Selfishness ruled the day. The leaders had become too rich. Life for them had become too easy. All over the empire, there were signs of unrest and possible rebellion. It was as if a gigantic boiling pot were ready to explode.

A New Leader

In a way Rome did explode, into wars of Roman against Roman. There was a large uprising of slaves that was brutally crushed by a Roman army. Soon there were civil wars (a civil war is a war between different parts of one country).

In this situation a new leader, Julius Caesar, appeared. He was a general

Julius Caesar.

who had conquered a huge new province called Gaul, which in later times would become France.

In a long and important civil war against another powerful general (named Pompey), Julius Caesar emerged victorious. The Roman Senate appointed him dictator, which means "absolute ruler."

As dictator, Caesar tried to make things better. He lowered taxes. He appointed many new senators. He replaced greedy governors in the provinces with honest men. He started programs to help the poor.

Despite all this, Caesar had many enemies. Some rich people were afraid of his plans to help the poor. Some people were worried that he was becoming too powerful.

Some were also angry at Caesar because of his involvement with Cleopatra, the Queen of Egypt. Egypt during these years was a rich and wonderful civilization, especially the capital city of Alexandria, an important center of trade and the arts. Before becoming dictator of Rome, Caesar had fought and won battles over the control of Egypt. But instead of making Egypt part of the Roman Empire, Caesar had declared that Egypt should be ruled by the beautiful and intelligent Cleopatra. When Caesar returned from Egypt to Rome, he sent for Cleopatra to join him. He even had a gold statue of her placed in a temple! Many Romans feared that Caesar was planning to rule Rome as a king, and that he would make Cleopatra his queen. That would mean giving Egypt some power over Rome, something the proud Romans would not allow.

The enemies of Caesar came up with a plan to stop him—by killing him. One day in March of the year 44 B.C. as Caesar met with the Senate, he was surrounded by a group of senators. From their robes they pulled out knives,

and then they stabbed Caesar to death. He was even stabbed by people he had once helped, including a young nobleman named Brutus. There is a famous story that, as Caesar was dying, he looked sadly at Brutus and asked, *"Et tu, Brute?"* which means, "You too, Brutus?"

Caesar dies at the hands of the Senate.

A Republic No Longer

Those Romans who were not Caesar's enemies were furious about Caesar's death. His grand-nephew, later called Augustus, promised to catch the murderers. One of Caesar's friends, Mark Antony, helped Augustus. The hunt for the murderers of Caesar led to another civil war and many Romans died, including Brutus.

Then Augustus and Antony divided the empire between themselves, giving a bit to another general who had helped them. But they were uneasy with each other. Augustus's sister, Octavia, tried to keep the peace by marrying Antony, but there was a third war. Augustus fought Antony and won.

Rome was so worn out with civil war that the Senate welcomed a period of calm. It was glad to let Augustus have several important titles all at one time. The Senate kept renewing his titles, giving them to him year after year. That made it seem as if the form of

Augustus.

government, the republic, hadn't changed. In fact, however, Augustus was a kind of king, and the republic was really gone. The Roman Republic had lasted about five hundred years.

Although Augustus wanted the Senate to share in ruling, there is one way to tell who was really the boss. Can you think what that is? Well, Augustus had control of the army. What do you think the army would have done if the Senate tried to fire Augustus from his job? That is why we say Augustus was the first emperor of Rome. He ruled the empire until he died. The Senate only helped.

An Exciting Day

Livia, the first Roman Empress.

Rome was lucky to have Augustus as its first emperor. He lived quietly, worked hard, and wanted to give the people peace and plenty. He wasn't a man who enjoyed violence and war. He hadn't even been a very good general. He had depended on his best friend, Agrippa, to win his battles.

To get an idea of what life was like in Rome, you can pretend to accept an invitation from Augustus to go to a horse race with him. You sit between him and his wife, Livia, in a special box in a great stadium called the Circus Maximus. "Circus"

The Circus Maximus.

makes you think of clowns and elephants, but in fact *circus* is Latin for "circle," and *maximus* is Latin for "greatest." And what a great circle this stadium is! Well, not quite a circle, you notice, but more of an oval. It holds more than three hundred thousand people, more than modern-day football stadiums. Just think, about three hundred thousand people in one place. How many people live in your own town or city? How many go to your school? (Another famous Roman stadium, the Colosseum, still standing in Rome, held fifty thousand people and could be flooded for ship battles.)

In the Circus Maximus, you enjoy the horse race. You think Livia is very kind. You notice that Augustus often asks her advice.

Cooling Off

Augustus loves racing and bets on his favorite horses. The crowd becomes more excited, the day warmer. Soon it is getting really hot, though, and you leave the races and follow Augustus and Livia to a large building with several swimming pools. Livia goes in one door to the ladies' pool, Augustus goes into another pool.

Inside you find out that people aren't swimming the way you ex-

This picture, an artist's reconstruction, gives you a sense of how large Roman baths could be.

These are the ruins of the Roman baths in Bath, England.

pected. It turns out that this is a bath. Also there are steam rooms and exercise rooms, and warm pools and cold pools. People are relaxing and enjoying themselves, and they are getting very clean. You are surprised to see that the Romans enjoy some of the comforts you can find in a modern home, like heat and hot water.

What Romans Are Really Like

When you finish your bath, you do not return to the Circus Maximus. Livia does not like the events being held that afternoon, which include bloody fights between wild animals and fierce battles between gladiators. Gladiators are men, usually slaves and criminals, who fight against each other with swords and spears, usually to the death. Augustus has tried to persuade the Roman people to go to plays and athletic games like the Olympic games of the Greeks you may have read about in Book Two of this series. But the people still prefer to see violent fights with real swords and spears.

Augustus goes to these fights sometimes, because otherwise the Roman people get annoyed at him. If that happens, they won't flutter their thousands and thousands of handkerchiefs when he enters his box. They usually cheer him and wave their handkerchiefs. That's their way of telling him he's doing a good job.

As you walk to his home, Augustus points out the huge warehouses he's built to store grain. Much of it is brought in ships from Egypt. You see the poor lining up for free grain he gives them to make bread. Olive oil is being given away, too. All over the city, more than two hundred thousand poor Romans are collecting free food.

Augustus tells you he is setting up farming colonies for the poor. If they do not have food, they will become angry with Augustus, and crowd the streets in protest. Augustus doesn't want to call in soldiers to break the crowds up because he will look like a dictator. He is also having many marble temples, forums, and colonnades built to please the people.

Augustus says he has convinced the Senate to pass laws to make the apartment buildings of Rome safer for the poor. He tells you he is following the example of Julius Caesar by passing laws to improve the lives of slaves.

A Big Family

Inside a Roman house.

While Augustus is talking, he is taking you to his home. You just haven't realized it because you've been walking up a fairly quiet, tree-lined road. You stop in front of a good-sized house. He says he is home, so you look around for his palace. But there isn't one! He lives in this house. Livia is waiting to greet you. She shows you to a little indoor pool and explains they still collect rainwater in the pool through the opening in the roof, just as their ancestors did. But recently, water was piped into the house from one of the many new fountains being built in the streets for the people.

Livia points to the little altars around the room with masks on them. The masks look like the faces of her father and mother and grandparents, and of Augustus's family, too. All of these people have died. She tells you many Romans believe they will meet their dead relatives in an afterlife.

Tasty Food

It is lunchtime, and a servant announces that dinner is ready. The Romans eat their big meal in the daytime. Livia leads you through a large, open courtyard into a smaller room with three couches. You see some little tables and wonder where the chairs are. But there aren't any chairs.

You are still looking for a chair when you see that everyone else is reclining on a couch! That's the way they're going to eat, halfway lying down. They copied that from the Greeks, too, Augustus tells you. Children usually sit down, though, so they bring a chair for you.

Augustus points out some important people who have been invited to dinner, including two famous poets. There is Horace, who often writes about the goodness of a simple life in the country. And there is Virgil, who is writing a great, long poem that tells the story of a legendary prince called Aeneas.

Food is now placed on the tables, which are drawn up within reach. Augustus says that many rich Romans eat huge amounts of food and spend hours at dinner, but he thinks Romans should spend their time and money in better ways. Meals in his house are fairly simple.

Fowl or fish is the usual fare. A roast, too, if anyone has been hunting. Of course, special days call for fancy sauces and stews and desserts. But this is an ordinary day with ordinary fruits and nuts for dessert. After that, Augustus and his guests brush their teeth with toothpaste made from ashes!

The legs on this three-legged Roman table represent woodland gods called satyrs. Satyrs have the ears, legs, and short horns of a goat and the body of a man.

Child's Play

After dinner you are taken to meet the rest of the family. Younger children are playing in the garden. The older children are with their teacher, a Greek who has been freed from slavery and lives in the household. They study history and mathematics every afternoon.

Several boys are so busy throwing a kind of ball to one another that they don't notice you in the garden. You haven't seen this game before. But another boy and a few girls seem to be playing a game a lot like jacks, using animal

This Roman girl is playing knuckles.

bones. They tell you the game is called "knuckles" and invite you to join them. They tell you that if Augustus can make himself set down for awhile the burdens of ruling a vast empire, then he might come out and play. He is very busy, though, and you think he looks tired.

You are invited to spend the night. The house is very big, so you are surprised when you see that your bedroom is small and has no window. You are told this is a large bedroom for a Roman house. Most of the space in Roman houses is used for courtyards, pools, and rooms where the family gathers or for company. People are not alone very much.

A Present for You

The next morning Livia comes for you. She is going down into the Forum to shop and she wants you to choose a going-away present for yourself before you go back to the modern world.

What sights you see in the Forum! Beautiful marble temples, a sacred spring, an outdoor hospital, huge arches built to honor victorious generals, and groups of all kinds of people. You see many foreigners, some in shaggy furs, some in silk. You see lawyers, senators in white robes called togas, and rich ladies carried on very fancy, special seats.

But you stop to think about who is doing all the carrying—slaves. Yes, Rome is full of splendid riches, but not everyone can enjoy them.

Livia directs your attention to the many shops around you: goldsmiths, silversmiths, one run by a red-haired Briton selling pearls, one selling Chinese silk, several Syrian jewel merchants. Even diamonds from India are for sale. You can see that the Roman Empire is in contact with the oldest civilizations of Asia and Europe.

Here's the Roman Forum as Livia saw it.

But you decide to choose something truly Roman. Livia buys you a leather belt with a metal wolf as the buckle because it reminds you of the legend of Rome's founding. You walk back from the Forum to say good-bye to Augustus, and he gives you a book of Latin poems and a bag of knuckles!

NOTE TO PARENTS AND TEACHERS: *Children enjoy learning about the kinds of clothes the Romans wore: tunics, togas, and stoles for the women. They can talk about how these differ from their own clothes. Discuss, for example, what kind of climate would allow people to wear such loose, light apparel. (You can compare this warm-weather wear to the clothes Romans wore in cold weather. Romans wore leg wraps in Britain and Gaul, and early togas were always wool: lightweight for summer, heavy for winter. Augustus, who felt the cold, often wore leg wraps.) Children also enjoy "crowning" the winners of games with wreaths of laurel or oak, and wearing parts of draped sheets at a simple party.*

The Bad Emperors

Now that you've returned to the present you'll want to know what happened to Rome after Augustus ruled the empire.

Fortunately, Augustus and Livia lived to be very old, so Rome had a long stretch of good government to recover from war and get the new empire started. To rule such a large empire, the Roman government had to grow. Augustus appointed many honest, new officials. Also, Livia's son followed his father as emperor. This son was a good general and a smart ruler. Even so, people didn't like him very much.

But then there were some really bad emperors. One seemed to go crazy and terrified everyone around him. The worst one of all was the last member of Augustus's family, Nero.

Nero was so cruel he ordered his teacher, his mother, and many others killed. He entertained himself more than he ruled. The nobles and army had no respect for him. Finally, when he ordered a powerful general to come to Rome, the general knew he'd be executed. So the general brought his army along, and forced Nero to kill himself instead.

After Nero, different armies fought to determine who would be emperor. This showed everyone that the armies were really in charge. Augustus's plan to have the Senate share in ruling was delayed for a long time and never worked well.

Some of our months, some of our holidays, and some of our customs come from Roman times.

With a grown-up's help, you could try to find out the origins of the names March, July, and August, for example.

Did the Romans start Christmas presents? Giving presents in December was a Roman custom. Read about the Saturnalia in a children's encyclopedia.

The Good Emperors

Just when it seemed that Rome's best days had passed, five really good emperors came along. Some of them came from Spain or from Gaul, where France is now. They ruled for almost a century. Rome even gained more land.

These emperors built walls and forts and kept the peace. They gave Rome's citizens more justice. More and more people in the empire were made citizens. There was a much larger Senate. Half of its members came from outside Italy.

Under these good emperors schools were built for poor children. Slaves were no longer made to work in the mines for life. If there was an earthquake somewhere, Rome sent help. More and more aqueducts and baths and theaters were built throughout the empire.

The End Is Near: Constantine

Rome's good emperors weren't perfect. They wasted men and money making the empire bigger. They spent too much money on themselves. There were other problems, too. From the east, the army brought back the plague, a terrible sickness that killed huge numbers of people. These mistakes and troubles left Rome weaker, and less able to defend the empire when warriors and vast tribes from north and east pressed the borders.

The warriors came again and again. At first they were kept out by soldier-emperors. Unfortunately, the emperors also fought with each other in civil wars. Their civil wars killed sol-

diers Rome needed to defend itself from the warriors. But then, around A.D. 310, an emperor named Constantine became powerful enough to rule the whole empire again.

Constantine and Christianity

Constantine was the first *Christian* Roman emperor. Do you remember the very big difference between the Roman and Christian religions? The Romans worshipped many gods, but the Christians worshipped just one. As you may have read in Book One, Christianity was begun by a Jewish teacher called Jesus. His followers spread his teachings throughout the Roman Empire. Sometimes the Romans tolerated Christianity as just one of many religions in the empire. But sometimes Christians were cruelly persecuted and even killed for refusing to worship the Roman gods and the Roman emperor.

But Constantine changed all of this. He allowed Christians and others to practice their religion freely. After a time, Christianity became the official religion of Rome. It grew in importance and gradually became the main religion of Europe.

Constantine himself was raised to follow the Roman religion, not Christianity. Legend has it that he became a Christian after he had a vision—a kind of waking dream—just before leading his soldiers into an important battle. In his vision, he saw a cross, the symbol of the Christian religion. He ordered his soldiers to paint crosses on their shields. When Constantine and his soldiers won the battle, he believed that the Christian god had helped them, and so he accepted the Christian religion.

The Byzantine Empire

Constantine built a great new city called Constantinople. He put it at the southern edge of Europe, where Europe and Asia meet. He hoped this city would protect the empire from invaders from east and west. Can you find Constantinople on the map of the Roman Empire? Constantine decided that this city would take the place of Rome as the new capital of the whole Roman Empire. And after Rome itself fell to invaders, that's exactly what happened. Constantinople became the capital of what was called the Byzantine Empire, and flourished for another thousand years. (It was called the Byzantine Empire because Constantinople was built on the site of an older city called Byzantium. You can read about works of art from the Byzantine Empire in the Fine Arts section of this book.)

The End of Rome

And what happened to Rome itself? North of Rome there lived Germanic tribes. These tribes began moving south, partly because they wanted the rich land and cities of the Roman Empire, and partly because the Germanic tribes were themselves being pushed by fierce warriors from Asia, called Huns.

Little by little the Germanic tribes took over the western part of the Roman Empire: Britain, France, Spain, North Africa, and Italy. Sometimes the tribes moved in peacefully; other times they invaded the cities, damaged buildings, stole treasure, set fires, and killed and injured Roman citizens.

Even the city of Rome could not hold off these powerful invaders. In A.D.

410, a tribe of people called Visigoths attacked Rome. In A.D. 455, Rome was attacked and looted by a people called Vandals. Ever since, the spiteful destruction of property has been called "vandalism."

Many of Rome's soldiers were killed in these battles, and her farms ruined. Ships no longer brought wheat across the Mediterranean Sea from Egypt. Hunger and disease killed more citizens. That was the end of the ancient city of Rome and her glory.

The modern city of Rome surrounds the ruins of ancient Rome.

After Rome Fell

Some Germanic chiefs tried to live in the Roman palaces and fine houses, but not enough people knew how to repair them anymore. Bit by bit they crumbled, especially after fires and earthquakes. The same thing happened to the aqueducts. Without water and food and builders there can be no cities. The fallen stones of the empire lay in ruins for hundreds of years before they were used again. But one thing did not come again. The Mediterranean world has never since had the centuries of peace that people enjoyed during the best years of the Roman Empire.

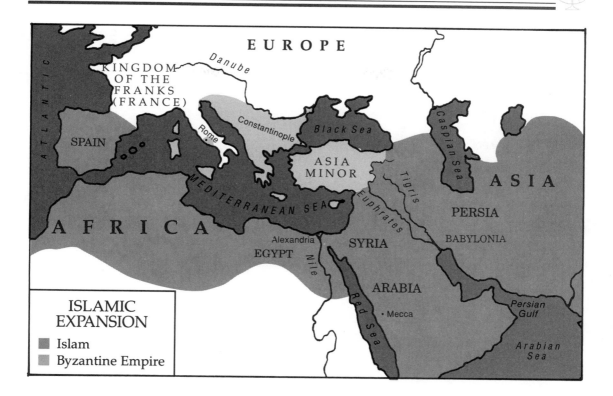

Islam: A New Civilization

For more than a thousand years, the eastern part of the Roman Empire continued to be ruled from Constantinople. It became the greatest city of Europe. Around A.D. 900 it contained over a million inhabitants of many races—as large as Rome itself was in earlier times. But Constantinople could not hold on to all the eastern lands of the old empire. Many of these lands were taken over by a new wave of people from the deserts of Arabia.

These people were different from most others in the ancient world. One of the main reasons they wanted to conquer new lands was to spread their religion. They were Arabs who believed in the religion of Islam. (We call people who believe in Islam, Muslims.) Can you find Arabia on the map? It's on the southwest edge of Rome's empire.

The Greeks and Romans and other ancient peoples had thought there were many gods. But Islam developed from the idea that there was only one god, whom the Muslims called Allah. The idea of one god had spread from the Jews and the Christians throughout the Roman Empire into Arabia.

This page from the Koran is written in Arabic.

The Muslims' holy leader, the prophet Mohammed, was born in Arabia hundreds of years after Jesus lived. Prophets are people who feel that God speaks through them. They tell God's message to other people. The sayings of Jewish prophets are recorded in the part of the Bible called the Old Testament. The Muslims believe Mohammed was the latest of these prophets. His sayings are recorded in the holy book of Islam, called the Koran. The Koran is to Muslims what the Bible is to Christians and the Torah is to Jews.

The Spread of Islam

Mohammed lived in Arabia, in Mecca. Mecca is the holiest city of Islam. Even to this day, millions of Muslims make a pilgrimage (a journey) to Mecca every year.

But back when Mohammed first started preaching the religion of Islam, many people in Mecca were not happy to hear him. His message about the one god, Allah, upset people who believed in various tribal gods. People also didn't like the strict conduct Mohammed demanded of followers of Islam. They got so angry with Mohammed that they drove him out of Mecca.

Still, he kept on preaching. All over Arabia he gathered followers who accepted him as the prophet, or messenger, of Allah. In A.D. 630, just eight years after he had been driven out of Mecca, he returned to the city with such a huge army that Mecca surrendered to him without even putting up a fight.

Mohammed led armies of Muslims in *jihads,* or holy wars, to spread the religion of Islam. The strong belief in Islam united many Arab tribes. All together they were able to take over much of the Eastern Roman Empire. Even after Mohammed's death in A.D. 632, Islam continued to spread rapidly. Only a dozen years later, all of Syria, Persia, Babylonia, and Egypt were Islamic, as the people of these ancient regions are to this day. Then the Muslims pushed west across North Africa and up into Spain. The Germanic tribes who had taken Spain from the Romans now lost it to the Muslims!

As the Muslims conquered, they added the wisdom of the Greeks and Romans to their own knowledge. Later, in the Middle Ages, when almost all Europeans had lost their knowledge of the ancient Greeks, it was from Muslims that they first learned about Greek science and philosophy. That's because the Muslims had preserved Greek writings by translating them into the Arabic language.

Muslims also made many scientific contributions, adding especially to the study of medicine. They developed very advanced mathematics. In fact, the numbers that we use today—1, 2, 3, 4, 5, and so on—were introduced to Europe by the Muslims, and are even today called Arabic numerals. These numbers are much better for solving problems in mathematics than are the Roman numerals I, II, III, IV, V, and so on.

An Arab village.

After hundreds of years, the religion of Islam spread through the whole of the Eastern Roman Empire, and finally Constantinople itself. The religion that Mohammed started continues throughout the world to this day.

Introduction to American Civilization

FOR PARENTS AND TEACHERS

In this book we tell stories about key points of American history, from American Indian civilizations through early English settlements, from the high civilizations of Africa to slavery, from the growth of the colonies to the Declaration of Independence. Parents and teachers will find suggestions for making the stories more memorable and vivid in activity boxes throughout the chapter.

Our treatment of these subjects reflects the improvements that are being demanded in the teaching of history. A public outcry has begun against watered-down social-studies textbooks whose chief goal has been to avoid offending anyone—even if that should mean removing all vividness and avoiding fundamental facts of history. The results of using such books are now manifest. Our children graduate from high school far too ignorant of our history, our traditions, and our ideals.

Prestigious commissions have recently called for real history to be taught in the schools, including coverage of non-European history in the Americas and the rest of the world. These are favorable signs for the approach we have taken to history in this series.

The first, and perhaps most important decision that our history advisory committees made was to include American and world history in the very earliest grades. Although some schools now wait until grade five to begin a significant study of American history, our best schools have always started earlier. They have proved that children in early grades are fascinated by stories of the American past—stories that go beyond "Why We Celebrate Thanksgiving."

The second, and perhaps most important reason for our decision to start early was our concern for fairness. Knowledge of American history and society is gained through the pores by children from advantaged families. It seemed unfair to our committees that children from less advantaged homes are now being denied basic knowledge which helps children understand the mainstream social and intellectual world around them. Social and cultural knowledge are built up gradually. An early, systematic exposure to history provides a framework for fuller understanding later on. It is simply unfair that the possession of such a framework should be determined by chance and luck rather than by good schooling.

Good luck in making the teaching and learning of American history great fun!

American Civilization

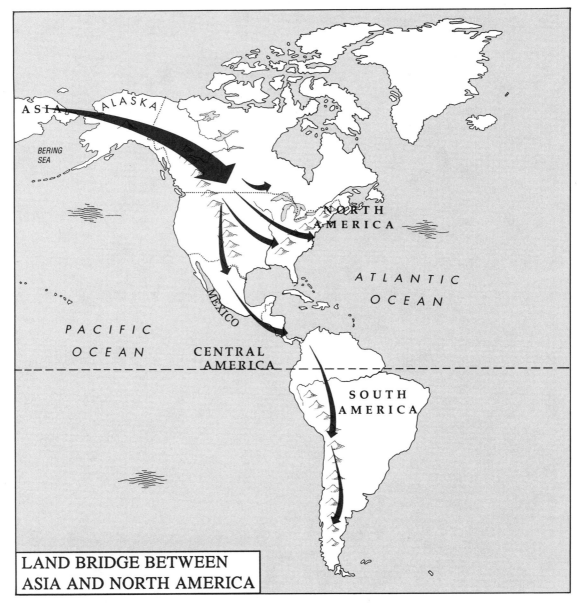

LAND BRIDGE BETWEEN
ASIA AND NORTH AMERICA

The arrows on the map show where ancestors of the American Indians journeyed.

The First Americans

The story of our country begins with the first people who lived here. As you may have read in the Geography section, these people are often called Indians because Columbus gave the people he met in the New World the wrong name. He thought he was in Asia, which he called "the Indies." In this book, we call these people by the term they usually use for themselves, American Indians. You may also hear them called Native Americans.

The ancestors of the American Indians came from Asia long, long ago. They came during the Ice Age when the oceans were lower and Alaska was attached to Asia by a land bridge. Then, about twelve thousand years ago, when the ice melted, the land bridge was covered by ocean water. Twelve thousand years ago! You can see how long the Indians have been in America— many centuries before the Greeks and Romans started their cities.

The first Americans who came over the land bridge probably followed the animals they hunted. They spread from Alaska to the tip of South America. These people were not all alike. They must have come from different parts of Asia. They must have come at different times. They certainly settled in different types of places in this New World and adapted themselves to the lands they settled. In Mexico and Central and South America they built cities and temples and called themselves the Maya, the Aztecs, and the Incas. You may have read about them in Book One of this series.

The Aztecs called the sun Royal Lord. They held ceremonies to strengthen the sun and thank it for giving light to the world.

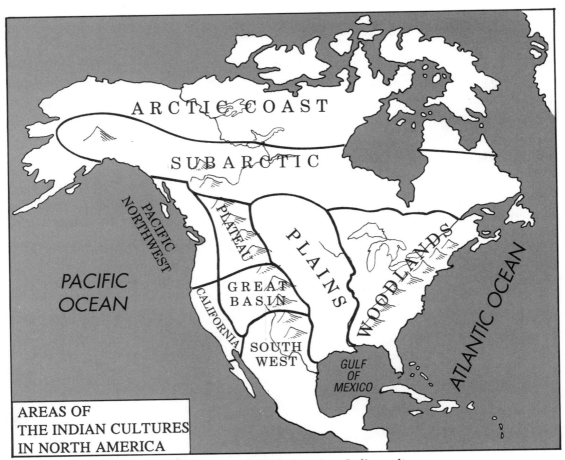

This map shows you where different types of North American Indian cultures flourished. Find where the Woodland Indian culture developed.

East of the Mississippi

Unlike the Plains Indians, who followed the buffalo over great distances, the tribes that lived east of the Mississippi tended to remain in smaller areas. They had what is called a Woodland culture. That means they found all of their food by fishing, hunting, and gathering berries, fruits, and nuts.

Later, as they began to plant and harvest crops, many of the Eastern tribes built homes out of the materials available around them, like mud or thatch. They planted beans, squash, and pumpkins, but corn or "maize" was the most important crop for most. The idea of growing corn might have come to them from the natives of Mexico.

Growing corn and other crops gave some Native American farmers a lot to eat, but it probably tempted others without farms to attack them for food. The farming tribes had to build stockades around their villages to protect themselves and their crops.

The planting and harvesting of the corn changed the lives of Indian women greatly. The women usually did all of the back-breaking work in the fields. They cleverly developed farming techniques that improved the life of the tribe. For instance, the Powhatans in Virginia used rakes made from deer antlers, and wooden hoes. More and more the men became warriors to protect the crops. They did the hunting and fishing, too, trapping fish in woven fences called weirs.

A weir fence leads fish into a maze-like trap.

There were different groups of Indians in different parts of the East. Some Indians, who traveled through the forests hunting, set up temporary wigwams and slept on mats. The wigwams were tents made of animal skins or bark. Others lived in more permanent dwellings, like the log-covered longhouses built by the Iroquois. One chief of the Natchez Indians had a wide bed with painted columns. And the explorer De Soto met Native Americans who built both summer and winter houses.

This is a sketch of an Iroquois village.

During the summer, the tribes who lived in what is now Florida often slept in wooden frames with roofs but no walls. In the winter they moved into houses with walls plastered in mud. These houses, when warmed by a fire, stayed hot all night.

Familiar Names

Here are names of some of the largest native tribes in the area of the Eastern United States. There were the Seminole; the Cherokee Confederacy; the Delaware; the Susquehanna; the Mohican, the Massachuset, and other coast tribes who spoke the Algonquin language; and there was the Iroquois Confederacy, which was an alliance in upper New York of five nations, the Mohawk, Oneida, Onondaga, Cayuga, and Seneca. Is your family descended from one of these tribes? Do you live in or near a town with one of these names? Have you heard of a stream or river or state or county named after these tribes? Can you find these names on the map?

The Iroquois Confederacy was by far the most powerful group in the area of the Eastern United States. The warrior chief Hiawatha is said to have started the Iroquois Confederacy by getting the five tribes to agree not to attack one another. Each tribe was to remain independent, but none could go to war without the agreement of all the others. Many later colonists, including Benjamin Franklin, admired their agreement.

The power of the Iroquois Confederacy grew as its member tribes took over neighboring lands. Later, the Tuscarora tribe joined the confederacy, and the whole group was called the Six Nations.

The Iroquois women planted corn, beans, and squash, and the men hunted. The men were great warriors, and when challenged, they made ruthless enemies. The young warriors, the "braves," were so fierce their chiefs complained they couldn't control them.

The Six Nations often fought against the French. Why? Because when the French had come to Canada, they had made friends with tribes that were enemies of the Six Nations. And that is also why the Six Nations sided with the British in 1754 when the British went to war with France in a war that came to be called the French and Indian war. The British were lucky to have the help of the Six Nations; their warriors were so fierce that they frightened other tribes and colonists. With the Six Nations on their side, the British were able to defeat the French and win control of most of Canada and the colonies.

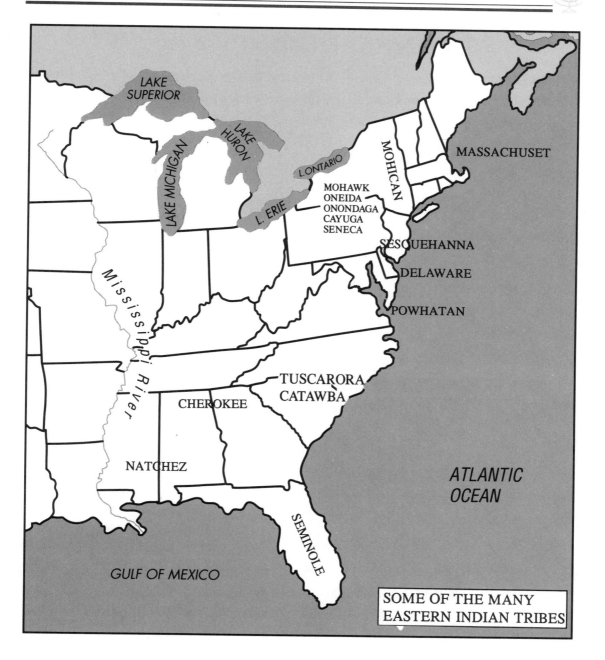

LAKE SUPERIOR

LAKE HURON

LAKE MICHIGAN

L. ONTARIO

L. ERIE

MOHICAN

MASSACHUSET

MOHAWK
ONEIDA
ONONDAGA
CAYUGA
SENECA

SESQUEHANNA

DELAWARE

POWHATAN

Mississippi River

TUSCARORA
CATAWBA

CHEROKEE

NATCHEZ

SEMINOLE

ATLANTIC OCEAN

GULF OF MEXICO

SOME OF THE MANY
EASTERN INDIAN TRIBES

A Day with Little Thunder

The first colonists who came from England met natives who spoke the Algonquin language. Let's pretend to meet an Algonquin boy of that time and see how he spends his day. We'll call him Little Thunder because Algonquin

boys were often named after things of the sky. Girls were named for things of the earth, such as Fast Stream. If you like, you can make up a name for one of Little Thunder's friends using a name for a thing of the earth or the sky.

Little Thunder is sleeping on a cozy bear skin. When he wakes up, he sees his tall, straight father, who is smearing red-dyed bear grease over his muscular arms. His father is going out to hunt, and this grease protects him from mosquitoes. The red color of the bear grease is the reason the English thought the natives were "red men." The first colonists in Virginia didn't know that a mosquito's bite could make them sick with a disease we now call malaria. So they didn't protect themselves, the way the Indians did, from that dangerous fever.

Little Thunder's father's hair is mostly shaved off to make it easier for bow hunting. To shoot, his father pulls the bowstring back to his cheek, squinting one eye close to the string for the best aim. Long hair could get caught or throw off the aim. Other warriors have many different hairstyles, but Little Thunder must wait until he's sixteen if he wants to let his hair grow long. He must also wait to get a tattoo of a wolf on his arm like his father has. This tattoo is worn by members of the Wolf Clan.

Little Thunder goes outside their dome-shaped wigwam of tree bark to watch his mother cooking breakfast over a fire. How good the smoke and food smell! He's going to have corn and venison (deer) stew!

Everyone Works

This morning, Little Thunder's mother and sister will work extra hard breaking up the earth for planting. Little Thunder is also going outside of the tall wood fence around the village. He will be checking his traps to see if any small animals are caught. He's taking his bow and arrow, just in case he sees some animals to shoot at.

He remembers to thread a long piece of leather through his lucky amulet, which is a round wooden disk with carving on it, and tie it around his neck before he goes out. His amulet has a coiled snake carved on it, because his special guardian is the spirit of the snake. He believes it will protect him from the dangers of the forest. All the Algonquin believe in the one Great Spirit, whom they will meet after death in a wonderful place. The Great Spirit does not notice what goes on every day on earth, though, so other spirit protectors are needed for events such as today's hunt.

As Little Thunder goes to the gate of the fort, he passes a wigwam where a very sick person lies. The women take good care of ordinary aches and pains with their herbs, but the very ill are tended by the medicine man or shaman. Little Thunder hears the shaman inside, singing and shaking a tortoise-shell rattle. He is trying to drive away the evil spirits that have made this person so sick.

At the Games

Little Thunder comes back early from his trapping. He has several squirrels to skin and he wants to finish his work in time to watch the games on the field in the center of the village. He knows that the highest chief of many tribes will be there. He is called the chief sachem and is a royal person. If he has no son, his daughter will become the next chief sachem. The most important thing is to keep the rule in the same royal family. That helps keep all the Algonquin tribes from fighting one another, because they all will do what the chief sachem says.

Little Thunder arrives at the games just as the crowd is cheering the winning wrestler. Next comes stick ball, the sort of game that trains young men for battle. (You may know this game as lacrosse; it was first played by American Indians.) Everyone watching gets very excited. The women are jumping and shouting, and one woman darts into the game and whips her husband with a switch so he will try harder! Little Thunder dances for joy when his favorite team wins.

Trouble Ahead

Suddenly the chief sachem stands and everyone is quiet. He has two things to say. First of all, he is going to punish someone from another village who has stolen from this one. The guilty man will have to work for this village for a month. Second, there is going to be a war dance tonight, for tomorrow they are going on the warpath against another nation. Little Thunder leaves for dinner wondering if his father will join the war party. He knows the warriors are great heroes, but he also worries that his father will be killed.

Shall We Go to War?

That evening over dinner Little Thunder's mother asks his father what he is going to do. Little Thunder can see from his mother's sad eyes that she is afraid he will go to war. But his father surprises them. He is not sure what he will do. He is worried because there are fewer and fewer Algonquin. He wishes they wouldn't fight so much. Native Americans are killing each other while disease from the white man is sweeping the land. Algonquin have been dying of disease in large numbers ever since the French first came to buy firs.

That night the family gathers with others around the huge campfire at the center of the village. The war dance has already begun. A drum is beating loudly and the war leader has a club in one hand and a tomahawk in another. (A tomahawk is a small ax used in fighting.) He raises his voice and sings of his brave deeds in the past. He starts dancing around a post, making special motions with his arms. He is pointing to the spirits of clouds and birds. More and more braves join in. Some of them are afraid, but they raise their weapons to show how they will fight and they beat the post furiously. By joining the dance they are getting up the courage to go on the warpath.

Everyone seems worked up to a fever of excitement. Little Thunder wishes he were old enough to be a brave. Then he sees that his father has gone back to their wigwam. Has he gone for his weapons so he can join the dance? A big lump forms in the little boy's throat. What will happen to his father? Will he ever come back to them?

He keeps his eyes on the doorway of his wigwam. Minutes pass. His father does not return. Finally the dance is over, and Little Thunder goes in to bed. He finds his father telling his little sister a story. Little Thunder goes happily to sleep. An exciting day is over, with his family still safe.

Try to find cities, towns, states, and rivers named after these native tribes on a map of the United States today. A grown-up can help you.

You might enjoy the following coloring books and projects about Indians: North American Indian Design Coloring Book *and* Indian Tribes of North America Coloring Book. *A good vacation or class project would be the Dover* Cut and Make North America Indian Masks. *To order call your local bookstore or write Dover Publications, 31 East Second Street, Mineola, NY 11501.*

Tobacco and the People of Pocahontas

Did you ever hear the story of Pocahontas? You may have read about her in Book One of this series. She was the Indian princess who was said to have saved John Smith, the leader of Jamestown, the first English colony.

Jamestown, on the river James in Virginia, was started in 1607. Later, Pocahontas married one of the English colonists, John Rolfe.

To Pocahontas and her people, tobacco was an important plant. Smoking tobacco in pipes was holy; it meant peace. Indians declared peace by smoking the peace pipe. But the English saw opportunities to sell tobacco in England.

Pocahontas's husband, John Rolfe, started planting tobacco, which helped the colony grow large and rich. Not knowing smoking to be harmful, he hoped that it would become popular in England. If that happened, Virginia would have a "cash crop" to send home, something to sell to make money. After all, the Jamestown colony was started by the Virginia Company for the purpose of making money.

Soon tobacco was planted up and down the riverbanks and even in the streets of Jamestown! Everyone in Europe seemed to want it. The colonists were happy, but Pocahontas's people were not. They saw thousands of Europeans arriving on ships and taking their land. The colonists, of course, thought there was plenty of land to go around. They didn't realize they were destroying Indian hunting grounds when they cut down trees to plant tobacco. And most of them didn't care what the natives thought. To them, people without either cities or the Christian religion were "savages."

As colonists grew more and more tobacco, they began to use slaves to care for the crops.

An engaging twenty-minute videocassette on colonial Jamestown may be borrowed from the Jamestown Yorktown Foundation. Because there are nominal postage and handling fees, we recommend that you first call the foundation at (804) 253-4939 to determine the fees and availability of the tape. You may then apply in writing to:

> *Jamestown Yorktown Foundation*
> *Education Office*
> *P.O. Box JF*
> *Williamsburg, VA 23187*

The Natives Go to War

In 1622 the natives attacked Jamestown, and almost pushed the invading colonists back into the sea. Many on both sides were killed. In 1627, twenty years after the founding of Jamestown, only about one thousand settlers were left of the fourteen thousand people who had originally crossed the sea to Virginia. Many people had died or gone back to England. The Europeans weren't doing very well living in this new place.

But some colonists hung on, and the colony grew. There were always many, many more coming from Europe than the natives could defeat. Why did the Europeans keep coming? Back in Europe there were terrible wars, and there were large numbers of people who were poor. People wanted land where they could live peacefully. More and more Europeans came and took the lands of the Indians.

The Chieftain's Spy

Some have said that Pocahontas's father, a chief named Powhatan, wanted to know how many more English might come. He supposedly sent a native spy on a ship going back to England to count how many Englishmen there were in the English tribe. The spy was given sticks and told to cut a notch for every English person he saw. The poor man hadn't been in England an hour before he threw the sticks away! There were just too many English to count. He was also surprised to find that the English "chief," King James, was so small and weak-looking. Let's find out more about the English people that the Indians met in America.

The Assembly: Something Special

Even in those early days, something very important for our future happened in Virginia. Because there had been so much trouble keeping the Virginia colony alive, the company that started it had to promise settlers a lot of rights to get them to come to the New World. The settlers would have the right to hold an assembly where they could decide how to run the colony. Later, when the colony of Virginia ran into hard times, the King took over the colony. But still, the settlers continued to make their own laws. Virginians became so used to governing themselves that much later on the colonists would decide they didn't need the King at all.

Plymouth

The second English colony was Plymouth in what is now Massachusetts. (Find it on your map.) The Pilgrims arrived here in 1620 on the *Mayflower*. Their reasons for coming were very different from the Virginia colonists' reasons.

The Pilgrims could not practice their religion in England without being punished, so they wanted to find a place where no one would bother them. They set sail for Virginia, but storms blew them much farther north, where they finally landed.

The Pilgrims elected William Bradford as their governor. While still on board the *Mayflower*, Bradford helped write a plan of government for the Plymouth Colony, called the *Mayflower Compact*. A "compact" is an agreement. The Mayflower Compact is important because it is one of the first

The Mayflower.

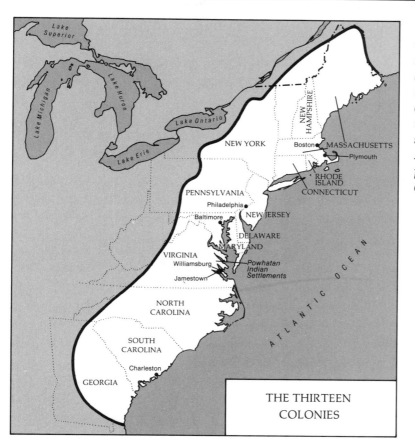

THE THIRTEEN
COLONIES

The thirteen original colonies were not exactly the same shape and size as the current-day states that have their names. Here you can see the colonies' original shapes and the shapes of the present-day states. See how the colony of Massachusetts included the present state of Maine? What other differences can you see?

times settlers in the New World freely agreed to write down the rules and laws by which they would govern themselves.

The people at Plymouth suffered like the first Virginians. They almost starved, and they too were helped by Algonquin-speaking natives, who gave them corn. The next year, 1621, they had a good crop and had a celebration to give thanks to God for helping them. The Indians always held a thanksgiving in the

The first Thanksgiving.

fall, when the crops were safely harvested, so the Pilgrims probably got the idea from them.

Can you see why everyone would be grateful to have a good crop of corn? What else could they eat all through winter? Do you eat corn on Thanksgiving? What else do you eat then?

A Bigger Colony

A few years later, another group of people, called Puritans, who were also being punished in England because of their religion, went to a third colony. It was called Massachusetts Bay, after an Indian tribe. Boston became the biggest town of this new colony.

The leaders of this Puritan colony were not poor like the Pilgrims. The first governor of Massachusetts, John Winthrop, was a wealthy man. The Puritans did not have such a terrible voyage over the ocean, but they did have hard times in the wild, new country.

The Puritans were very strict with themselves. They sat in freezing cold churches hour after hour listening to religious leaders advising them how to behave. They were not supposed to dance, or sled, or play cards, or swim. They even had a law to whip anyone who celebrated Christmas! That holiday began, they said, in "evil" Rome and was not in the Christian Bible.

John Winthrop.

Splitting Up

The majority of Puritans were hard on other Puritans who did not agree with them. One who disagreed was Roger Williams. He said they were wrong in taking the Indians' land and in passing laws that made everyone behave the same way. He was put on trial and sentenced to be sent back to England. But Governor Winthrop let him slip away, and he began a settlement in what became Rhode Island.

Another person who argued with the Puritan leaders was Anne Hutchinson. She, too, was driven out of Massachusetts Bay, and she also started a new settlement in Rhode Island.

The hard work of the Puritans made their colony very prosperous. In the next few years, during a war in England, Puritans and others poured into Massachusetts by the thousands. They moved into what became Connecticut and New Hampshire. Their numbers reached almost twenty thousand!

Anne Hutchinson preaching. Some Puritan leaders did not like Anne Hutchinson's ideas and thought it wasn't proper for a woman to preach.

Warpath Again

As all these people moved in, they took over the hunting grounds of the Indians and built farms. The Indians struck back, and there was a terrible fight. Colonists were killed, kidnapped, and burned out of their homes. They, in turn, savagely attacked even the friendly Indians in Rhode Island. The colonists had better weapons, and when the battles were over, Indian strength in New England was gone forever.

More Colonies

Soon there were many other colonies between Massachusetts and Virginia, and in the area south of Virginia. All of these colonies got their start in one way or another from the King of England. Even the colony that the Dutch began was taken over by the English King's brother, the Duke of York, who later became king. Look at the map of the thirteen colonies and listen to the names of the colonies. Which one belonged to the Duke of York?

Puritans were not the only people who left England because of their religion. Catholics and Quakers were also punished in England for their religious beliefs. Many went to two colonies, Maryland and Pennsylvania. These were started as places of safety where people would not be punished for their religious beliefs. Maryland was started by a Roman Catholic, Lord Baltimore, and Pennsylvania was started by a Quaker, William Penn. As safe places to practice the religion of their founders, they were like Massachusetts. But Maryland and Pennsylvania allowed much more freedom to practice different religions.

William Penn and scenes of the Delaware River, Pennsylvania.

A Safer Place

Because of better land and easier laws, these new colonies between Virginia and Massachusetts quickly became as wealthy as the older colonies. They also became a safe haven for people from *many* different countries, not just for the English. Sephardic Jews (Jews from Spain and Portugal) found a home with the Dutch of New York. People from almost every country in Europe went into New Jersey, Delaware, and Pennsylvania.

Did you, your parents, or your grandparents come to this country from another place? Find out how and why you or your ancestors came to live in the United States.

Farther South

The last British colony, Georgia, was started as an idealistic experiment by James Oglethorpe. British prisons were overcrowded with poor people, whose only crime was being in debt. Oglethorpe wanted these debtors to have a second chance and he invited them to settle his new colony. But few debtors wanted to try life in the hot, swampy land across the sea.

The people who did come to Georgia didn't like the laws Oglethorpe had made forbidding them to own slaves and possess huge farms. So as time went on and Georgia grew, bit by bit these laws were changed until some people there owned slaves and huge farms, called plantations, just as their neighbors in South Carolina did.

North Carolina and South Carolina began as one English colony given to eight friends of the English king. But the first town in North Carolina was actually started by French Protestants, who were forced by the Catholic King to leave France. South Carolina was known for allowing greater religious

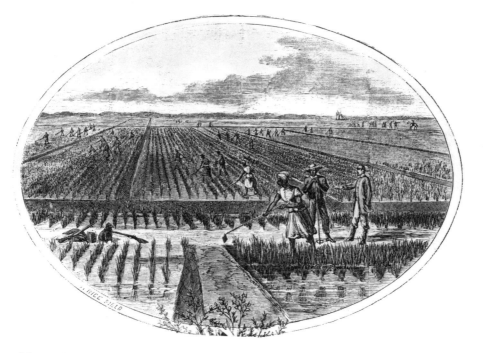

Many rice plantations were this large. Can you see why growing rice required the labor of so many people?

freedom than almost any other colony. The Carolina settlers had a hard time surviving until they stopped relying on trading with the Native Americans and began planting rice. They learned how to grow rice from the Africans who worked as slaves in their fields.

Hard Labor

One large group of people who came to the colonies did not want to come. They were brought from Africa as slaves.

When these people from Africa were put on ships for America, their lives changed overnight. They were taken from their families and countries, and they had such terrible voyages to the New World it's hard to believe anyone stayed alive.

The first group of Africans arrived at Jamestown. Like many poor people who came from England, these Africans probably came as indentured servants, not slaves. Being indentured usually meant they had to work hard several years for a wealthy man who had paid for their passage to America. They received food, clothes, and shelter but no money. When their years of service were up, they were given

This picture shows the inhumanely cramped conditions on a slave trade ship.

tools, and they went off to find land of their own as best they could.

But big landowners weren't happy when their indentured servants left. They wanted more and more workers to plant tobacco. Workers were also needed on the big rice plantations farther south, and also on some farms in the North. Pretty soon, laws were passed in Virginia and elsewhere that said the Africans would have to spend their entire lives working for the man who "owned" them. After that, almost all Africans who came to the United States were brought as slaves. Later in this series we will talk about why that happened and how slavery ended.

Songhai

Many of the people who came to this country from Africa said they came from Timbuktu, which you can find on the map below. Let's find out more about Timbuktu.

Timbuktu was an important city in Songhai, one of several large African kingdoms south of the Sahara. Songhai was on a trading route where camels crossed the desert from North Africa. For centuries, the North African Muslims had brought gold and ivory and slaves back from Timbuktu. Then, around the time of Columbus, the King of Songhai journeyed to Arabia.

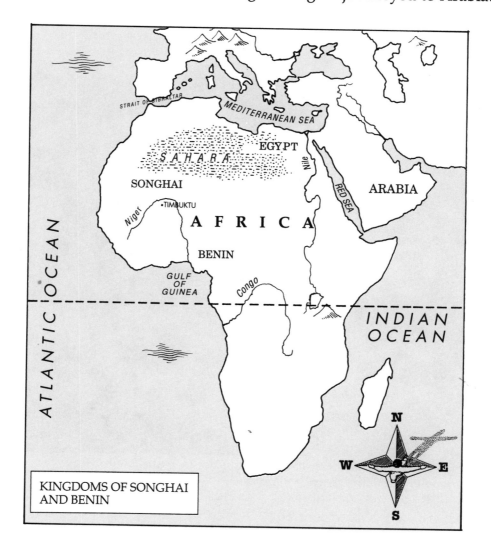

KINGDOMS OF SONGHAI AND BENIN

This king, Askia Muhammad, went to Arabia because he believed in Islam. His nobles were Muslim, too. They built schools and Muslim places of worship, called mosques, in Timbuktu. But when his sons rebelled against him and then fought against one another, invaders were able to take over parts of the kingdom. African-Americans who said they were from Timbuktu may have been descendants of Muslims still living in the area of old Songhai.

Much of the time, the people of Songhai farmed and traded with other farmers. In towns like Timbuktu, craftsmen worked in gold, copper, iron, and bronze, merchants traded in busy markets, and servants ran the homes of the wealthy. Long canoes carried many things up and down the long, wide river called the Niger. And none of these people knew any more about Europeans than the Europeans knew of them.

You can see that long canoes are still being used today by looking at this present-day picture of the Niger's riverbank.

Benin

Farther south, another African kingdom, Benin, was well known for its beautiful ivory and wood carvings and brass statues. The "oba" (the king and religious leader) lived in a large palace, and his city was surrounded by stone walls. It reminded the few Europeans who went there of cities in Europe.

The Benin artist who made this small ivory mask laid metal pieces in the eyes and forehead. Notice how smooth and softly rounded the face is.

The ancestors of many African-Americans came from this area. It was called the "slave coast" because other kingdoms around Benin fought and captured their enemies to sell to the captains of the slave ships. As in ancient Egypt, Persia, Greece, and Rome, prisoners taken in war were almost always made slaves. Africans kept many of their prisoners as slaves, but sold some to Europeans.

The people of Benin had religious beliefs we describe as "animistic." In this they were similar to many other peoples, including the Greeks, the Romans, and the American Indians. Animists believe that spirits live in everything, in men and mountains, in

This bronze plaque shows sentries guarding the palace of the oba, or king. The snake symbolizes the oba's power. What do you think this plaque might feel like? Look at all its textures.

animals and ancestors. Many beliefs, songs, and dances of these religions were remembered by the slaves, and joined other customs to make the new culture of the United States.

Can you imagine how frightened the Africans who came to America as slaves must have been when they arrived? At first many did not know a single word of English. But they learned everything they could, while they lived by themselves in rough cabins and worked hard every day at difficult farm jobs. One thing that comforted them was to share with one another the songs and stories they had brought from Africa.

The Africans brought their games with them, too. You might enjoy playing Fox is the Warner, which was played by African-American children in early Virginia. One player, chosen to be the fox, stands in a "den," a circle marked on the ground. When the fox is ready to come out, he or she sings aloud:

> *This is the morning,*
> *The fox gives warning.*
> *I'm coming out!*
> *So watch out!*

Then the fox tries to get out of the den while the other players try to keep him in. To win his way out the fox has to tap another player with a stick or rolled-up paper he holds while he hops about on one foot. If he can hit someone, that person must be caught by the other players and forced into the den to become the next fox.

Sarah Sees a "Walking"

Now we are going to meet a colonial girl. Let's say her name is Sarah, because people in colonial times often took names from the Bible. Sarah lives on a farm just north of Philadelphia. Her parents and older brothers work very hard, their land is good, and they all eat well. They are even able to buy cloth in Philadelphia to make their clothes. For her birthday, Sarah received a wonderful surprise—a pair of leather shoes with buckles!

This is what it might have looked like inside Sarah's house.

The colony Sarah lives in was started by William Penn, who named it Pennsylvania. Pennsylvania means "Penn's Woods." William Penn's father had once loaned the King of England a lot of money, and Penn collected on this loan by being granted a very large piece of wooded land between Maryland and New York. Penn wanted the land to become a safe place for people of his religion, called Quakers, to live. Quakers were often punished in England because they believed *all* people were equal and because they refused to fight in wars.

How the "Walk" Began

At first, the Quakers got along well with the Delaware Indians because Penn was careful to buy from them the land he wanted. He didn't take it just because the King of England told him he could. There was plenty of land, and the Indians moved north and west.

William Penn and the Delaware signing their treaty in 1682.

But now Penn is dead, and his sons are claiming more land than the Delaware thought they had sold. Penn's sons say he bought all the land around the upper Delaware River for as far as a man could walk in a day and a half. They have hired three athletes to walk as fast as they can. Sarah is going to watch the walkers.

It is September 1737, and Sarah has gotten up early. She washes her face in a basin of cold water with soap she helped to make out of ashes and the fat from cooking. Next, she goes out to feed the chickens and collect eggs for breakfast. She also gathers the sticks she is supposed to take to school to keep the one-room schoolhouse warm in winter. She calls good-bye to her mother, who reminds her to wear her bonnet and shawl.

It is still early when Sarah starts out for town, but she hurries. She knows the walkers are coming through today, and she is the only one in her family who has time to see them.

What Sarah Saw

Sure enough, here they come, but they already look tired. That's because they're half-running. The Indian witnesses are saying the whole "walk" is unfair. They say a Delaware would have walked a few miles, rested a bit, perhaps shot a squirrel. They refuse to witness any more. As Sarah goes on to school, she wonders why people from different cultures have such a hard time understanding each other.

About a month later Sarah is eating supper with her family when her father tells them how the "walk" turned out.

One of the hired men was able to keep going for a day and a half. He walked fifty-five miles! When the Delaware protested, Penn's sons threatened to ask their enemies, the Iroquois, to come fight them. The Delaware were shocked. They had always been welcome in Penn's city, Philadelphia, which means the "city of brotherly love."

This is a painting of Lapowiasa, a Delaware Indian.

Sarah's father says he doesn't think William Penn would have done this. He is afraid the Delaware will be wandering and fighting until there are few left. And he will turn out to be right.

Sarah goes to bed soon after dark. She thinks about the Delaware, hoping they will find other lands. She won't forget them.

Dover Publications *has an* Everyday Dress of the American Colonial Period Coloring Book, *which shows colonial occupations as well as apparel. Parents and teachers may wish to underscore the vast difference in modes of living between colonial times and today to help children understand that ideas and events flow from life as it is lived. Dover also has a* Cut and Assemble the Mayflower: A Full-Color Paper Model of the Reconstruction at Plymouth Plantation. *For a free catalogue write Dover Publications, 31 East Second Street, Mineola, NY 11501.*

Children of colonial times played many games that you know, such as Blind Man's Buff, London Bridge Is Falling Down, and Here We Go 'Round the Mulberry Bush. If you'd like to play any of these and don't remember how, an adult can help you find out. (Parents: libraries stock books of games which you and your children can enjoy. Many of these teach the games of different lands and time periods.)

The Colonies Grow Up

We have heard how hard it was for the first colonists in Virginia and Massachusetts just to get started. We know they were helped by the Indians, but then turned around and fought them. We've also heard how the first colonies grew and how more colonies were started. By 1763 there were around two million people in the thirteen English colonies!

Cities were slowly growing. New York City, Boston (in present-day Massachusetts), and Charleston (in present-day South Carolina) were busy trading centers. From them tobacco, wheat, lumber, rice, and furs were exported mostly to Britain, and into them came manufactured goods from Britain. Philadelphia, designed by William Penn to be a "green country town" with five parks, by 1775 became the second-largest city in the British Empire. Only London was bigger.

So you might think of Britain and her thirteen colonies as being like a mother with children who have grown up. The colonies had been getting along with one another and the mother country fairly well. Also, the colonies had helped Britain fight the French in America, although not as much as Britain wanted. In return, Britain protected the colonies.

The Parent Says "No"

Yes, by 1763 the colonists thought themselves to be grown-up. They were happy that the French were finally gone. Imagine their annoyance when Britain suddenly told them not to do something *very* important: not to move westward anymore! The Indians were to keep the land west of the Appalachian mountains; Britain was going to take over France's place in buying furs from them.

Also, Britain wouldn't have to fight the Indians so often if the colonies stopped growing and taking more Indian lands for farms. Britain was tired of fighting and tired of paying for it.

Britain Wants Money

There was another big problem. To pay for the wars it was fighting elsewhere, Britain wanted more money from the colonies and began increasing taxes. Earlier on we read about how Britain first gave Virginians the right to have an assembly where they could decide how to run the colony. By 1763, all the colonists were used to electing their own assemblies, and said that no one could tax them except their own representatives in their own legislatures. (A legislature is a group of people with the power to make laws.) The British also started passing other laws that the colonists found unfair. The colonists were told they had to find houses for British troops, for example. Many of the colonists began to believe the British government and its King, George III, were trying to take away their rights.

In the Language Arts section of this book you can read about what one colonist, Patrick Henry, said about a tax called the Stamp Act. Like Patrick

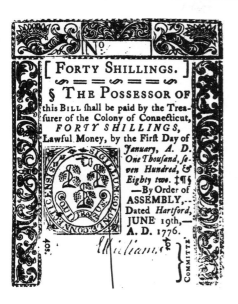

Henry, colonists from all classes, from lawyers to laborers, were angry. Many refused to buy British goods until Parliament took away one of the taxes, the Stamp Tax. The British gave way and removed the tax, but the argument grew worse anyway. The British sent home the legislature of New York, and they sent British soldiers, called "Redcoats" for the color of their uniforms, to Boston.

Does this look like money to you? It's a picture of paper money from colonial times.

The "Boston Massacre"

The trouble started at Boston Harbor on a cold day in March 1770. Some British soldiers were standing guard duty. A group of colonists began to throw snowballs at the soldiers and call them names. A crowd gathered, and in the crowd was a man named Crispus Attucks, who had escaped from slavery when he was young and became a sailor. We don't know exactly what Attucks and the other colonists did when they gathered at Boston Harbor. But we do know that at some point the Redcoats fired their guns, killing five colonists including Crispus Attucks, and wounding eight more. That's why the incident is called the "Boston Massacre."

The Boston Tea Party

News of this "massacre" shocked all the colonies. It even caused the British to take back, or repeal, more of their taxes. Things were fairly quiet for a while, but then a new British government gave an unfair advantage to a British tea company so it could sell its tea to the colonists at a cheaper price than anyone else. To stop that in December 1773, some Bostonians disguised themselves as

The Boston Tea Party.

Indians and dumped chests full of the company's tea into Boston Harbor. Colonists joked that they had given a "Boston tea party."

The British were furious and closed off Boston's port until the colony paid for the tea. They also took away some of the other rights of Massachusetts.

Colonists everywhere were shocked again, and they sent help to Massachusetts. They also sent leaders to meet in Philadelphia to talk about what to do next. This gathering in September 1774 was called the Continental Congress. The Congress decided the colonies would not buy British goods until the British government repealed the many acts that upset the colonists. The colonists wanted the Stamp Act repealed and the Boston Harbor reopened. They were tired of feeding and housing British soldiers. And they felt they should not be taxed by the British legislature (Parliament) because they had no say, or representation, in Parliament's decisions. The cry of "no taxation without representation" swept through the colonies.

The Pot Boils Over

Important members of Parliament wanted to soothe the colonies, but most insisted that the colonies *were* represented by the Parliament. King George III

King George III of England.

and his chief advisers sent more Redcoats to Massachusetts. Do you think that made things better or worse?

If you said "worse," you would be right. There were many people in Massachusetts who were ready to be free of Britain entirely. Some of them began to collect weapons.

The Shot Heard 'Round the World

In April of 1775, British troops were sent to the town of Concord, Massachusetts, to capture the weapons the colonists had stored there. The colonists were warned of their approach, though, when Paul Revere made his famous ride through Massachusetts countryside. He called out: "The British are coming!"

A band of colonists, called minutemen because they could be ready to fight within minutes, faced the soldiers at the town of Lexington. Shots were fired, and eight colonists were killed. The larger British forces continued their mission to Concord.

The Battle of Lexington.

While most of the British soldiers searched Concord, minutemen attacked and scattered a small group of Redcoats left to defend a bridge. The British in Concord, finding no large store of supplies, turned back to Boston. And all along their way, they were fired on from every side by angry colonists hiding behind trees and walls along the road. When the day was over, 273 British and 90 colonists had been killed or wounded. The American Revolution had begun.

Years after the battles at Concord and Lexington, the famous American poet Ralph Waldo Emerson wrote a poem to celebrate a monument built to honor the minutemen. His poem is called the "Concord Hymn." Some of the words in the poem may sound unusual to you, but a dictionary can help them make sense. Here's the poem:

By the rude bridge that arched the flood,
    Their flag to April's breeze unfurled,
Here once the embattled farmers stood
    And fired the shot heard round the world.

The foe long since in silence slept;
Alike the conqueror silent sleeps;
And Time the ruined bridge has swept
    Down the dark stream which seaward creeps.

On this green bank, by this soft stream,
    We set to-day a votive stone;
That memory may their deed redeem,
    When, like our sires, our sons are gone.

Spirit, that made those heroes dare
    To die, and leave their children free,
Bid Time and Nature gently spare
    The shaft we raise to them and thee.

American Now

We can start thinking of the colonists as being more American than British after the fights at Concord and Lexington. A month after the fighting in Massachusetts, the Continental Congress met in Philadelphia for the second time. It named George Washington as commander in chief of a Continental army and sent him to help Boston. Even before he arrived, the British and Americans had fought again in a battle called Bunker Hill. In this battle the minutemen were so low on ammunition that one of their commanders ordered, "Don't fire until you see the whites of their eyes." Even so, the untrained minutemen held off two attacks by the far more skilled British soldiers, only to lose a third when they ran completely out of gunpowder.

There was also fighting going on in Canada and South Carolina. In fact, there was so much fighting that King George III planned to send more troops. More and more of America's men and women agreed with the words of a man named Thomas Paine: "The blood of the slain . . . cries, *'tis time to part*." Paine, who had come to the colonies from England only a few years earlier, became a leading advocate for breaking with Britain. In a famous pamphlet called *Common Sense*, he pointed out that it was silly for a little country like Britain to own a big continent like North America—that would be like the moon owning the earth! Here's how he said it:

In no instance hath nature made the satellite larger than its primary planet; and as England and America, with respect to each other, reverse the common order of nature, it is evident that they belong to different systems.

The Declaration of Independence

A Virginia delegate to the Second Continental Congress was the first to call for American independence. It was important that Virginia was ready to do this. As the first and biggest colony, Virginia gave the call for independence a strong and believable voice. A group headed by another Virginian, Thomas Jefferson, was asked to write down the reasons for independence. Men from other large colonies, such as Benjamin Franklin of Pennsylvania and John Adams of Massachusetts, helped him.

The signing of the Declaration of Independence. Do you recognize anyone in this picture?

They wrote the Declaration of Independence, a famous document in the history of liberty that is still quoted all over the world. The declaration states that all people have rights that no one should take away:

> We hold these truths to be self-evident, that all men are created equal, that they are endowed by their Creator with certain unalienable* Rights, that among these are Life, Liberty and the pursuit of Happiness.

The Declaration was accepted by the whole Congress on July 4, 1776. Now you know why we celebrate the Fourth of July every year. It's a birthday party for our country. What do you do on that day?

*not able to be taken away

A New Flag

Now that there was a new country, a new flag was needed. It would be carried by the Continental army in good times and in bad.

There is a story that the first flag was made by Betsy Ross. She lived in Philadelphia and her business was making clothes. Maybe she made George Washington's clothes. He is supposed to have asked her to make a new flag.

He gave her his ideas about stars and stripes, and she may have added a few of her own. She sewed thirteen stars on a dark blue background, one for each of the colonies in 1776. When a new colony was added, another star could be sewn on. Then she sewed thirteen strips of red and white fabric so the number of the original colonies in 1776 would always be known.

We can't be certain this story is true, but we do know that a flag with thirteen stripes of red and white and thirteen stars on a dark blue background became the first flag of the new United States of America.

Here's how one artist imagined the story of Betsy Ross and the flag.

"Give Me Liberty . . ."

Just because America declared independence did not mean that the mother country would let her "grown-up children" go. The British thought they had the most freedom of any people in the world. But the colonists didn't believe they were sharing in that freedom. Most of the colonists were willing to risk their whole future to gain true freedom, and many thought that Britain would not voluntarily let them have the land and the trade they wanted.

Can you imagine what a tremendous step these new Americans were taking? They were going to have to fight one of the most powerful countries in the world. They had often been proud to be Britain's colonies. Their language was English, and many of their ideas of freedom had come from England. It must have been hard to break away.

If they failed, the men and women who led the American Revolution would lose their wealth and probably their lives. On any day, an American soldier could be killed. Patrick Henry must have spoken for them when he told his fellow Virginians to "give me liberty, or give me death!"

Choose the name of a person who you know from colonial and Revolution-ary times and learn something extra about him or her. Then draw something to symbolize that person (such as a kite for Benjamin Franklin). See if your friends can guess who it is. Be sure to tell them what you've learned if they can't guess.

Using crayons or colored paper and paste, you can make a flag showing the thirteen stars and stripes of the first U.S. flag. Would you like to design a flag for your family or your school? What sort of questions would you ask yourself to get started?

NOTE TO PARENTS AND TEACHERS: *A good discussion for both the world and American history sections in this book would focus on the misery that wars and great migrations cause the human race. Discussion topics could include the fall of Rome to the Germanic tribes, the Indian removals and African slave transportations resulting from European migration to the New World, or the hardships faced by the colonists and the poverty and persecution they escaped in Europe.*

III.

FINE ARTS

Introduction
to the Fine Arts

FOR PARENTS AND TEACHERS

Here we focus on the concepts of rhythm in music, and on shape, pattern, rhythm, and texture in the visual arts. We offer reproductions of some well-known works of art, giving the child a frame of reference for experiencing and conversing about music and visual arts.

To be enjoyed, art needs to be experienced. The best way for a child to explore art is to learn to play an instrument, sculpt, make paintings and drawings, act in plays, and write. In these books we cannot hope to substitute for those experiences, or to provide extensive music and art training. But the explanations and illustrations we provide can enhance the child's appreciation and perception of the arts.

To make the most of the foundation this book provides, we make these recommendations:

• When you are working with the child, relate artworks and art ideas to the literature, history, and science sections of this book, and to life experiences.

• Use the suggested activities to develop additional art activities.

• Encourage the child to comment on what he or she has learned in connection with the child's latest art project.

• Learn to see the value of your child's work even when it appears naive to you.

• Continue to build on the basic vocabulary this book provides by exploring art books, encouraging art projects (even messy or noisy ones!) at home and at school, and enrolling your child in art and music programs.

Several excellent music programs are available for schools, two of the most prominent being the series published by Silver Burdett, and by Holt, Rinehart and Winston. In addition, many have found the Kodaly and Orff teaching approaches to music to be of great value.

Many fine books or series on visual art, especially designed for children, are available at bookstores and libraries. *Looking at Paintings*, published by the Van Nostrand Reinhold Company and copyrighted by Marshall Cavendish, Ltd., is an excellent guide to paintings. David Macaulay has published a series on various kinds of architectural works. For more information on famous artists and their best-known works, you may want to look up the series *Come Look with Me*, published by Tomasson-Grant.

Actively encouraging children's involvement with art not only gives them new and delightful ways of experiencing the world but also gives them confidence in their own abilities. Making art for themselves, whether in music, painting, sculpting, or writing, allows them to express their individuality, and helps enhance their self-esteem. Experiencing fine art contributes to their future development by giving them a basis for responding to the ideals, perceptions, and insights embodied in works of art from various parts of the world.

Music

Rhythm

Have you ever wanted to clap your hands or dance when you heard some music? What makes you want to do that? It's the beat of the music—the *boom-boom-boom-boom* or *rat-a-tat-tat* that happens over and over again. The beat is part of the rhythm of a song.

Rhythm is a part of music. Some music—like that of some African and American Indian tribes—is made up mainly of rhythms. You can hear rhythms everywhere around you, if you try. Listen to your heart: ba-*boom*, ba-*boom*, ba-*boom!* Even *you* have a rhythm!

Donna Graham, leader of the African-American dance troupe Chihamba (chah HAHM bah), dances to the accompaniment of African drum music.

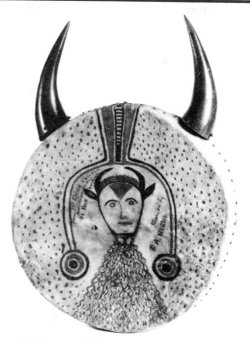

*A Sioux medicine man, or healer, used
this drum in healing ceremonies.*

The words you speak have rhythm, too. Here's a word with a two-beat rhythm:

1 2		1 2		1 2		1 2
magic	|	magic	|	magic	|	magic

Can you hear the *one*-two, *one*-two when you say it over and over? Try a word with three beats:

1 2 3		1 2 3		1 2 3		1 2 3
wonderful	|	wonderful	|	wonderful	|	wonderful

Many states with long names have four beats and are fun to say over and over.

1 2 3 4		1 2 3 4		1 2 3 4		1 2 3 4		1 2 3 4
Mississippi	|	Minnesota	|	Alabama	|	Massachusetts	|	Indiana

Can you hear how we divide each of the state names into four parts as we say them? This is the way we count out most songs, too. The most common way of counting out music is with *four* beats. Let's try a song with four beats now, one you're probably quite familiar with. It's lots of fun to clap on the first beat (marked *1*), and sing louder where we've underlined.

3 4	1 2 3 4	1 2 3 4	1 2 3 4	1 2 3 4
She'll be	comin' round the	mountain when she	comes, ———	She'll be
	1 2 3 4	1 2 3 4	1 2 3 4	1 2 3 4
	comin' round the	mountain when she	comes, ———	She'll be
	1 2 3 4	1 2 3 4	1 2 3 4	1 2 3 4
	comin' round the	mountain, she'll be	comin' round the	mountain, she'll be
	1 2 3 4	1 2 3 4	1 2 3 4	1 2 3 4
	comin' round the	mountain when she	comes. ———	(She'll be)

Did you notice that there are times when you don't sing? Right after "when she comes," for example? These times when you don't sing are called rests.

Meter

When we count the beat, we are marking what is called meter. The counting is a way of measuring out the time of the song, just as the ticking of the clock measures out time. The counting tells you when to sing and when to take a rest. Each set of four beats in "She'll Be Comin' Round the Mountain" is called a measure, because it measures out the song.

Most notes in our song fit the counting exactly, and take just one beat each. But some words are more important, so you sing them longer than the other ones. You sing "comes" much longer than anything else, for four whole beats. That's one reason you need a rest afterward. Try singing the first line again and notice how you sing "comes" for four beats, and then rest for two beats afterward.

1 2 3 4	1 2 3 4	1 2 3 4	1 2 3 4
She'll be	comin' round the	mountain when she	comes ———

Could you hear it? Let's try the whole second verse. This time let's clap on *first* and *third* beat of every measure.

3 4	1 2 3 4	1 2 3 4	1 2 3 4	1 2 3 4
She'll be	drivin' six white	horses when she	comes, ———	She'll be
	1 2 3 4	1 2 3 4	1 2 3 4	1 2 3 4
	drivin' six white	horses when she	comes, ———	She'll be
	1 2 3 4	1 2 3 4	1 2 3 4	1 2 3 4
	drivin' six white	horses, she'll be	drivin' six white	horses, she'll be
	1 2 3 4	1 2 3 4	1 2 3 4	1 2 3 4
	drivin' six white	horses when she	comes. ———	(She'll be)

You often hear drums in popular songs playing this rhythm: 1 2 3 4, 1 2 3 4. "She'll Be Comin' Round the Mountain" is a pretty fast song, but there are also slower songs that you can count out in fours.

Tempo

How slow or fast a song is sung is called the tempo. Here's a famous African-American spiritual that has a medium-slow tempo. It sounds good to clap on the first and third beat on this song, too.

1 2 3 4	1 2 3 4	1 2 3 4	1 2 3 4
We shall o-ver	come, ———	We shall o-ver	come, ——
1 2 3 4	1 2 3 4	1 2 3 4	1 2 3 4
We shall o-ver	come, some	day.———	Oh-oh
1 2 3 4	1 2 3 4	1 2 3 4	1 2 3 4
Deep in my	heart, ———	I do be-lieve, ———	
1 2 3 4	1 2 3 4	1 2 3 4	1 2 3 4
We shall o-ver	come some	day.———	

Second Verse: We shall walk in peace, etc.

Songs that have four beats to each measure are the most common ones. But another popular type of song is sung to a count of three: 1 2 3, 1 2 3. Here is a very slow song that is sung to this count of three.

1	2	3	1	2 3	1	2 3	1	2	3	1	2 3	1	2 3
Down	in	the	val ——		ley ——		val ley	so		low ——		——	

1	2	3	1	2 3	1	2 3	1	2	3	1	2 3	1	2 3
Hang	your head		o ——		ver, ——		hear the wind			blow.——		——	

Songs that have three beats in each measure are often called waltzes, because that is the kind of dance that is done to them. "On Top of Old Smokey" is another famous song in this meter. Try counting it out in three's as well.

On Top of Old Smokey

On top of Old Smokey
All covered with snow,
I lost my true lover
For courtin' too slow.

Here is what we've learned so far: meter is a way of counting out a song. It tells you when to sing and when to take a rest. In simple songs, most notes take one beat each and fit the counting exactly. But some notes may not fit the count of the meter exactly; they vary the rhythm to make it more fun. The first beat is usually the loudest, telling us we've begun a new measure, so you can clap on the first beat.

African and Latin Rhythms

Other songs have complicated rhythms. The words in these songs don't fit the count very easily, but they're even more fun to sing once you get their rhythms. Two kinds of complicated rhythms that have influenced American music are African rhythms and rhythms from Latin America, called Latin rhythms. Both have had an influence on the music we call jazz, and on much of the popular music you can hear on the radio. We'll tell you more about them in later books. But here is a simple song from Mexico that gives you the feel of some delightful Latin rhythms:

La Cucaracha
(The Cockroach)

When a fellow loves a maiden
And that maiden doesn't love him,
It's the same as when a bald man
Finds a comb upon the highway.

The cucaracha, the cucaracha,
Doesn't want to travel on
Because she hasn't,
Oh no, she hasn't,
Fried bananas for to eat.

Instruments That Keep Rhythm

A drum, a cymbal, even a pot or anything else you can hit, can be used to play the beat. Some rhythm instruments like drums are called percussion instruments.

Can you find the bass drum and cymbal in this picture?

There are many different kinds of drums, as you can see. The biggest drums, like the bass drum and the kettle drum, usually give off the lowest, loudest sounds, like *boom, boom, boom.* Smaller drums generally give off higher, sharper sounds, like *tok, tok, tok.* Other percussion instruments give off crashing sounds, like the cymbal, or a bright, tingling sound, like the triangle. Maracas, which come from South America, are made from large, dried plant shells called gourds. They are like a baby's rattle. You shake them and they make a fine, scratchy sound.

Kettle drum.

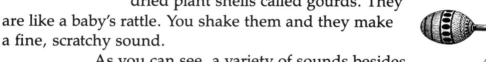

Snare drum.

Maracas.

As you can see, a variety of sounds besides clapping can be used to keep the beat. Some percussion instruments like steel drums make pitches as well as beats. (Pitch is a term we use to indicate the highness or lowness of a sound. A train whistle's sound has a high pitch; a gong has a low pitch.) Steel drums were invented in the Caribbean, when the people living there took empty oil barrels and turned them into musical instruments!

This drum set includes a snare drum, a tom-tom, a crash cymbal, a bass drum, a triangle, and a tambourine.

Musicians can also keep rhythm on string instruments like guitars or bass fiddles by plucking or strumming the strings. And the bass notes on a piano are often used to keep the rhythm.

Rhythm is a very old part of music, and drums are some of the oldest kinds of musical instruments. People have been beating out rhythms on drums and other things almost as far back as we can tell.

Triangle.

You can make your own percussion instruments very easily—just banging two sticks or two stones together can make percussion music! Try using an oatmeal box or a coffee can with a lid as a drum, or fill them with rice or dried beans to make a rattling instrument. Two pot lids make great cymbals, and one by itself can be a gong. If you make and gather enough of these, you and your friends can have a parade.

The Rhythm the Drums Play

When you hear drums playing in the background of a song on the radio, they are generally counting out the meter of the song. But drums can do so much more than hitting "one two three four," or "one two three," over and over again. Drummers vary the beat several different ways. They can hit some beats louder than others, the way we sang the first and third notes louder. Or they can hit some beats and not hit others at all, the way we clapped only on the first and third beats. Or they can even hit twice as many beats in some places, and make them fit into the meter. To tell you that an important part of a song is coming up, they can get louder and louder and build up to a great crash. These are all parts of the rhythm of a song, too. Listen for the drums playing the meter and other rhythms the next time you listen to a song.

Rhythm: A Review

When you hear songs on records and tapes, songs played by bands, you can most easily find the beat by listening to the drums. You can hear them in the background pounding away. When you listen to a song on the radio or on a tape, try to listen for the beat in the background. Does the song have three-beats or four-beats? Can you tell? Can you count along with it?

Let's review what we learned about rhythm. Rhythm is a major part of music and is found throughout the world. It is usually played on percussion instruments. The most common percussion instruments are drums.

Notation: How Music Is Written Down

The way music is written down is called notation. Notes are placed on a set of lines called a staff to show how high or low you sing them. This is a picture of a staff:

You can think of the staff as a kind of ladder that the melody climbs up, or goes down, or jumps around on. Notes are placed on the lines of the staff and on the spaces between the lines, and the higher you sing the notes, the higher up the staff the notes are written. Often notes are written on two staffs together like this:

The top one, called the treble or G clef, is used for higher notes, while the lower one, called the bass or F clef, is used for lower notes.

This is the treble or G clef.

This is the bass or F clef.

This is what the notes of the C major scale look like, playing from a low-sounding C in the bass clef to a C octave higher in the treble clef. (Remember, an octave is a set of eight notes.) Because middle C is at the center of the keyboard on a piano, it is in the middle of the two clefs on a line all its own, as you can see.

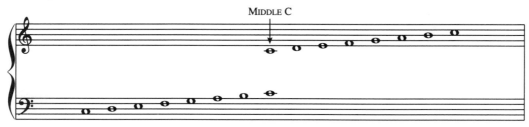

MIDDLE C

The written notes also tell you how long to sing them. In the most common meter, called 4/4 (you say "four, four"), a note called the quarter note

is held for one beat, and it takes four of them to fill up a measure. The half note   lasts half a measure, and two of them fill up a measure.

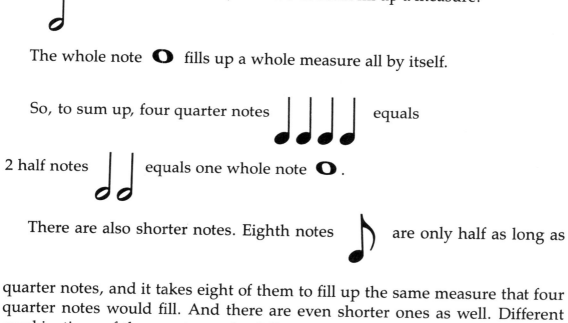

The whole note **O** fills up a whole measure all by itself.

So, to sum up, four quarter notes   equals

2 half notes   equals one whole note **O** .

There are also shorter notes. Eighth notes   are only half as long as

quarter notes, and it takes eight of them to fill up the same measure that four quarter notes would fill. And there are even shorter ones as well. Different combinations of these notes make different rhythms in music. Rests, such as

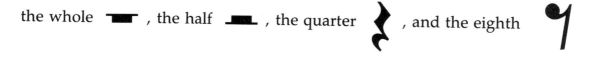

the whole ▬ , the half ▬ , the quarter   , and the eighth

tell you when and how long not to sing.

Learning to read notes from printed music takes a lot of practice. But it is a great tool, just like learning to read words, because the world of music is opened up to you when you simply look at a page of sheet music. You'll find an example to practice with on the next page.

She'll Be Comin' Round The Mountain

Traditional

2. She'll be drivin' six white horses when she comes,   (etc.)

3. Oh, we'll all go out to meet her when she comes,   (etc.)

4. Oh, we'll kill the old red rooster when she comes,   (etc.)

Visual Arts

Elements of Art

In Book Two we talked about some of the elements artists use in creating paintings, sculptures, and works of architecture. Remember this painting by Jan Vermeer from Book Two? Vermeer was especially fascinated by the element of light, which he represented by brightening his colors in certain places. Can you find the light in Vermeer's painting?

Let's take a closer look at his painting to see how he uses light and lines together. Notice which direction the light is coming from and where it is pointing. Do you see how the vertical and horizontal lines of the window and table direct our attention to the places where the light falls most strongly? Vermeer used lines and strong light to help us pay attention to the woman in the picture and make her seem special.

In art, "design" is the way elements work together to please us, to show emotion, tell a story, or give us new ways to see. Vermeer's painting shows that he gave a lot of thought to how light and lines would work together. But there are many more things he had to think about, and in this section we will learn some of them.

Lines Make Shapes

Have you ever made a drawing? What materials did you use? A famous artist named Paul Klee (pronounced CLAY) once described drawing as taking a line for a walk! Many different materials can be used to make a drawing, but artists often use pencil or charcoal on paper.

Look at this picture by the Japanese artist Hokusai (HOE coos eye). What did Hokusai draw? You may not know exactly, but you might recognize the image of a person holding a musical instrument that looks a little bit like a banjo.

Like Hokusai, artists often use lines to indicate shapes. In fact, Hokusai named his drawing *Tuning the Samisen* (SAM ee sohn), so this is a drawing of a Japanese musician preparing an instrument to play properly. Do you think the musician cares about the samisen and the music it will play? What makes you think that?

In Hokusai's drawing, you see shapes made with lines. Let's find out how artists think about the shapes they draw. Look at these drawn shapes.

Cone   *Star*   *Box*

Inside the lines are a cone, star, and box. Outside the lines is another space. We see shapes when we notice that lines divide the space inside a cone, star, and box from another space that is outside. Artists call the line that divides spaces from one another an "outline." Can you see that Hokusai uses an outline to show the shape of the samisen?

Find all the outlined shapes you can in Hokusai's drawing. Take your own pencil for a walk over a piece of paper to make the outline of any shape you can imagine!

Shapes with Straight and Curved Lines

Look closely at the lines in Hokusai's drawing. Compare the lines making the samisen to the lines that make the musician's clothes. Are the lines that make the samisen mostly straight or curved? What about the lines that make the musician's clothes? Shapes that are drawn with mostly straight lines are called "rectilinear." *Recta* is a Latin word for straight, so rectilinear means "straight lined." Shapes like the musician's clothes that are drawn with mostly curved lines are called—can you guess?—curvilinear.

Rectilinear shapes often look more precise and orderly than curvilinear shapes, which tend to look more free and flowing. Look out the window and name things you see that look orderly, then things that look flowing. What kinds of things seem to have more rectilinear shapes? What kinds of things seem to have more curvilinear shapes? Look back at Hokusai's drawing. Do the musician's clothes look more precise or more flowing to you?

Lines Can Show Emotion

Draw a thin straight line across the page. Now draw a line that gets thicker and then thinner again. Compare the two kinds of lines. You might say the thin line is more calm or careful because it looks very much the same in all of its parts, and that the other line is more lively or active because it changes. Look back at the drawing by Hokusai. Notice that he uses fine lines to draw the samisen, the head of the musician, and the hands of the musician. Notice that the parts of the musician's body covered by clothes are drawn with lines that get thick and thin.

Why does Hokusai draw the musician's body with lively thick and thin lines, and the musician's face, hands, and instrument with calm, thin lines? Many works of art use lines as part of a way to tell a story or give us a feeling about what we see. Hokusai may have used calm lines for the samisen and the musician's head and hands to show that the musician is using great care to make the instrument ready to play. Maybe Hokusai used lively lines for the musician's clothes to make the thin lines seem even more calm. What do you think? Make up a story about this musician.

A Different Way to Make Shapes

Looking at Hokusai's drawing, you saw how artists use lines to make shapes. We are going to look at quilts to learn another way artists make shapes. But first let's find out what quilts are.

In the history section of this book, you can read about how the American colonists settled the eastern shore of this continent. Did you know that the colonists also made art? In the next two pages are photographs of quilts that were made in the colonies of Pennsylvania and Boston. Quilts are warm bedcovers made by sewing together layers of cloth. We think of these quilts as works of art because they were made so carefully to create a pleasing design.

Most colonial quilts were made by women for their families or for gifts. Sewing the layers together is called quilting. The Double Irish Chain quilt on page 176 is called a piecework quilt because many small pieces of cloth were sewn together to make the material for the top of the quilt.

There is a story about how piecework started. When the first colonists came to America, they could not easily get material from Europe to make clothes. So they had to try and make all cloth last as long as possible. Instead of throwing away clothes that were starting to wear out, women cut up the sturdiest parts of old dresses and shirts and other clothes into smaller pieces to make different things. Often they made quilts with the smaller pieces.

When there were lots of pieces, the women carefully planned how to sew them together in designs to make a big piece of material for the top layer of the quilt. Often, all the women in the town would get together to sew the piecework top to the other layers of the quilt. They would turn their work into a big party called a quilting bee. After the quilting bee, the men might join the quilters for music and dancing. Making this kind of art could be fun for the whole town!

Quilts are still being made today, but not as often as they were by the colonists. In fact, some people say quilting is a dying art because there are fewer and fewer people who know how to do it, and many who know how to make quilts no longer take the time. Because quilts are becoming so rare, people often hang them on walls now, instead of putting them on beds. That way the careful sewing and lovely patterns can be seen more easily.

What Quilts Tell Us About Shapes

The quilts you see here are not only beautiful and useful, they can help us figure out some fascinating things about the way we see shapes. Let's look at the Willow Oak quilt. Instead of sewing square pieces together in a pattern,

This appliqué quilt design is called Willow Oak. We don't know who made it.

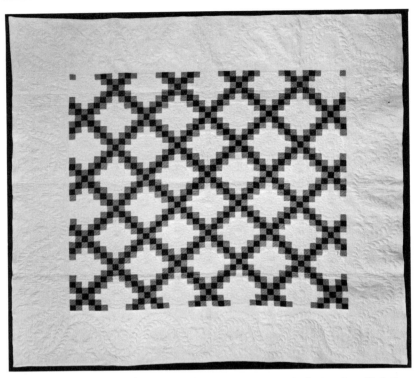

*This quilt was made by Margie Gorrect. Its piecework design is called the
Double Irish Chain.*

the artist cut the material into shapes that were then sewed onto the top of the
quilt. This way of making a quilt design is called appliqué. The Willow Oak
quilt was made with dark appliqué pieces sewed onto a light material. See if
you can find the dark shapes made by the appliqué pieces. What do these
shapes remind you of?

Remember how an outline helped your eyes see shapes in Hokusai's
drawing? There are no outlines in these quilts, but you can still see shapes.
When dark and light materials are put next to one another, our eyes see shapes
even when there are no outlines.

In the Willow Oak quilt, do you notice that you pay attention to the dark
shapes rather than the light ones? To see the white shapes, you have to
concentrate. The shapes that you notice first are called the figures, and shapes
that you *don't* pay attention to at first are called the ground.

Now look again at the Hokusai drawing. Does it have figure and ground?
Yes! Look at the space between the musician's clothes and the top of the

samisen. The dress and the samisen are figure, and the little space between them is ground. You can see that the ground is a shape too. But you didn't notice that shape first, because instead you were paying attention to the figures of the musician and the samisen.

This painting is by a clever artist named M. C. Escher. Why do you think Escher might have named this painting *Sky and Water*? Do you notice how the dark shapes are figures at the top of the painting, but gradually become ground at the bottom?

*Y*ou can make your own quilt. You'll need cloth scraps, pins, a needle, and thread. Cut a large scrap to make a square the size of a piece of writing paper. This will be your quilt top. Think about a design for it. Cut up the other cloth scraps into pieces and arrange them into your design on the quilt top. Use pins to fasten the pieces to the quilt top. Then use a needle and thread to sew the pieces to each other and to the quilt top. To sew the pieces, you can use slash stitches like this: \ Or you can use a cross-stitch, like this: **X**

You can try making both piecework patterns and appliqué patterns.

Using Shapes to Show Emotion

The American artist Mary Cassatt made this painting about one hundred years ago. In earlier times, people didn't always take a bath in a bathtub. They didn't always have running water. Children were sometimes bathed with a washcloth in a small basin with water from a pitcher, like the little girl in Cassatt's painting.

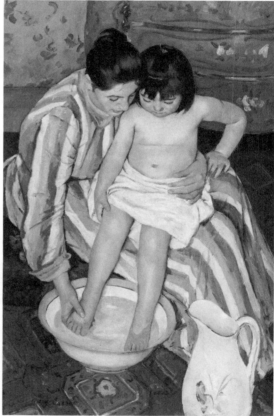

Even though Cassatt has filled the canvas with lots of paint, one of the ways she helps you see shapes may remind you of a drawing. For example, look at the arm that the little girl has pressed against the woman. Cassatt helps you see the shape of the arm by outlining it. Find some other outlined shapes.

Remember how you saw shapes when dark and light materials were put next to each other in the quilts? Cassatt also helps you see shapes by putting dark and light parts next to one another in the painting. For example, look at the light-colored basin full of water. Cassatt helps you see the bottom of the basin by the contrast between the light color of the basin and the dark color of the rug. Find another light figure against a dark ground. Find a dark figure. (Hint: what about the hair of the two people?)

In this painting, Cassatt uses lines and figure and ground to make shapes that speak to us about emotions. How does she do this? Many people's eyes tend to go first to the shape of the little girl's tummy because it is so light and has so few lines in it compared to other parts of the painting. It's important that our eyes go there, because it makes us look at the faces of the woman and little girl. We notice how close their heads are together. Because the woman and little girl have their heads close together and are looking at the same spot, we tend to feel that they like being close to one another. Cassatt often pictured women and children enjoying things in daily life together.

A Painting About an Idea

Shapes in paintings don't only speak to us about emotions, they can tell us stories or tell us about important ideas! This painting by Edward Hicks, called *The Peaceable Kingdom*, is about the founding of the Pennsylvania colonies. It is called *The Peaceable Kingdom* because the Quakers who founded the colony hoped their new homes would be so peaceful that even animals that are usually enemies of each other and of people would become friends.

In America, there aren't any lions exactly like the one in the picture. Why did Hicks show an African lion? It was because the picture wasn't supposed to show an actual scene. It was supposed to show an *idea* of peace. In the Bible, there is a passage the Quakers knew very well. It was from the book of the Bible called Isaiah. It predicted a wonderful new world. Isaiah says:

> The wolf shall dwell with the lamb, and the leopard shall lie down with the kid; and the calf and the young lion and the fatling together; and a little child shall lead them.

You may see other versions of The Peaceable Kingdom. *Edward Hicks was so fascinated by the idea it portrays that he painted about fifty different versions.*

How many of these creatures do you see in the painting? Very often, you have to know something about the people who made pictures and the things they knew and cared about in order to "see" what they meant the picture to say.

Shapes in Architecture

This picture is of a work of architecture built about two thousand years ago! It is an aqueduct built by the Romans in Nîmes, France. It's name, Pont du Gard, means "the bridge of Gard" (Gard is the region where the aqueduct stands). You may have read, in the World Civilization section of this book, that the Romans had excellent architects and built many different kinds of structures, including aqueducts like the Pont du Gard. The main purpose of an aqueduct wasn't to make a pretty design, of course, any more than the main purpose of a quilt was. An aqueduct took water over very long distances to places where people needed the water. But sometimes useful shapes for things like bridges and buildings are very beautiful shapes too, and builders often try to use these shapes to make their works look pleasing.

This aqueduct is a good example of Roman architecture because it shows us a shape that Romans used a lot, the round arch. Do you see the many half-circles in the Pont du Gard? These half-circles are round arches, and they are useful because they make it easier for the other parts of the aqueduct to carry weight. To see how an arch works, try this. Put your thumb and first finger in an arch shape on top of a table. Hold them in that shape, and press down with your other hand on top. Do you notice that the round arch puts equal weight on your thumb and finger? The arch makes each part of the aqueduct hold the same amount of weight, so no part does too much work.

If you could touch the Pont du Gard, you could feel the shape of the arches.

But you are looking at it in a photograph. The photographer did not draw lines or use paint so that you could see the shapes of the arches, but many of the elements that help you see shape in paintings also help you see shape in a photograph. Can you see how the shadows seem to outline the arches? Point to where darkness and light create figure and ground in this photograph.

Notice that there are many arches in this photograph of the Pont du Gard. Even though some arches are different sizes, the Romans used the same kind of shape over and over again. The Romans also put the shapes at the same distances from one another. We say that the shape of the arch is repeated (or that there is a repetition of the shape) in this piece of architecture. When our eyes see repeating shapes, we see pattern. Look back at the colonial quilts. Now that you know what pattern is, can you find the patterns in these works of art?

Shapes and Rhythm

The photograph of the Pont du Gard that you have just been looking at was taken right in front of the aqueduct. This picture is also of the Pont du Gard, but it was taken from above and to one side of it. Looking at this picture, many people's eyes will follow the *line* made by the beams from the right-hand side of the picture to the left-hand side. But the *shapes* of the arches also help our eyes move this way.

Looking at this photograph, our eyes tend to do two things. They tend to see the pattern created by the repeating arches, and also to follow the arches across the photograph. When repeating shapes make patterns that help our eyes move around a work of art, we say the pattern creates a rhythm. Much Roman architecture had the kind of rhythm you see in this aqueduct because the Romans used arches so often in their buildings.

You can make outlines and figure patterns using potatoes and paints. Cut a raw potato in half. On the smooth, cut surface of one of the potato halves, carve shapes into the potato. On the other half of the potato, cut away everything except the shape you want to see. Coat the potato surfaces with paint, and then use them as stamps on a piece of paper. Use your imagination to make patterns with your potato stamps!

Sponges make wonderful stamps. Use your imagination to cut sponges into shapes. See what kinds of patterns the sponge stamps make.

You can also make stamps out of parts of your hands! Coat the fingertip of your thumb with paint and press it on paper to make patterns. If you have enough paint and paper, you can use your whole hand as a stamp.

All Kinds of Horses

Did you notice how strong and still the aqueduct looked? The arch shapes in the Pont du Gard are repeated so that the only differences are the sizes of the arches. The constantly repeated shapes help give the feeling that the Pont du Gard is steady and secure. But when shapes are varied, the result can be anything but still. For example, here's lots of action! The work of art on the next page, painted by the English artist Walter Crane, shows the god Neptune with the horses that draw his chariot. What realm was Neptune supposed to rule over?

How do you feel when you look at this painting? Can you imagine the pounding of the horses on the beach? Repetition helps us enjoy the pattern of the horses and helps our eyes follow the rhythmic movement the shapes create. Have you ever seen the sea when strong waves were coming in? As they reach the shore they curve over toward the beach, like the bodies of the horses do in this painting.

Even though this painting looks very lively and excited, if you look closely at it and think about what you have learned so far, you will see that Crane

must have planned shapes very carefully. Can you find where Crane uses outline to help us see shapes? Where does he use figure and ground to help us see shapes?

Let's compare the effect repetition and rhythm have in this painting to the effect created by the repeated shapes in the aqueduct. In Crane's painting, the *variety* in the horse shapes tends to make the rhythm of this painting feel changeable and violent compared to the steady, calm rhythm of the Pont du Gard. We may tend to feel that Crane's painting is as lively as the aqueduct is still.

Pictures Like Puzzles

The special kind of artwork shown on the next page, mosaic, makes pictures using features of both architecture and painting. Mosaics are made of small squares of colored glass, jewels, and precious metals fitted together like a puzzle and set into the wall of a building. Because mosaics were made of such hard, lasting bits of material, many are as bright today as when they were first made. They were meant to last as long as the religious buildings they were in, and many have.

The picture you see on the next page is a small part, or detail, of the mosaics covering all the walls in the church of San Vitale in Ravenna, Italy. It shows the Empress Theodora and her court. You may have read about Theodora's city, Con-

stantinople, in the World Civilization section of this book. About two hundred years after Constantine died, Theodora's husband, the Emperor Justinian, ruled the city of Constantinople and the lands that had made up the eastern part of the Roman Empire. These lands, and the civilization that flourished there from the 400's to the 1400's, are known as the Byzantine Empire. Because the art of these people has its own special style, it is called Byzantine art.

Some of the best-known Byzantine art, like these mosaics, were in churches or were about religious subjects. This is because the Christian religion was an important part of these people's daily lives, and art could be used to tell the stories of religion to those who could not read. The Empress Theodora is in this mosaic because during Justinian's reign (A.D. 527–65) she and her husband built churches so that many could have a place to worship.

This photograph of the mosaic makes it look as though it is black, white, and gray, but if you were in San Vitale you would be struck by the brilliant colors of the mosaic. You would also be amazed by the way the mosaic looks as though it is filled with light. Light is so important in the mosaics at Ravenna that a poem on the wall of a building in Ravenna says, "Light was either born here, or captured, and reigneth here freely."

The mosaic looks filled with light because much of the background is made of gold, which catches and reflects the light coming from windows or candles. The Byzantines used this beautiful material because the images they made were supposed to make people think of the perfect things of heaven. You must use your imagination to think how it would feel to be in a very large room whose rounded walls are covered with all the colors of the rainbow and glowing with light!

Slow Rhythms

When you look at the mosaic, what do you notice first—the border, the fountain, or Theodora and her attendants? Many of us notice the people first. The reason is not hard to find, now that you know about how artists help our eyes see shapes. Notice how the artist has used outline to help your eyes see the shapes of the people. Are the shapes mostly the same or mostly different? If you said mostly the same, you were right! Because the shapes are so strongly outlined and because they are repeated, we tend to take notice of them.

How do Theodora and her attendants look? They are all standing very straight and seem to be paying close attention to what's in front of them. Even the folds of their clothes fall in straight, vertical lines! The strong outlines and the straightness of the figures tend to help us appreciate them more as perfect shapes than as pictures of real, imperfect human beings. This makes sense because people used to think that kings and queens were holy people, almost like saints.

The repeating shapes of the people make a rhythm in this mosaic. When you look at the shapes, do you tend to feel as though the mosaic is more steady and calm, Like the Pont du Gard, or more changeable and lively, like *The Horses of Neptune?* Because the shapes are so much the same, you may find that your eyes tend to look for longer periods at one figure at a time. You might say that the rhythm slows down the movement of your eyes so that you must spend more time looking at the mosaic.

Why would the artist want the rhythm to have this effect? Remember that the mosaic is built in a church, San Vitale. The design of the mosaic is meant to help people slow down and spend time concentrating on the things of heaven.

Make your own mosaic by tearing up colored paper into small squares. Arrange the small squares into shapes or patterns on a piece of cardboard or paper. Glue the squares down on the paper. You can experiment with other kinds of material beside colored paper, like bottle caps, feathers, sequins, or string.

Make a mosaic sand cast. Get the following materials: plaster of paris, water, clean sand in a box, a container and spoon to mix plaster, and decorative objects to make the mosaics (for example, buttons, shells, pebbles, bits of wood, glass). Wet the sand and press something into it to make an impression. Put the decorative objects face down in the impression so that there is as little space between them as possible. Mix the plaster of paris according to the box instructions. Pour the plaster onto the decorative objects in the impression, and let it harden (it will take about fifteen or twenty minutes). As the plaster hardens, it should stick to the decorations. Remove the plaster cast from the impression and brush loose sand from the surface.

In front of this mural, you can see the railing put up so that people cannot touch and damage it. If you were standing at the railing, it would probably reach up to your chest. That means that each human figure on the mural is as big as you are—or bigger!

Paintings That Are Part of Walls

This large picture, painted on a hospital wall in Mexico City, was made in 1953 by the Mexican artist Diego Rivera. Large pictures painted on walls are called murals, from the Latin word for wall, which is *murus*. The mosaics at Ravenna are also called murals because they are very large artworks made directly on a wall or ceiling.

Rivera made his mural in the fresco style, which means that he painted onto a wall covered with damp plaster. Then, as the plaster dried, the paint became part of the plaster. One of the reasons that Rivera wanted to paint frescos is that it was an artform of ancient Mexico, but he learned about murals and the techniques of fresco painting from both Mexican and Italian artists.

The Mexican Muralists

Works by great Mexican muralists like Rivera are often found on public buildings in Mexico because their works show stories about things that have affected Mexico's people.

If you have read the American Civilization sections of Book One and Book Two of this series, you may have already learned about one of the great Mexican civilizations—the Aztec civilization—that existed in Mexico before Europeans came there. This mural tells the history of Mexican medicine by showing the kind of medicine practiced by the Aztecs as well as the medicine practiced in modern times. It is called *The History of Medicine in Mexico: The People's Demand for Better Health.*

A Mural That Makes a Message

Look closely at the central figure in *The History of Medicine in Mexico.* This is Rivera's picture of the Aztec goddess who was believed to make things clean by touching them. Can you think why Rivera would put a symbol of cleanliness in a mural about medicine?

To the left of the goddess, Rivera has painted modern medical instruments and people dressed in modern clothing to show his vision of modern medicine. To the right of the goddess, Rivera has painted ancient instruments and people dressed as they were in the time of the Aztecs to show his vision of the Aztec people's medicine. Notice that many of the people on either side of the goddess have similar-looking faces. Can you think what this might mean? It may show that even though people are dressed differently and use different devices to help them be healthy, they are basically the same.

Now look at the way people are grouped together. On the modern side, there are lots of people crowded together at the top, but as you look further down, box-like rooms hold few people. Where there are lots of people there seem to be few doctors. Where there are few people there seem to be lots of doctors. The boxes and the way people are arranged make a division between many and few, and between the number of doctors for every patient.

How are people arranged on the Aztec side? People are in many small groups arranged in a circle, and there seems to be a healer for every sick person. What do you think Rivera means by showing modern medicine and Aztec medicine this way? Perhaps he means that modern medicine does not treat people with the kind of equality that the Aztecs did.

Shapes That Frame a Picture

Now look at the whole mural. Even though Rivera has painted many shapes crowded together on this mural, notice that at the edges of the mural are big shapes that are either very dark or very light—two light trees on either side, a band of dark serpents at the base (bottom), and a dark sky on top. Compared with all the shapes in the middle of the mural, these edges look simple. You could say that the shapes Rivera has painted around the edges of the mural make a kind of frame.

A frame acts in many ways, including setting the scene for a painting or picture. The frame of this mural includes things of nature like the sun and moon, and things of the imagination like winged serpents. What kind of feeling do you think this frame gives? Many would say it is the feeling of being in a dream, where things seem both real and imaginary. This makes sense because the mural partly shows Rivera's dream for the health of the Mexican people.

Now look at the whole mural again. Rivera has put ancient and modern times in the same frame, as if to say that all of Mexico's people have a part in the story of good health. Also, the goddess holds out her hands in blessing over both the modern and ancient practice of medicine. What might this mean? Perhaps that Rivera hopes Mexico can improve people's health by finding a way to bring together the best of both ancient and modern medical practice.

Y*ou can read about Diego Rivera's childhood in a colorful picture book called* Diego *by Jeanette Wintes (Knopf, 1991).*

Pattern and Texture

This is a work of art that is meant to be worn! It is a mask made by an Iroquois artist. Do you ever wear masks? In the American Civilization section of this book, you read about the first Americans—the Native Americans. The Iroquois are one of the peoples that American colonists met in the New World. This mask was made for a member of the Iroquois Husk Face Society. Can you tell what the mask is made of? (The name of the society may give you a clue.)

The Iroquois wore these masks several times a year, in special ceremonies held for the care of crops. When they wore the masks, Iroquois people played the parts of harvest spirits. Why do you think the Iroquois would want to ask the spirits for help with crops? The dancers in the Husk Face Society were men, but women also had an important role in the ceremonies— women were the artists who made the masks.

Even though the Iroquois mask is very different from the Byzantine mosaics, comparing the two artworks helps us learn about each. Look at the mask and at the close-up photo of the San Vitale mosaic on page 191. (Remember that the woman in this detail of the mosaic is the Empress Theodora.) If you look closely at each picture, you will notice that repeating shapes are important in both the mosaic and the mask. See how the little squares of the mosaic are put together to make up Theodora's face? In a similar way, the face in the mask is made from many braids. Think back to the way Le Pont du Gard repeated shapes. Can you remember the name for repeating shapes in art? Pattern! Both the mosaic and the mask use small shapes to create the pattern of a face.

Can you almost imagine how the squares of glass and the corn braids would feel if you ran your hands over them? Do you think one would feel colder than the other? When you answer these questions, you are describing the texture of the artworks. Artists use the word texture to describe how the surface of an artwork feels, or how we imagine it feels when we look at it.

In art, we call repeating shapes texture if they tend to make us imagine how they would feel if we ran our fingers over them. There is both pattern and texture in the mosaic and the mask. Do you pay more attention to pattern or texture when you look at the mosaic? What about the mask? There are no right or wrong answers to these questions, but many people would say the mosaic emphasizes pattern, while the mask emphasizes texture.

You can make a mask of your own. Cut a piece of cardboard into a round shape big enough to cover your face. Make round holes in the cardboard in the appropriate places for your eyes and mouth (also for your nose, if you want to). Make a little hole close to each edge of the mask. Put heavy string through each hole and tie the string so that the mask will stay snug on your face when you wear it. Use your imagination to decorate the mask. You can draw on the mask. You can glue all sorts of things onto the front of the mask—like crumpled, colored tissue paper, tinfoil, or even corn husks! You can glue knitting wool onto the mask for hair (or a beard and mustache). You can even poke holes into patterns in the cardboard. Then wear your mask and pretend you are a character in a story you have made up!

What Have You Learned?

Think of all the new things you have learned about design! You have learned how lines make shapes. You have learned how we see shapes in an artwork even when there are no lines. You have discovered that lines and shapes can tell stories and show emotion. You have found out about how shapes create rhythms. And you have learned how shapes can make pattern and texture. But best of all, you have made artworks yourself that use all these elements!

IV.

MATHEMATICS

Introduction to Mathematics—Grades One Through Six

Americans do not pay enough attention to mathematics in the early grades. As a proportion of total class time, we spend less time on mathematics and more time on language arts than other countries do. Yet those other countries outshine us not only in math, but also in language arts. Their children's reading and writing levels are as high as or higher than ours by seventh grade. Do they know something we don't know?

It is almost impossible for children *not* to practice the use of language. Their out-of-school practice in speaking and listening helps their performance in reading and writing, since there's a lot of overlap between listening, talking, reading, and writing. But with so little time spent on math, it is all too easy for children to neglect practicing mathematics, which is a kind of language. Just as English should become second nature to our children, so should math.

Because of our poor math showing in international comparisons, discussion about the teaching of math in the United States is in ferment. Experts are debating whether we should burden young children with mental computation, or encourage the use of calculators to relieve children of drudgery and free their minds to understand math concepts. The experts we consulted may disagree about the best techniques for teaching math, but they do agree that we must define with great clarity the outcomes we want to achieve in each grade. The main purpose of the math chapters in this series is to describe these outcomes with clarity and specificity. Achieving these clearly delineated goals will require expert teaching and, of course, many more exercises and problems than we have room to include.

We have arrived at our summary of outcomes by consulting

the goals that have been promulgated by the National Research Council and the National Council of Teachers of Mathematics. We have, in addition, coordinated the recommendations of these bodies with the math standards of the nations that produce top results in math achievement at the elementary level—especially France and Japan. The math curriculums of those nations have stood the test of time with millions of young students. France, in particular, with one of the greatest mathematical traditions in human history, continues to produce world-class mathematicians both in early grades and, later on, in post-graduate research. We must not ignore such achievements, but rather build upon the most successful educational sequences wherever they are to be found.

Every successful program for teaching math to young people follows these three cardinal rules of early mathematics education: 1) practice, 2) practice, and 3) practice. Not mindless, repetitive practice, but thoughtful and varied practice. Problems need to be approached from a variety of angles, and where possible connected with intuition and facility at quickly estimating correct results. The scientific literature on skill acquisition shows unambiguously that practice is the key to proficiency in *all* skills. Well-meaning persons who want to protect the joy of the childhood years wrongly fear that practice in mathematics portends a soul-killing approach to schooling.

Nothing could be further from the truth. Math is potentially great fun, and math skill yields a sense of mastery and self-esteem. The destroyer of joy in mathematics is not practice but anxiety—anxiety that one is mathematically stupid, that one does not have that special numerical talent. But math talent is no more rare than language talent. The number of great mathematicians and the number of great poets per million of population are roughly the same. Yet people experience math anxiety to a much greater degree than language anxiety. Why? Because their early training has denied them systematic familiarity with the vocabulary, grammar, and spelling of mathematics. Those of us adults who experience math anxiety must resolve not to let this same educational wound be inflicted upon our children.

The basic operations of math must be familiar before the principles behind those operations are well understood. Again, an analogy with language learning is pertinent. Most people agree that it's important to learn the alphabet at an early age, before one understands the full significance of the alphabet. (A deep understanding of the alphabet is confined to professors of linguistics.) Being instantaneously familiar with the sums and differences of any two digits is even more basic than knowing the alphabet. Such knowledge is on a par with knowing basic sentences of English—which is a stage prior to knowing the alphabet.

While practice is the watchword of math, intelligent, fun practice is the hallmark of good math teaching. One teaching hint is worth remembering at all levels of math. Children should be encouraged to practice the same operation or types of problems from several different angles. This is a very useful way to begin to grasp the relationships behind math operations.

Since intelligent practice and problem-solving activities are essential to learning math, we must stress again that the math section of this book must be regarded as a supplement, not as a sufficient vehicle for teaching mathematics. The section is, in effect, a detailed *summary* of the math that should be mastered in this grade. We have thought it important in this series to include these detailed summaries to help parents and teachers ascertain that children have in fact learned the math they should know in each grade. The math sections should be used in conjunction with problems and activities taken from workbooks, from standard math texts, or from the imaginations of teachers and parents.

Familiarity-through-practice in the early grades is a sure road to making mathematics fun, and it's the only road to conquering fear and anxiety in mathematics. Those who follow this very basic teaching principle in the early grades will win the gratitude of their children in later years.

Introduction to Third-Grade Mathematics

FOR PARENTS AND TEACHERS

In the first and second grades, students should have gained a firm base in addition and subtraction, and should have already begun to learn multiplication. In third grade, students should add considerably to their understanding of the following elements of arithmetic.

They should memorize the multiplication table up to 9×9. They should be able to find quickly and accurately each related division fact. (For example, the division facts related to $2 \times 9 = 18$ are $18 \div 2 = 9$ and $18 \div 9 = 2$.) They should understand clearly that multiplication and division are opposite operations. They should learn the algorithms for doing multiplication and division where the multiplier or divisor is a one-digit number.

In the third grade, students should start mentally solving addition and subtraction problems that have two digits. They should extend their work with equations that have a missing value. They should begin working with graphs, and continue their work in basic geometry. They should learn equivalences among different units of measurement, and should practice word problems extensively, particularly those involving several steps.

It is unfortunate that some of these skills and concepts are not as firmly established as they should be during third grade in U.S. schools. It may seem that time can be made up in fourth grade, if the multiplication and division facts are not securely learned and practiced. In reality, however, there are many new topics to master during fourth grade that depend on mastery of the third-grade material. There will *not* be time to use that year for lengthy repetition of material already taught. By fifth grade in countries like Japan or France, students are already at work on a sophisticated curriculum, quite different in its demands from their work in third and even fourth grade. Students still learning multiplication facts in fourth grade would not be prepared for such demands.

Thus, while aspects of this chapter may seem more challenging than what is usually asked of American third graders, such material is an essential part of the curriculum for students in countries that are more successful at teaching math than we are. Our students need to have a flexible and secure understanding of this material as a basis for their future work, and the best way to ensure this mastery is to challenge students with varied approaches. It is important, for example, that students understand clearly the relationship between opposite operations such as addition and subtraction, and multiplication and division. They should learn these reciprocal relationships both in solving problems with a missing value and in checking their work. They should regularly solve challenging word problems involving several steps. With regular practice, students can be well prepared for math in the fourth grade and beyond.

Third-Grade Mathematics

Multiplication

Multiplication Words

In the equation $2 \times 5 = 10$, 2 and 5 are factors, and 10 is the product. You can multiply factors in any order without changing the product.

$$2 \times 5 = 10 \quad \text{and} \quad 5 \times 2 = 10$$

Multiplying Vertically

$4 \times 5 = 20$ can also be written

$$\begin{array}{r} 5 \\ \times\ 4 \\ \hline 20 \end{array}$$

You read both as "four times five equals twenty." Notice that when you read a vertical multiplication problem, you begin with the number next to the multiplication sign and read up.

Showing Multiplication

You can make a "picture" of a multiplication problem using graph paper. For example, you can show 3×5 by a rectangle with 3 rows and 5 columns.

If you count the squares by the rows, you have

5 + 5 + 5, which is 3 × 5

If you count the squares by the columns, you have

3 + 3 + 3 + 3 + 3, which is 5 × 3

Either way, there are 15 squares in all.

You can also show 3 × 5 by a rectangle with 5 rows and 3 columns.

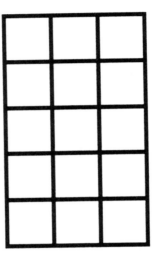

*N**ow have some fun making at least three other multiplication facts into graph paper pictures like 3 × 5.*

Multiplication is a quick way of doing repeated addition. Practice writing multiplication as repeated addition, and repeated addition as multiplication. For example, 4 × 5 can also be written 5 + 5 + 5 + 5. And, 3 + 3 + 3 + 3 + 3 + 3 can also be written 6 × 3.

The Multiplication Table

Last year you learned the multiplication tables up to 5. Here are the rest of the multiplication tables.

6 as a factor	7 as a factor	8 as a factor	9 as a factor
$0 \times 6 = 0$	$0 \times 7 = 0$	$0 \times 8 = 0$	$0 \times 9 = 0$
$1 \times 6 = 6$	$1 \times 7 = 7$	$1 \times 8 = 8$	$1 \times 9 = 9$
$2 \times 6 = 12$	$2 \times 7 = 14$	$2 \times 8 = 16$	$2 \times 9 = 18$
$3 \times 6 = 18$	$3 \times 7 = 21$	$3 \times 8 = 24$	$3 \times 9 = 27$
$4 \times 6 = 24$	$4 \times 7 = 28$	$4 \times 8 = 32$	$4 \times 9 = 36$
$5 \times 6 = 30$	$5 \times 7 = 35$	$5 \times 8 = 40$	$5 \times 9 = 45$
$6 \times 6 = 36$	$6 \times 7 = 42$	$6 \times 8 = 48$	$6 \times 9 = 54$
$7 \times 6 = 42$	$7 \times 7 = 49$	$7 \times 8 = 56$	$7 \times 9 = 63$
$8 \times 6 = 48$	$8 \times 7 = 56$	$8 \times 8 = 64$	$8 \times 9 = 72$
$9 \times 6 = 54$	$9 \times 7 = 63$	$9 \times 8 = 72$	$9 \times 9 = 81$

Only the sixteen multiplication facts that are purple are actually new. The others you already know. For example, if you know $9 \times 5 = 45$, then you know $5 \times 9 = 45$. Learn each of these new tables, so that you can say them easily. Also be able to give the product of any single fact quickly, without making any mistakes.

Remember that you can skip-count to get to the next fact in a table.

$8 \times 6 = 48$, so 9×6 is 6 more or 54.
$7 \times 7 = 49$, so 8×7 is 7 more or 56.

When you know all the multiplication facts well, practice filling in a table with all of them.

x	0	1	2	3	4	5	6	7	8	9
0										
1										
2										
3					15					
4										
5								35		
6								42		
7										
8										
9										

Parentheses, Multiplying Three Numbers

The symbols ( ) are parentheses. You do what is inside parentheses *first.*

You add $(2+3)+5$ like this:
$$(2+3)+5=$$
$$5\ +5=10$$

You add $2+(3+5)$ like this:
$$2+(3+5)=$$
$$2+\ \ 8\ =10$$

Notice that whether you put $2+3$ in the parentheses or $3+5$ in the parentheses, the sum is the same. No matter how you group addends with parentheses, the sum stays the same.

You can also multiply three or more numbers using parentheses:

Multiply $(3\times2)\times4$ like this:
$$(3\times2)\times4=$$
$$6\ \ \times4=24$$

Multiply $3\times(2\times4)$ like this:
$$3\times(2\times4)=$$
$$3\times\ \ 8\ =24$$

Notice that the product is the same both times. No matter how you group factors, the product is the same.

Division

Operations

Addition, subtraction, and multiplication are called operations. They are three of the four operations of arithmetic. The fourth operation is division.

You already know that subtraction is the opposite of addition. We say that addition and subtraction are opposite operations. The opposite operation of multiplication is division. Let's see how division works.

An Example of Division

Peter has 18 stamps. He wants to divide them into groups of 3. How many groups will he have?

$$18 \div 3 = 6$$

This is a division problem because you need to divide the 18 stamps into groups of 3 to solve it. How many groups of 3 are there in 18? There are 6 threes in 18. So Peter will have 6 groups of stamps. We write this division problem: $18 \div 3 = 6$. We read it: "Eighteen divided by three equals six." The sign $\div$ means "divided by" and shows that you are dividing.

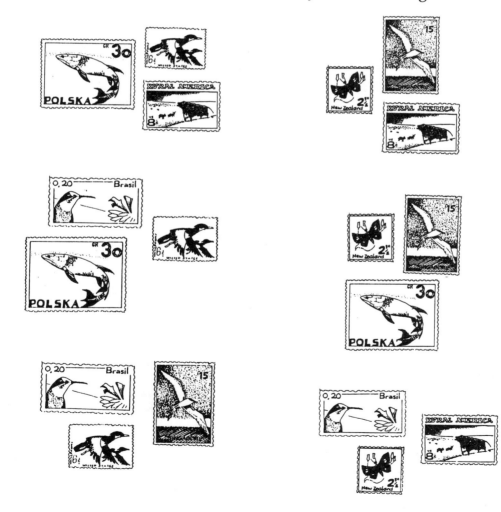

Solving Division Problems

Division and multiplication are opposite operations. The easiest way to solve a division problem is to think of a multiplication problem. Here is an example. What is $30 \div 6$? You want to know how many sixes there are in 30. **Think:** what times 6 equals 30? $5 \times 6 = 30$. So $30 \div 6 = 5$. The thirty spools of thread are divided into 5 groups with 6 spools in each group.

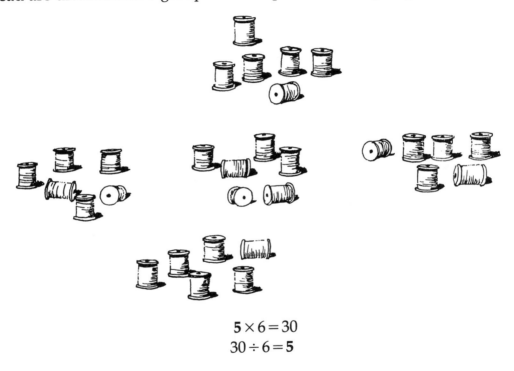

$$5 \times 6 = 30$$
$$30 \div 6 = 5$$

Here is another example. What is $54 \div 9$? You want to know how many nines there are in 54. **Think:** what times 9 equals 54? $6 \times 9 = 54$. So $54 \div 9 = 6$.

Division Words

The answer to a division problem is called the quotient. The number you are dividing is called the dividend. The number you are dividing by is called the divisor.

Learn to use these words to describe the numbers in a division problem. For example, in $12 \div 4 = 3$, 12 is the dividend, 4 is the divisor, and 3 is the quotient.

There are two ways to write division. You can write it like this:

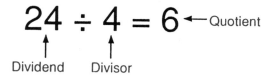

or like this:

$$\text{divisor } 4\overline{)2\ 4} \quad \begin{array}{l} \text{quotient} \\ \text{dividend} \end{array}$$

with the 6 over the 4.

Notice that the answer, the 6, goes over the ones' place. Learn to write division in both ways. For example:

$$8 \div 2 = 4 \quad \text{is the same as} \quad 2\overline{)8}$$

$$8\overline{)56} \quad \text{is the same as} \quad 56 \div 8 = 7$$

Division Facts

Learn the basic division facts. These facts will help you solve any division problem.

You can use the multiplication facts you already know to find the quotient of each division fact. We'll talk more about this later. Here are the division facts with 2, 3, 4, and 5 as divisors.

2 as a divisor	3 as a divisor	4 as a divisor	5 as a divisor
$0 \div 2 = 0$	$0 \div 3 = 0$	$0 \div 4 = 0$	$0 \div 5 = 0$
$2 \div 2 = 1$	$3 \div 3 = 1$	$4 \div 4 = 1$	$5 \div 5 = 1$
$4 \div 2 = 2$	$6 \div 3 = 2$	$8 \div 4 = 2$	$10 \div 5 = 2$
$6 \div 2 = 3$	$9 \div 3 = 3$	$12 \div 4 = 3$	$15 \div 5 = 3$
$8 \div 2 = 4$	$12 \div 3 = 4$	$16 \div 4 = 4$	$20 \div 5 = 4$
$10 \div 2 = 5$	$15 \div 3 = 5$	$20 \div 4 = 5$	$25 \div 5 = 5$
$12 \div 2 = 6$	$18 \div 3 = 6$	$24 \div 4 = 6$	$30 \div 5 = 6$
$14 \div 2 = 7$	$21 \div 3 = 7$	$28 \div 4 = 7$	$35 \div 5 = 7$
$16 \div 2 = 8$	$24 \div 3 = 8$	$32 \div 4 = 8$	$40 \div 5 = 8$
$18 \div 2 = 9$	$27 \div 3 = 9$	$36 \div 4 = 9$	$45 \div 5 = 9$

Learn to find the quotient of each division fact quickly, without making any mistakes.

Here are the division facts with 6, 7, 8, and 9 as divisors.

6 as a divisor	7 as a divisor	8 as a divisor	9 as a divisor
$0 \div 6 = 0$	$0 \div 7 = 0$	$0 \div 8 = 0$	$0 \div 9 = 0$
$6 \div 6 = 1$	$7 \div 7 = 1$	$8 \div 8 = 1$	$9 \div 9 = 1$
$12 \div 6 = 2$	$14 \div 7 = 2$	$16 \div 8 = 2$	$18 \div 9 = 2$
$18 \div 6 = 3$	$21 \div 7 = 3$	$24 \div 8 = 3$	$27 \div 9 = 3$
$24 \div 6 = 4$	$28 \div 7 = 4$	$32 \div 8 = 4$	$36 \div 9 = 4$
$30 \div 6 = 5$	$35 \div 7 = 5$	$40 \div 8 = 5$	$45 \div 9 = 5$
$36 \div 6 = 6$	$42 \div 7 = 6$	$48 \div 8 = 6$	$54 \div 9 = 6$
$42 \div 6 = 7$	$49 \div 7 = 7$	$56 \div 8 = 7$	$63 \div 9 = 7$
$48 \div 6 = 8$	$56 \div 7 = 8$	$64 \div 8 = 8$	$72 \div 9 = 8$
$54 \div 6 = 9$	$63 \div 7 = 9$	$72 \div 8 = 9$	$81 \div 9 = 9$

Division Rules for 0 and 1

Here are some rules for dividing with 0 and 1.

Rules for 0.
1. 0 divided by any number (except 0) equals 0.
$$0 \div 8 = 0 \qquad 0 \div 5 = 0$$

2. You cannot divide by 0.
$$5 \div 0 \text{ is an impossible problem.}$$

Rules for 1.
1. Any number (except 0) divided by itself equals 1.
$$8 \div 8 = 1 \qquad 6 \div 6 = 1$$

2. Any number divided by 1 equals that number.
$$5 \div 1 = 5 \qquad 7 \div 1 = 7$$

These rules can help you learn the division facts. For example, the last rule makes it easy to learn all the division facts that have 1 as a divisor: $0 \div 1 = 0$, $1 \div 1 = 1$, $2 \div 1 = 2$, $3 \div 1 = 3$, $4 \div 1 = 4$, $5 \div 1 = 5$, and so on.

Division Word Problems
Here are two kinds of division problems. Learn to solve both kinds.

1. Margaret has 35 green peppers. She wants to put 5 into each basket. How many baskets does she need?

You want to know how many groups of 5 there are in 35. You write $35 \div 5 = 7$. She needs 7 baskets. (What other way can you write $35 \div 5$?)

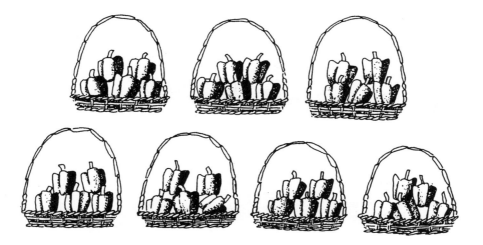

2. Mrs. Fletcher has 27 roses. She wants to divide them equally into 3 vases. How many roses should she put into each vase?

You want to know how many will be in each group, if you divide 27 into 3 groups. You write $27 \div 3 = 9$. She should put 9 roses into each vase.

Sometimes you want to know how many groups, sometimes you want to know how many are in each group. You solve both kinds of problems in the same way.

Picturing Multiplication and Division Facts

As you've just read, multiplication and division are opposite operations. For example, the opposite of multiplying by 9 is dividing by 9. The opposite of $7 \times 9 = 63$ is $63 \div 9 = 7$. Here is a picture of how this works:

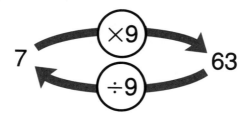

Here is another example:

The opposite of $48 \div 6 = 8$ is $8 \times 6 = 48$

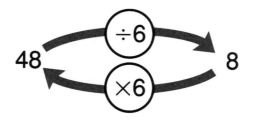

Learn to draw pictures like these to show opposite multiplication and division facts. When you can do this, you can find opposite multiplication and division facts.

Picturing Multiplication and Division Facts with Blank Spaces

Learn to fill in the blanks in pictures like these.

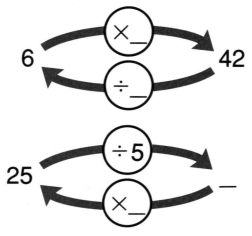

You should also be able to do the same thing with equations that have blank spaces.

_____ $\times 5 = 40$　**Think:** What times 5 equals 40? 8. So $8 \times 5 = 40$.

Division and Fractions

When something is divided into three equal parts, each part is $\frac{1}{3}$.

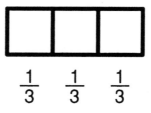

$$\frac{1}{3} \quad \frac{1}{3} \quad \frac{1}{3}$$

If you want to find $\frac{1}{3}$ of 24, you divide 24 into 3 equal parts. To divide 24 into 3 equal parts, you divide by 3:

$$24 \div 3 = 8$$

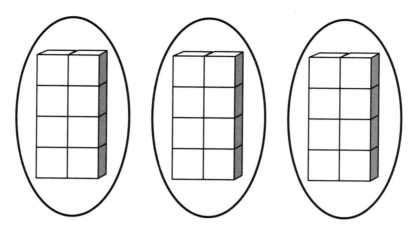

In the same way, if you want to find $\frac{1}{4}$ of 36, you divide 36 by 4. $36 \div 4 = 9$, so $\frac{1}{4}$ of 36 equals 9.

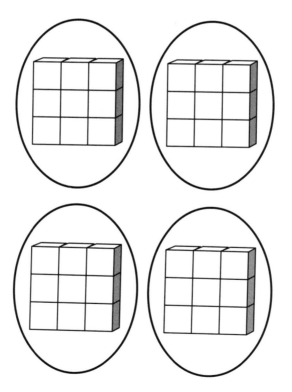

Using the division facts, learn to find the fractions $\frac{1}{2}$, $\frac{1}{3}$, $\frac{1}{4}$, $\frac{1}{5}$, $\frac{1}{6}$, $\frac{1}{7}$, $\frac{1}{8}$, and $\frac{1}{9}$ of different numbers.

Numbers Through Hundred Thousands

Numbers to Ten Thousand

We have been learning how to build and recognize numbers. You can count to 100. Now let's count by 100s, like this: 100, 200, 300, 400, 500, 600, 700, 800, 900. What comes next? 1,000. Remember that 10 hundreds are the same as 1,000.

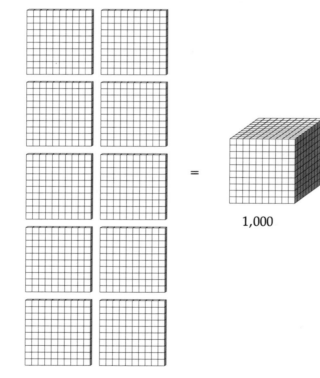

Ten hundreds   =   1,000

The number 1,000 has four digits. Learn the place value of the digits in a four-digit number. Let's look at the four-digit number 2,453.

thousands	,	hundreds	tens	ones
2	,	4	5	3

The 2 in the thousands' place is 2,000.
The 4 in the hundreds' place is   400.
The 5 in the tens' place is   50.
The 3 in the ones' place is   3.

You read 2,453 as, "two thousand, four hundred fifty-three."

Make a place-value chart and practice putting four-digit numbers in it. 1,965 would look like this:

thousands	,	hundreds	tens	ones
1	,	9	6	5

Reading and Writing Four-Digit Numbers

In digits, the thousands are written 1,000; 2,000; 3,000; 4,000; 5,000; 6,000; 7,000; 8,000; 9,000. In words, the thousands are written: one thousand, two thousand, three thousand, four thousand, five thousand, six thousand, seven thousand, eight thousand, nine thousand.

Learn to read any four-digit number, beginning with the thousands' place. For example, 8,329 is read "eight thousand, three hundred twenty-nine."

Learn to write any four-digit number in digits or in words. For example, in digits, "two thousand, seven hundred thirty-three" is written 2,733. In words,

6,364 is written "six thousand, three hundred sixty-four." Notice that you always put a comma between the thousands' place and the hundreds' place. This comma makes it easier to read large numbers.

If we were to fill in the place-value chart with some numbers we have learned so far, it would look like this:

thousands	,	hundreds	tens	ones
				1
			1	0
		1	0	0
1	,	0	0	0

The place-value chart can show numbers so big we couldn't fit the whole chart on the page. For now, let's learn these two new place values.

Ten Thousands and Hundred Thousands

The next two place values we will learn are the ten thousands' place and the hundred thousands' place.

hundred thousands	ten thousands	thousands	,	hundreds	tens	ones
2	6	7	,	3	5	3

The 2 in the hundred thousands' place is 200,000.
The 6 in the ten thousands' place is   60,000.
The 7 in the thousands' place is   7,000.
The 3 in the hundreds' place is   300.
The 5 in the tens' place is   50.
The 3 in the ones' place is   3.

You read 267,353 as "two hundred sixty-seven thousand, three hundred fifty-three."

Learn to read and write five- and six-digit numbers. For example, you read 864,374 as "eight hundred sixty-four thousand, three hundred seventy-four."

You write six hundred thousand, eighty-four in digits as 600,084. You write 450,057 in words as, "four hundred fifty thousand, fifty-seven."

Expanded Form

287 is in standard form. Remember that the expanded form of 287 is $200 + 80 + 7$. Learn to write numbers with places in the thousands in expanded form.

4,325 in expanded form is $4,000 + 300 + 20 + 5$.
50,802 in expanded form is $50,000 + 800 + 2$.

Practice writing many large numbers like these in expanded form. Also practice writing numbers that are in expanded form in standard form. In standard form, $700,000 + 5,000 + 600 + 7$ is 705,607.

Counting with Thousands

You count from one thousand to the next thousand by counting all 999 numbers in between. From 1,000 to 2,000 the numbers are 1,001; 1,002; 1,003 . . . 1,999; 2,000. The three dots . . . mean "and so on."

It takes too long to count from one thousand to the next. Practice counting in short stretches. Count from 4,994 until you reach the next thousand: 4,994; 4,995; 4,996; 4,997; 4,998; 4,999; 5,000. Or count backward from 56,003 like this: 56,003; 56,002; 56,001; 56,000. Can you count forward from 7,899 to the next thousand and backward from 23,010 to the nearest thousand?

Counting forward is the same as adding 1 each time. Learn to add 1 quickly in your head to numbers like this:

$$3,999 + 1 = 4,000 \quad 62,099 + 1 = 62,100 \quad 124,999 + 1 = 125,000$$

Counting backward is the same as subtracting 1 each time. Learn to subtract 1 quickly in your head from numbers like this:

$$3,000 - 1 = 2,999 \quad 94,260 - 1 = 94,259 \quad 300,000 - 1 = 299,999$$

Also practice writing the numbers that come before and after a number. Here are the numbers that come before and after 76,609.

Before   After

76,608 ← 76,609 → 76,610

Skip-Counting with Thousands

Learn to continue a line of numbers either forward or backward, counting by tens, fives, evens, or odds. Here are some examples.

counting by tens: forward—7,210; 7,220; 7,230; 7,240
                             backward—7,210; 7,200; 7,190; 7,180

counting by odds: forward—23,995; 23,997; 23,999; 24,001
                             backward—23,995; 23,993; 23,991; 23,989

counting by fives: forward—8,005; 8,010; 8,015; 8,020
                             backward—8,005; 8,000; 7,995; 7,990

> **P**ick numbers in the thousands to practice skip-counting by fives and tens and by either evens or odds. Practice going both forward and backward from that number.

Rounding Numbers

Sometimes it is easier to say *about* how much something is instead of *exactly* how much it is. For instance, you might say that the night sky looks like it contains "about 100,000" stars, not "128,347." This is called rounding numbers. You round a number to show about how large it is. You can round a number to the nearest ten, hundred, thousand, or hundred thousand.

To round a number to the nearest ten, you make it into the ten that is closest. Take the number 23, for example. 23 is between 20 and 30.

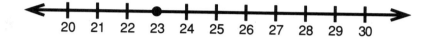

It is closer to 20. So 23 rounded to the nearest ten is 20. 27 is also between 20 and 30. It is closer to 30. So 27 rounded to the nearest ten is 30.

There is a rule you need to learn about rounding: when a number is exactly between two numbers, you round up, to the greater number. For example, take 25, which is exactly between 20 and 30. You round 25 up to 30.

You round to the nearest hundred or thousand in the same way. Round 362 to the nearest hundred. 362 is between 300 and 400. It is closer to 400, so 362 rounded to the nearest hundred is 400. Round 8,257 to the nearest thousand. 8,257 is between 8,000 and 9,000. It is closer to 8,000. So 8,257 rounded to the nearest thousand is 8,000.

You do not always round numbers to the highest place value. 7,048 rounded to the nearest ten is 7,050. 6,152 rounded to the nearest hundred is 6,200.

Comparing and Ordering Thousands

When you compare two numbers to see which is greater, always compare the digits in the largest place value first. That means you start from the left. Then compare the number in the next largest place value, and so on. As soon as you find that a number is greater in a place value, the entire number must be greater. Of course, any number that has thousands is greater than any number that just has hundreds. For example, 1,002 > 998. In the same way, 100,002 > 99,908.

Let's look at an example that will help you see how to figure out whether <, >, or = belongs between two large numbers. Our numbers are 4,827 and

4,900. If you think of them arranged by place values, you can set them up like this:

thousands	,	hundreds	tens	ones
4	,	8	2	7
4	,	9	0	0

↑ The hundreds are different.

↑ The thousands are the same.

First compare the thousands' place. 4,000 equals 4,000. The thousands are the same. So far the numbers seem equal. Then compare the hundreds' place. 800 < 900. So 4,827 < 4,900.

Now, you compare 53,505 and 53,089.

ten thousands	thousands	,	hundreds	tens	ones
5	3	,	5	0	5
5	3	,	0	8	9

Remember that you can order numbers from least to greatest. To order 4,567; 5,892; 3,853; 5,889 from least to greatest, you would write: 3,853; 4,567; 5,889; 5,892.

You can also order numbers from greatest to least. These six numbers are ordered from greatest to least: 58,694; 58,599; 46,822; 46,083; 1,003; 99.

Order these numbers from least to greatest: 65; 96; 4,560; 4,575; 4,556; 45,765; 79,243; 67,221. Now find numbers all over your house, at least six of them and order them from greatest to least. (Hint: appliance serial numbers are fun, so are grocery store product code numbers.)

Equations and Inequalities

Remember that a number statement that uses an equals sign is an equation. $5+4=9$ and $221=221$ are both equations.

A number statement that uses the signs $>$ or $<$ is called an inequality. An inequality shows in what way numbers are *not* equal. $4,827 < 4,900$ and $1,002 > 997$ are both inequalities.

Ordinal Numbers Through One Hundredth

Remember that ordinal numbers give the place of something in an order. For example, June is the *sixth* month of the year.

Learn to write out the ordinal numbers through one hundredth. You know the ordinal numbers to thirty-first. The ordinal numbers continue in the same way to one hundredth: thirty-first, thirty-second, thirty-third, thirty-fourth, thirty-fifth, thirty-sixth, thirty-seventh, thirty-eighth, thirty-ninth, fortieth, forty-first . . . ninety-ninth, one hundredth.

You don't always have to write ordinal numbers out; sometimes they can be abbreviated. Here's a chart that gives you a few examples of the ways to abbreviate them.

Ordinal Number	Abbreviation	Ordinal Number	Abbreviation
First	1st	Thirty-first	31st
Second	2nd	Thirty-second	32nd
Third	3rd	Thirty-third	33rd
Fourth	4th	Thirty-fourth	34th

All the ordinals that end in "th" are abbreviated in the same way as fourth and thirty-fourth.

Addition and Subtraction

Column Addition

Learn to add four or more numbers in a column. Here is an example. Begin by adding the ones column down.

Add the ones.
Regroup if necessary.

```
 t  o
 2
 1  2
 1  9      2+9=11
 3  8     11+8=19
+6  4     19+4=23
————
    3
```

Add the tens.

```
              t  o
              2
2+1= 3        1  2
3+1= 4        1  9
4+3= 7        3  8
7+6=13       +6  4
             ————
             13  3
```

To do column addition, you often need to add combinations like $11+8=19$ or $19+4=23$ in your head. You also often have to regroup more than 1 ten. 23 ones is the same as 2 tens, 3 ones.

When you do a math problem you should always check your work. With column addition, to check you add up from the bottom. Here's a check of the problem we just did.

Add the ones.

```
 t  o
 2
 1  2     21+2=23
 1  9     12+9=21
 3  8      4+8=12
+6  4
————
    3
```

Add the tens.

```
             t  o
11+2=13      2
10+1=11      1  2
 9+1=10      1  9
 6+3= 9      3  8
            +6  4
            ————
            13  3  ✔
```

Mental Addition

Remember that you can use parentheses to group addends in different ways without changing the sum.

$$(8+2)+3=13 \qquad 8+(2+3)=13$$

You can also add numbers in a different order without changing the sum.

$$2+3=5 \qquad 3+2=5$$

So, when you are adding many numbers together, you can group them, and then add them, in the easiest way. To find the sum of $8+6+2+9+4$ easily, group the pairs of numbers that add to 10, like this:

$$\begin{aligned} 8+6+2+9+4 &= (8+2)+(6+4)+9 \\ &= 10 + 10 +9 \\ &= 29 \end{aligned}$$

When you are adding two-digit numbers in your head, look for two numbers that make an even 10. To add $28+35+12$ easily, group the numbers like this:

$$\begin{aligned} 28+35+12 &= (28+12)+35 \\ &= 40 +35 \\ &= 75 \end{aligned}$$

More Mental Addition Methods

Here is another method to help you add numbers in your head. When you are adding a number that ends in 9, you can make it an even ten, and then subtract 1 from the final sum.

For example, to add $37+29$, you can think $29=30-1$.

Think: $37+29=37+30-1=67-1=66$.

You can make an addend an even hundred, and then subtract in the same way. To add 253 and 198, you can think $198=200-2$.

Think: $253+198=253+200-2=453-2=451$

When you are adding in your head, it is often easier to add a number in two parts. To find the sum of $84 + 28$, you can think: $84 + 16$ makes an even hundred. So make 28 into $16 + 12$.

Think: $84 + 28 = 84 + 16 + 12 = 100 + 12 = 112$

Here is another example.

Think: $365 + 411 = 365 + 400 + 11 = 765 + 11 = 776$

Practice doing many mental addition problems using these methods whenever they will help you.

Estimating Sums and Differences

To estimate means to find *about* what an answer is. When you do not need to know an answer exactly, you can estimate to find out quickly what the approximate answer is. You can estimate the sums of two-digit numbers by rounding each number to the nearest ten, and then adding. Here is an example.

$$
\begin{array}{ccc}
 & \text{rounds to} & \\
29 & \longrightarrow & 30 \\
+45 & \longrightarrow & +50 \\
\hline
 & & 80
\end{array}
$$

$29 + 45$ is about 80.

You can estimate the differences of two-digit numbers in the same way.

$$
\begin{array}{ccc}
 & \text{rounds to} & \\
87 & \longrightarrow & 90 \\
-41 & \longrightarrow & -40 \\
\hline
 & & 50
\end{array}
$$

$87 - 41$ is about 50.

You can estimate the sums and differences of three-digit numbers by rounding to the nearest hundred, and then adding or subtracting.

$$\begin{array}{c} \text{rounds to} \\ \begin{array}{r} 559 \\ +318 \\ \hline \end{array} \quad \xrightarrow{\qquad} \quad \begin{array}{r} 600 \\ +300 \\ \hline 900 \end{array} \end{array}$$

$$\begin{array}{c} \text{rounds to} \\ \begin{array}{r} 419 \\ -187 \\ \hline \end{array} \quad \xrightarrow{\qquad} \quad \begin{array}{r} 400 \\ -200 \\ \hline 200 \end{array} \end{array}$$

Practice adding and subtracting by estimating. Since you can add and subtract very quickly when you estimate, you can also use estimation as a quick way to check an answer. But estimation can only tell you if your answer is about right; it is not a sure way to check.

More Than One Operation

Sometimes you have to do more than one operation in a problem. For example, sometimes you have to both add and multiply. When there is more than one operation, always do the operation inside the parentheses first. Here is an example.

$$7 \times (12 - 8) = 7 \times 4 = 28$$

Practice doing many problems with different kinds of operations. Here are some more examples.

1. $(10 + 2) - (6 + 2) =$
   $12 - 8 = 4$

2. $(43 - 38) \times (5 + 3) =$
   $5 \times 8 = 40$

3. $(9 \times 4) + (6 \times 5) =$
   $36 + 30 = 66$

Practice using $>$, $<$, or $=$ in problems like these, which use more than one operation.

$$8 \times 6 < 82 - 31 \qquad 63 \div 9 > 3 \times 2 \qquad 21 + 11 = 4 \times 8$$

Remember that $8 \times 6 < 82 - 31$ and $63 \div 9 > 3 \times 2$ are inequalities. $21 + 11 = 4 \times 8$ is an equation.

Mental Subtraction

Here is a method to help you subtract numbers in your head. When you are subtracting a number that ends in 9, you can subtract an even ten instead, and then add 1.

For example, to take 19 away from 54, you can think: subtracting 19 is the same as subtracting 20, then adding 1.

Think: $54 - 19 = 54 - 20 + 1 = 34 + 1 = 35.$

You can make a number you are subtracting an even hundred in the same way. For example, to subtract 198 from 426 you can think: subtracting 198 is the same as subtracting 200, then adding 2.

Think: $426 - 198 = 426 - 200 + 2 = 226 + 2 = 228.$

When you are subtracting in your head, it is often easier to subtract a number by first taking away part of the number, then taking away the rest. For example, to subtract 23 from 48, you can first subtract 20, then subtract 3 more.
Think: $48 - 23 = (48 - 20) - 3 = 28 - 3 = 25$

To solve $125 - 29 = \underline{\quad}$, you can think: $125 - 25$ makes an even hundred. So think of taking away 29 as first taking away 25, then taking away 4 more.
Think: $125 - 29 = (125 - 25) - 4 = 100 - 4 = 96$

Practice doing many mental subtraction problems, using these methods whenever they will help you.

Sums and Differences of Four-Digit Numbers

Adding with Thousands

Sometimes when you add, you need to regroup hundreds as thousands. When you add vertically, always work from right to left. To find this sum, add the ones, then the tens, then the hundreds, then the thousands. Let's find the sum of 2,635 + 3,728.

```
  th  h  t  o              th  h  t  o
                            1     1
  2 , 6  3  5               2 , 6  3  5
+ 3 , 7  2  8             + 3 , 7  2  8
─────────────             ─────────────
                           6 , 3  6  3
```

In the same way you have learned to regroup ones as tens, regroup when necessary as you move to the left. In this problem, you do not need to regroup tens as hundreds, but you do need to regroup hundreds as thousands. 6 hundreds plus 7 hundreds equals 13 hundreds. You regroup 13 hundreds as 1 thousand 3 hundreds. Then you add the thousands. The sum equals 6,363.

Practice finding sums with three or more addends, as well as with two addends. Sometimes when you are adding four-digit numbers, you need to regroup thousands as ten thousands.

```
 ten                       ten
 th  th  h  t  o           th  th  h  t  o
                            1  2   2  2
     5 , 6  2  7                5 , 6  2  7
     7 , 4  8  2                7 , 4  8  2
            3  8                       3  8
 +      9   7  5           +       9   7  5
 ───────────────          ───────────────
                           1 4 , 1   2  2
```

You write 14 thousands as 1 ten thousand, 4 thousands.

You often have to add numbers together that have a different number of digits. Given a problem like 3,584 + 723 + 19 + 250, practice writing the numbers in columns and then adding them. Make sure to keep the numbers in the correct place-value column.

```
th   h   t   o
     1   1   1
 3,  5   8   4
         7   2   3
             1   9
 +       2   5   0
 4,  5   7   6
```

In general, practice doing addition in columns until it is easy for you and you are very good at regrouping. With three addends, add up to check. With only two addends, rewrite the addends in a different order, and add again. Also practice estimating, to see if the sum is about right.

To estimate the sum of four-digit numbers, round to the nearest thousand.

```
                 rounds to
    5, 3 3 4     ──────▶      5, 0 0 0
 +  2, 9 2 6     ──────▶    + 3, 0 0 0
                             8, 0 0 0
```

5,334 + 2,926 is about 8,000. So, you know that the sum of 5,334 + 2,926 should be *about* 8,000.

Subtraction: Regrouping More Than Once

Sometimes when you subtract you need to regroup more than once. When you subtract vertically, work from right to left.

Since you cannot take 9 from 4, regroup.	Subtract the ones.	Since you cannot take 8 tens from 1 ten, regroup again.	Subtract the tens. Subtract the hundreds.

$$
\begin{array}{r}
5\ 2\ 4 \\
-\ 3\ 8\ 9 \\
\hline
\end{array}
$$

$$
\begin{array}{r}
1\ 14 \\
5\ 2\ 4 \\
-\ 3\ 8\ 9 \\
\hline
5
\end{array}
$$

$$
\begin{array}{r}
11 \\
4\ 1\ 14 \\
5\ 2\ 4 \\
-\ 3\ 8\ 9 \\
\hline
5
\end{array}
$$

$$
\begin{array}{r}
11 \\
4\ 1\ 14 \\
5\ 2\ 4 \\
-\ 3\ 8\ 9 \\
\hline
1\ 3\ 5
\end{array}
$$

The difference is 135.

Make up subtraction problems in which you have to regroup more than once, and practice them many times.

Subtracting Across Zeros

Sometimes when you need to regroup, there is a zero in the next place. Then you need to regroup in a different way. Here is an example. Find the difference of 304 and 187.

$$
\begin{array}{r}
h\ \ t\ \ o \\
3\ \ 0\ \ 4 \\
-\ 1\ \ 8\ \ 7 \\
\hline
\end{array}
$$

Subtract the ones. Since you cannot take 7 from 4, you need to regroup. But there are no tens to regroup. You need to go to the hundreds' place. Change 3 hundreds 0 tens to 2 hundreds 9 tens 10 ones. You can also think: change 30 tens to 29 tens. Now you can add the extra ten to the ones' place.

$$
\begin{array}{r}
2\ 9\ 14 \\
3\ 0\ 4 \\
-\ 1\ 8\ 7 \\
\hline
\end{array}
\qquad
\begin{array}{r}
2\ 9\ 14 \\
3\ 0\ 4 \\
-\ 1\ 8\ 7 \\
\hline
1\ 1\ 7 \\
\end{array}
$$

Let's see how this process works when you have to subtract across several zeros. When subtracting four-digit numbers, first subtract the ones, then the tens, then the hundreds, then the thousands.

$$
\begin{array}{r}
4\ 0\ 0\ 0 \\
-\ 2\ 8\ 9\ 6 \\
\hline
\end{array}
$$

Think: you need an extra ten for the ones' place. Change 400 tens to 399 tens, and add the extra ten to the ones' place. Then subtract the ones, the tens, the hundreds and the thousands, column by column.

$$
\begin{array}{r}
3\ 9\ 9\ 10 \\
4\ 0\ 0\ 0 \\
-\ 2\ 8\ 9\ 6 \\
\hline
\end{array}
\qquad
\begin{array}{r}
\text{Subtract} \\
3\ 9\ 9\ 10 \\
4\ 0\ 0\ 0 \\
-\ 2\ 8\ 9\ 6 \\
\hline
1\ 1\ 0\ 4 \\
\end{array}
$$

Four-Digit Subtraction

Practice subtracting with four-digit numbers until you can do it easily, especially across zeros. Practice writing a subtraction problem in columns and then subtracting. Here is an example. Find the difference of 3,037 and 1,682.

```
                        2 9 13        2 9 13        2 9 13
  3 0 3 7      3 0 3 7    3 0 3 7      3 0 3 7      3 0 3 7
- 1 6 8 2    - 1 6 8 2  - 1 6 8 2    - 1 6 8 2    - 1 6 8 2
                     5        5 5        3 5 5      1 3 5 5
```

Remember to check each subtraction problem by addition like this:

```
    2 9 13
    3 0 3 7          1 3 5 5          1 1
  - 1 6 8 2        + 1 6 8 2        1 3 5 5
    1 3 5 5                         + 1 6 8 2
                                     3 0 3 7  ✔
```

You can also check to see if the difference of four-digit numbers is about right by estimating. Round each number to the nearest thousand and then subtract.

```
                    rounds to
      3 0 3 7      ⟶        3 0 0 0
    - 1 6 8 2      ⟶      - 2 0 0 0
                             1 0 0 0
```

$3,037 - 1,682$ is about $1,000$.

Adding and Subtracting Amounts of Money

You add and subtract amounts of money the same way you add and subtract other numbers. Here are two examples.

```
                      7 17                                       2 1
1.  $ 8 5. 8 7     $ 8 5. 8 7      2.  $ 5 1. 6 8      $ 5 1. 6 8
  - 1 3. 4 8     - 1 3. 4 8              2. 8 0          2. 8 0
                 $ 7 2. 3 9              0. 5 6          0. 5 6
                                      + 1 2. 8 4      + 1 2. 8 4
                                                      $ 6 7. 8 8
```

Do not forget to write the dollar sign and the cents point in your answer.

Mental Addition and Subtraction

You can add and subtract thousands the same way you add and subtract ones.

$$7+2 \quad = 9$$
$$7{,}000 + 2{,}000 = 9{,}000$$

$$60 - 20 \quad = 40$$
$$60{,}000 - 20{,}000 = 40{,}000$$

learn to add and subtract thousands mentally in problems like these.

$$6{,}000 \; + \underline{\qquad} = \quad 9{,}000$$
$$54{,}000 \; - 24{,}000 = \underline{\qquad}$$
$$350{,}000 + \underline{\qquad} = 450{,}000$$

Also practice adding the amount it takes to make the next thousand. This will help you learn place value.

$$9{,}990 + \underline{\qquad} = 10{,}000$$
$$39{,}900 + \underline{\qquad} = 40{,}000$$
$$59{,}980 + \underline{\qquad} = 60{,}000$$

Time, Money, and Graphs

Time to the Minute

Learn to tell time to the minute quickly. Remember that the minute hand moves from one number to the next in 5 minutes. On many clocks there is a short mark for each minute in between. In 1 minute, the minute hand moves from one of these short marks to the next.

It is 9:20.   Now it is 9:21.

In the next picture the minute hand is on the third mark between 1:45 and 1:50.

It is 1:48

Practice writing time in minutes before and after an hour. Subtract how many minutes it is after the hour from 60, to find how many minutes it is before the next hour. 2:38 is 22 minutes before 3:00.

$$\begin{array}{r} {}^{5}\,{}^{10} \\ \cancel{6}\ \cancel{0} \\ -3\ 8 \\ \hline 2\ 2 \end{array}$$

Elapsed Time in Minutes

Learn to find how much time has elapsed in minutes. From 10:15 to 10:45 is 30 minutes because $45 - 15 = 30$.

Find how many minutes it is from 2:35 to 3:18. You need to do this problem in two steps. First find how many minutes it is from 2:35 to 3:00. 25 minutes, because $60 - 35 = 25$. Then add 18 more minutes for the time from 3:00 to 3:18. 25 minutes + 18 minutes = 43 minutes. From 2:35 to 3:18 is 43 minutes.

Working with the Calendar

Let's learn how to find a date that comes weeks before or after another date. Here's how.

Remember that a week has 7 days. One week before December 12th is December 5th because $12 - 7 = 5$. What is 2 weeks after December 12th? There are 14 days in 2 weeks, because $2 \times 7 = 14$. $12 + 14 = 26$. So 2 weeks after

DECEMBER

SUNDAY	MONDAY	TUESDAY	WEDNESDAY	THURSDAY	FRIDAY	SATURDAY
		1	2	3	4	5
6	7	8	9	10	11	12
13	14	15	16	17	18	19
20	21	22	23	24	25	26
27	28	29	30	31		

December 12th is December 26th. Learn to find the date weeks before and after another date.

You can also find out which day of the week a date comes on. Here are two examples. If May 10th is a Sunday, May 17th, a week later, will be a Sunday also. What day of the week will it be 10 days after Wednesday? In 7 days it will be Wednesday again. Thursday is the 8th day, Friday the 9th, and Saturday the 10th. So 10 days after Wednesday will be Saturday.

MAY

SUNDAY	MONDAY	TUESDAY	WEDNESDAY	THURSDAY	FRIDAY	SATURDAY
					1	2
3	4	5	6	7	8	9
10	11	12	13	14	15	16
17	18	19	20	21	22	23
24/31	25	26	27	28	29	30

Money

Learn these new bills.

A five-dollar bill.
$5.00
500¢

A ten-dollar bill.
$10.00
1,000¢

A twenty-dollar bill.
$20.00
2,000¢

Learn to write amounts of money in dollars or in cents. $8.45 is 845¢.
1,127¢ is $11.27.

Learn how to make change. Alice buys a granola bar for 54¢. She gives the clerk a dollar bill. The clerk makes change by counting forward from the cost of the granola bar. One penny is 55¢, a dime 65¢, another dime 75¢, a quarter $1.00. So the clerk gives Alice a penny, two dimes, and a quarter. (Alice can check her change with subtraction. $1.00 minus 54¢ is 100¢ − 54¢ = 46¢. So Alice will get 46¢ in change.)

You always make change by counting forward from the cost of what was bought to the amount paid for it. You should use as few coins or bills as possible when making change. Always start with the coins or bills of least value, and work toward the coins or bills of greatest value. For example, a customer gives Roberta $20.00 for a book that costs $11.43. What change should Roberta give? Two pennies come to $11.45. A nickel comes to $11.50. Two quarters come to $12.00. Three one-dollar bills make $15.00. A five-dollar bill makes $20.00. Roberta makes change by counting forward like this, using as few coins and bills as possible.

P*ractice making change using as few bills and coins as possible. You can make up your own examples but here's one to get you started. How much change does Ron get from a hundred-dollar bill if his groceries cost $73.18?*

Reading Graphs

A graph is a way of showing information in a diagram. Learn to read line graphs and bar graphs.

Here is a bar graph.

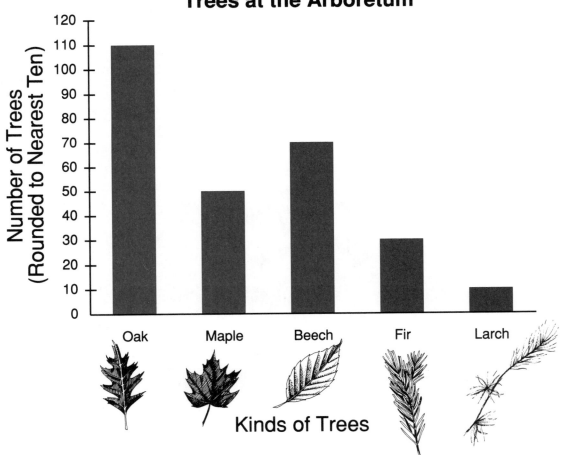

This bar graph shows how many of each kind of tree there are at the arboretum, rounded to the nearest ten. Each bar, or rectangle, on the graph shows about how many trees of a certain kind there are. For example, there are about 70 beeches. About how many more oaks than maples are there? 60 more oaks, because $110 - 50 = 60$.

Here is a line graph.

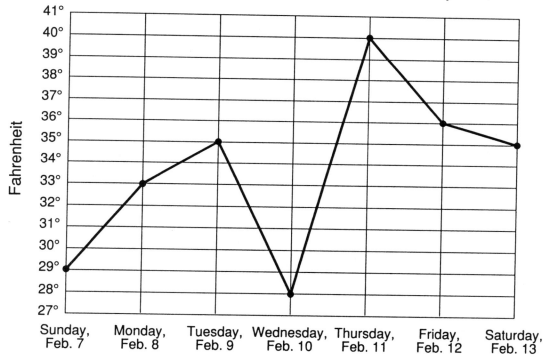

Daily High Temperatures for the Week of February 7–13

This line graph shows the daily high temperatures for the week of February 7–13. Each point shows the high temperature on that day. The line segments connect the points to show how the high temperature changed from day to day. The change in high temperature from Wednesday to Thursday was 12° F. How much warmer was the high temperature of Friday than Sunday? 7°F., because $36 - 29 = 7$.

Measurement

The U.S. Customary System and the Metric System

In the United States, we use two systems of measurement: the U.S. customary system and the metric system. You may already be familiar with both systems from your work in science.

Here are some of the units used to measure length, weight, and capacity in each system. Capacity means how much something can hold. The abbreviation for each unit is in parentheses.

U.S. Customary System		
Length	Weight	Capacity
mile (mi)	pound (lb)	gallon (gal)
yard (yd)	ounce (oz)	quart (qt)
foot (ft)		pint (pt)
inch (in)		cup (c)

Metric System		
Length	Weight	Capacity
centimeter (cm)	gram (g)	liter (l)
meter (m)	kilogram (kg)	
kilometer (k)		

Learn to change a measurement from one unit in a system to another. Here are some equations to show you how to change units in the U.S. customary system.

1 ft = 12 in   1 lb = 16 oz   1 gal = 4 qt
1 yd = 3 ft   1 qt = 2 pt
                                                    1 pt = 2 c

Here are three examples of changes between units in a system.

1. Since 1 ft = 12 in, to find out how many inches in 3 feet, you can add 12 in + 12 in + 12 in 12 + 12 + 12 = 36, so 3 ft = 36 in.

2. You can find out how many quarts there are in 6 gallons of cider by multiplying:

$$1 \text{ gal} = 4 \text{ qt}$$
$$6 \times 4 = 24$$
$$6 \text{ gal} = 24 \text{ qt}$$

3. To find out how many pints are in 8 cups, you can divide by 2, since $2 \text{ c} = 1 \text{ pt}$:

$$8 \div 2 = 4$$
$$8 \text{ c} = 4 \text{ pt}$$

In the metric system, it is even easier to change units because it is just like working with place value. Here are some equations for changing units in the metric system.

$$1 \text{ m} = 100 \text{ cm} \qquad\qquad 1 \text{ kg} = 1,000 \text{ g}$$
$$1 \text{ km} = 1,000 \text{ m}$$

Each meter is 100 centimeters. So 5 meters are 500 centimeters, because $5 \times 100 = 500$. Each kilometer is 1,000 meters. So 6 kilometers are 6,000 meters, because $6 \times 1,000 = 6,000$. In the same way, $9 \text{ kg} = 9,000 \text{ g}$.

Measurement Word Problems

Learn how to solve problems that involve units of measurement. For example, Mrs. Johnson has a kilogram of flour. She uses 500 grams to make

two loaves of bread. She uses another 250 grams to make some brownies. How many grams of flour does she use, and how many does she have left?

$$500 \text{ g} + 250 \text{g} = 750 \text{ g}$$

So Mrs. Johnson uses 750 grams of flour. She started with 1 kilogram of flour. 1 kg = 1,000 g.

$$
\begin{array}{r}
0\ 9\ 10 \\
\cancel{1}\ \cancel{0}\ \cancel{0}\ 0 \text{ g} \\
-\quad 7\ 5\ 0 \text{ g} \\
\hline
2\ 5\ 0 \text{ g}
\end{array}
$$

So Mrs. Johnson has 250 grams of flour left.

Practice problems like these, in which you first have to add, then subtract. Be careful in measurement problems to remember which units you are working with. Always write the units you are working with in your answer.

Geometry

Polygons

Remember the difference between closed figures and open figures?

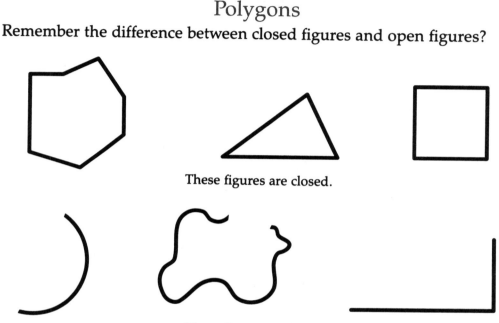

These figures are closed.

These figures are open.

A closed figure can be formed entirely with line segments. Here is line segment TS or ST. A line segment gets its name from the letters assigned to its endpoints.

S   T

A closed figure that is formed by line segments is called a polygon. Triangles, rectangles, and squares are polygons; circles are not polygons.

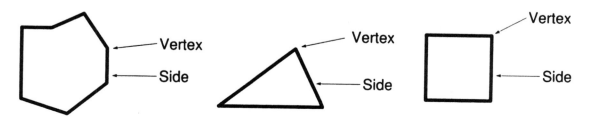

In a polygon, each side is a line segment. The point where two line segments meet is called a vertex. (The plural of vertex is vertices or vertexes.)

Like all points, vertices are named by letters. You name a polygon by starting at one vertex and naming all the other vertices in order. Here are two examples.

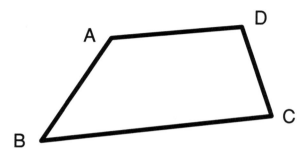

Starting at point B, you could name this polygon polygon BADC; you could also name the vertices in the other direction: polygon BCDA. Or you could start with any of the other points, and name the vertices in order in either direction. Altogether there are eight possible names for this polygon. Can you write all of them?

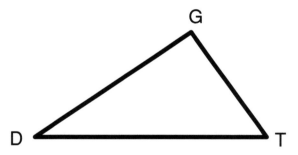

Here are the six possible names for the triangle above: triangle DGT, triangle DTG, triangle TGD, triangle TDG, triangle GTD, triangle GDT.

Have fun with polygons. Draw a polygon with a certain number of sides, say five. Now draw another polygon with five sides that looks very different. See how many polygons you can make with five sides. Now try this with a ten-sided polygon.

Angles

Whenever two sides of a polygon meet they form an angle.
Here's an example of an angle.

angle

This polygon has four sides, four vertices, and four angles.

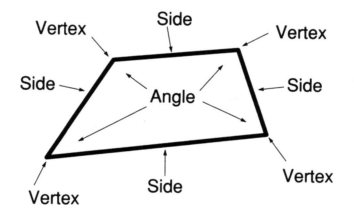

A right angle is an angle that forms a square corner.

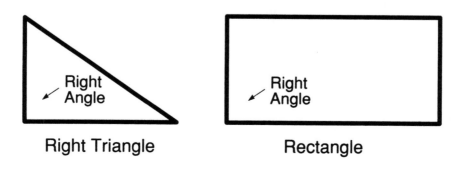

Right Triangle   Rectangle

Squares and rectangles have four right angles.

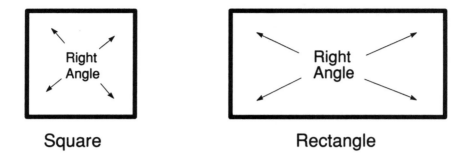

Square   Rectangle

Congruent and Symmetric Figures

Two figures that are exactly the same shape and size are said to be congruent. Sometimes you have to turn a figure around to see if it is congruent.

These two triangles are congruent.

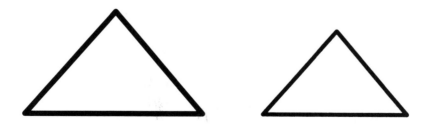

These two triangles are not congruent.
They have the same shape, but not the
same size.

Remember that when you fold a figure along a line of symmetry, the two halves of the figure match. A figure that has a line of symmetery is said to be symmetric. Sometimes figures have more than one line of symmetery. For example, a square has four lines of symmetry.

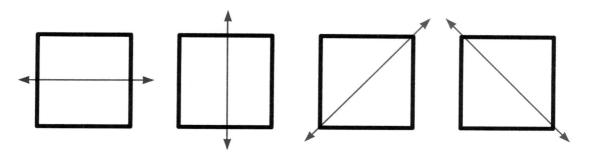

A circle has more lines of symmetry than you can count.

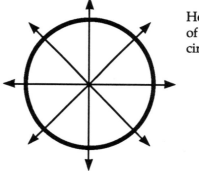

Here are some of the lines of symmetry for this circle.

You can fold figures to see if they are symmetric. If they are symmetric, you can see how many lines of symmetry they have.

Make a Geometry Mobile

What sort of symmetrical figures would you like to see floating in the air? All triangles, or an assortment of hearts, circles, and cones? Make four or five symmetrical shapes out of construction paper. Use a hole puncher or poke a hole in each. Then cut string or thread into 12-centimeter lengths, and tie the threads through the holes in your figures. You can use sticks or popsicle sticks to hang the figures. The hard part is finding the right lengths for each string to make the pieces balance each other in a pattern you like.

Perimeter

Perimeter is the distance around a figure. To find the perimeter of a figure, you add the lengths of its sides together.

Practice measuring the sides of polygons to the nearest inch or centimeter; then add the lengths together to find the perimeter of the polygon in inches or centimeters. Here is an example in centimeters.

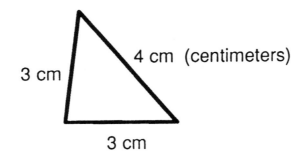

3 cm + 4 cm + 3 cm = 10 cm. The perimeter of the triangle is 10 cm.

Area

The area of a figure is the number of square units that cover its surface. A square unit has sides that are each one unit long. For example, this is a square centimeter.

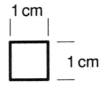

This polygon has an area of 11 square centimeters. You write 11 square centimeters as 11 cm².

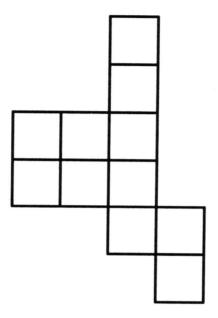

This rectangle has an area of 6 square inches. You write 6 square inches as 6 in².

Learn to find the area of a figure by counting square units. Make sure always to write your answer in square units, such as in² or cm².

Solids

Three-dimensional figures are often called solids.

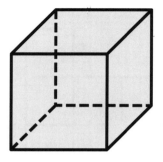

A flat surface on a solid is called a face. The line segment where two faces meet is called an edge. Edges come together at a vertex.

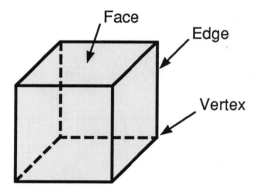

Learn to count the number of faces, edges, and vertices on solid figures. Notice that the point of a cone is a vertex.

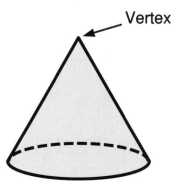

Learn this new solid: a rectangular prism. A rectangular prism has six sides that are rectangles.

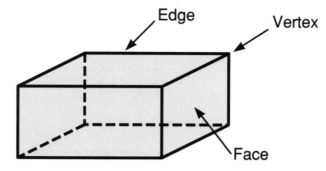

Multiplication—Part Two

Multiplying Tens, Hundreds, and Thousands

It is easy to multiply tens, hundreds, and thousands. Use the multiplication facts you already know.

3×2 **tens** $= 6$ **tens** 4×7 **hundreds** $= 28$ **hundreds**

$3 \times 20 = 60$ $4 \times 700 = 2,800$

$$\begin{array}{r} 20 \\ \times\ 3 \\ \hline 60 \end{array} \qquad\qquad \begin{array}{r} 700 \\ \times\ \ 4 \\ \hline 2,800 \end{array}$$

3×6 **thousands** $= 18$ **thousands**

$3 \times 6,000 = 18,000$

$$\begin{array}{r} 6,000 \\ \times\ \ \ \ 3 \\ \hline 18,000 \end{array}$$

Practice solving problems like these quickly. Remember that you are multiplying tens, hundreds, or thousands. Be sure to keep the right number of zeros in the product!

A Way to Multiply

Learn a way to multiply 3×16 by breaking 16 into smaller numbers. Graph paper can help us see how this works. On graph paper draw a rectangle with 3 rows and 16 columns.

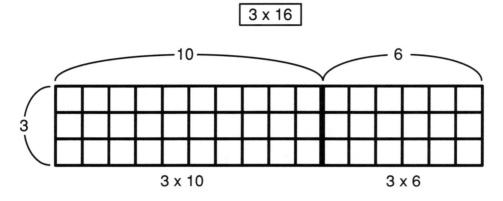

You can see from the picture that 3×16 is the same as $(3 \times 10) + (3 \times 6)$. So you can multiply 3×16 like this:

$$3 \times 16 = (3 \times 10) + (3 \times 6) = 30 + 18 = 48$$

You can also write this multiplication problem vertically, like this:
$$\begin{array}{r} 1\ 6 \\ \times\ \ 3 \\ \hline \end{array}$$

When you multiply vertically, you start with the ones and move to the left to the greater values.

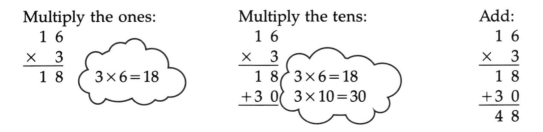

Notice how you write in the 0 to show that 3×10 is 3 tens, not 3 ones.

You can multiply 6×28 in the same way. First draw the problem on graph paper in rows and columns. Then write it vertically, and multiply. Notice that first you multiply $6 \times$ the ones, then you multiply $6 \times$ the tens.

$$
\begin{array}{r}
2\ 8 \\
\times \quad 6 \\
\hline
4\ 8 \\
+\ 1\ 2\ 0 \\
\hline
1\ 6\ 8
\end{array}
$$

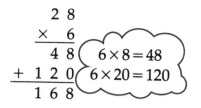

$6 \times 8 = 48$
$6 \times 20 = 120$

Practice multiplying this way, making a separate product for the ones and the tens, and then adding.

The Short Way to Multiply

Now learn the short way to write multiplication. With this method, you write the products on the same line. Let's use 23×3 as an example.

First we write it vertically.

Next we multiply $3 \times$ the ones in 23.

Then we multiply $3 \times$ the tens in 23 and write the product on the same line.

$$
\begin{array}{r}
2\ 3 \\
\times \quad 3 \\
\hline
\end{array}
\qquad
\begin{array}{r}
2\ 3 \\
\times \quad 3 \\
\hline
9
\end{array}
\qquad
\begin{array}{r}
2\ 3 \\
\times \quad 3 \\
\hline
6\ 9
\end{array}
$$

Often when you multiply this way, you need to regroup. See what happens when you multiply 6×28 this way.

Multiply 6×8 ones. Regroup 48 as 4 tens, 8 ones. Carry the 4 to the top of the tens' place.

Multiply 6×2 tens, then add the 4 tens.

$(6 \times 2) + 4 = 12 + 4 = 16$

$$
\begin{array}{r}
4 \\
2\ 8 \\
\times \quad 6 \\
\hline
8
\end{array}
\qquad
\begin{array}{r}
4 \\
2\ 8 \\
\times \quad 6 \\
\hline
1\ 6\ 8
\end{array}
$$

Multiplying Three-Digit and Four-Digit Numbers

You can multiply a three-digit number by a one-digit number by writing separate products for the ones, tens, and hundreds. Then you can add the separate products.

$$
\begin{array}{r}
2\ 8\ 4 \\
\times\quad 7 \\
\hline
2\ 8 \\
5\ 6\ 0 \\
+\ 1\ 4\ 0\ 0 \\
\hline
1\ 9\ 8\ 8
\end{array}
$$

$7 \times 4 = 28$
$7 \times 80 = 560$
$7 \times 200 = 1400$

The product of 7×284 is 1,988.

Practice multiplying three-digit numbers this way. Then learn to multiply a three-digit number the quick way, writing the products on one line.

Multiply 7 × the ones. Regroup 28.

$$
\begin{array}{r}
2 \\
2\ 8\ 4 \\
\times\quad 7 \\
\hline
8
\end{array}
$$

Multiply 7 × the tens. Add the 2 tens. Regroup 58 tens.

$$
\begin{array}{r}
5\ 2 \\
2\ 8\ 4 \\
\times\quad 7 \\
\hline
8\ 8
\end{array}
$$

Multiply 7 × the hundreds. Add the 5 hundreds.

$$
\begin{array}{r}
5\ 2 \\
2\ 8\ 4 \\
\times\quad 7 \\
\hline
1\ 9\ 8\ 8
\end{array}
$$

Here is an example where one of the digits in the number you are multiplying is 0. Remember that the product of any number and 0 equals 0.

$$
\begin{array}{r}
4 \\
5\ 0\ 7 \\
\times\quad 6 \\
\hline
3\ 0\ 4\ 2
\end{array}
$$

In this example, 6×0 tens $= 0$. You add 0 and the 4 tens you carried to the tens' place.

Learn to multiply a four-digit number. You multiply from right to left. First you multiply the ones, then the tens, then the hundreds, then the thousands.

Often you have to regroup. Here is an example.

$$
\begin{array}{r}
53 \\
1,7\,0\,4 \\
\times8 \\
\hline
1\,3,6\,3\,2
\end{array}
$$

The process of regrouping, multiplying in the next place, and then adding takes time to learn, and you need to practice it a lot. Practice multiplying one-digit numbers times two-digit, three-digit, and four-digit numbers. You can make up your own numbers to multiply. Be sure to practice with numbers that have zeros in them. Practice writing multiplication problems in place-value columns yourself.

Checking Multiplication

One good way to check multiplication is to estimate to see if the product is about right.

When you are multiplying a two-digit number, find the two tens that the number is between. You found that $8 \times 26 = 208$. To check this product, think 26 is between 20 and 30. So 8×26 should be between 8×20 and 8×30. $8 \times 20 = 160$. $8 \times 30 = 240$. 208 is between 160 and 240.

You can write this check like this:

$$8 \times 20 < 8 \times 26 < 8 \times 30$$
$$160 < 208 < 240 \quad ✔$$

A number statement like $8 \times 20 < 8 \times 26 < 8 \times 30$ is called a double inequality because there are 2 inequality signs.

When you are multiplying a three-digit number, check the product by finding the two hundreds that the number is between.

To check $6 \times 507 = 3,042$, you can think: 507 is between 500 and 600.

$$6 \times 500 < 6 \times 507 < 6 \times 600$$
$$3,000 < 3,042 < 3,600 \quad ✔$$

When you are multiplying a four-digit number, find the two thousands that it is between to check. Does $8 \times 1,704 = 13,632$?

$$8 \times 1,000 < 8 \times 1,704 < 8 \times 2,000$$
$$8,000 < 13,632 < 16,000 \qquad ✔$$

Check each multiplication problem by estimating in this way.

Another Way to Write Expanded Form

Remember that the expanded form of 7,836 is $7,000 + 800 + 30 + 6$. Now that you know how to multiply tens, hundreds, and thousands, you can write the expanded form of a number in another way.

$$7,000 = 7 \times 1,000$$
$$800 = 8 \times 100$$
$$30 = 3 \times 10$$

So you can write $7,000 + 800 + 30 + 6$ like this:

$$(7 \times 1,000) + (8 \times 100) + (3 \times 10) + 6$$

Practice writing numbers in this new expanded form. For example, write 3,604 as $(3 \times 1,000) + (6 \times 100) + 4$. Write 9,078 as $(9 \times 1,000) + (7 \times 10) + 8$.

Division—Part Two

Remainders

Mrs. Hughes wants to divide 33 sheets of construction paper among seven students, so that each student has the same number of sheets. If she gave each student 4 sheets, she would use 28 sheets ($4 \times 7 = 28$). If she gave each student 5 sheets, she would use 35 sheets ($5 \times 7 = 35$). She has only 33 sheets: she has enough to give 4 sheets to each student, but not enough to give 5 sheets. Since

$33 - 28 = 5$, there will be 5 sheets left over if she gives 4 to each student. Here is how you write this division problem.

Mrs. Hughes wants to divide 33 sheets of construction paper among her seven students:

$$7 \overline{)33}$$

What is 33 divided by 7? 7 doesn't go into 33 evenly. The closest we can come is $7 \times 4 = 28$. So we write 4 in the ones' place for the quotient. Then we put 28 below the 33 (or the dividend), and subtract it, to show how many we have left over: 5. Our remainder is 5. So we write R5 next to the quotient 4, like this:

	4 R5	Quotient (with Remainder)
Divisor	7)33	Dividend
	−28	Product of 7×4
	5	Remainder

Notice how you multiply the divisor and the quotient, and then subtract this product from the dividend to find the remainder.

When you do a division problem like this, make the quotient as big as you can. If the problem were 23 divided by 5, what would your quotient be? 3 or 4? It would be 4 because $3 \times 5 = 15$ and $23 - 15$ gives you 8 left over. Since you can subtract 5 from 8, you know that your quotient can be 1 greater. $4 \times 5 = 20$ leaves you 3 left over. Because you can't take 5 away from 3, you know you've found the greatest quotient.

When you find the quotient, multiply the divisor and the quotient and subtract this product from the dividend to find the remainder. You can always check your work by making sure that the remainder is less than the divisor. If the remainder is not less, you need to try again, with a larger quotient. Here is an example.

$$
\begin{array}{r}
5 \ R9 \\
8\overline{)\ 4\ 9} \\
-4\ 0 \\
\hline
9
\end{array}
\qquad\qquad
\begin{array}{r}
6 \ R1 \\
8\overline{)\ 4\ 9} \\
-4\ 8 \\
\hline
1
\end{array}
$$

Subtract 8×5 Subtract 8×6

$9 < 8?$ $1 < 8$ ✔

NO

Practice doing problems like $41 \div 6$ or $58 \div 7$, finding the quotients and the remainders. Remember that $6\overline{)41}$ and $41 \div 6$ are the same problem.

Dividing Tens, Hundreds, and Thousands

Sometimes you can divide tens, hundreds, and thousands easily using the division facts.

$9 \div 3 = 3$ $35 \div 7 = 5$ $18 \div 6 = 3$

and   and   and

$90 \div 3 = 30$ $3,500 \div 7 = 500$ $18,000 \div 6 = 3,000$

Notice how the quotient has the same number of zeros as the dividend. Practice doing problems like these in your head.

Two-Digit Quotients

Sometimes when you divide a two-digit number, the quotient has two digits. Divide 64 by 2. Remember, in division, you start with the highest place value in the dividend and move right. So in 2)64, we first divide the tens:

$$2\overline{)6\ 4}$$

Subtract 2×3

$0 < 2$

$$\begin{array}{r} 3 \\ 2\overline{)6\ 4} \\ -6 \\ \hline 0 \end{array}$$

Make sure the remainder is less than the divisor.

Then bring down the 4 ones in 64. Divide the ones.

$$\begin{array}{r} 3\ 2 \\ 2\overline{)6\ 4} \\ -6 \\ \hline 0\ 4 \end{array}$$

Subtract 2×2

$0 < 4$

$$\begin{array}{r} -\ 4 \\ \hline 0 \end{array}$$

Make sure the remainder is less than the divisor.

You can tell that $64 \div 2$ will have a two-digit quotient because you can divide 6 tens by 2. In the same way, $84 \div 5$ has a two-digit quotient because you can divide 8 tens by 5. $47 \div 8$ has a one-digit quotient because you cannot divide 4 tens by 8. You need to divide 47 ones by 8 instead.

Here is a problem with a two-digit quotient and a remainder.

Divide the tens.

Divide the ones.

$$\begin{array}{r} 1 \\ 5\overline{)8\ 4} \\ -5 \\ \hline 3 \end{array}$$

Subtract 5×1

Check $3 < 5$

$$\begin{array}{r} 1\ 6\ \text{R}4 \\ 5\overline{)8\ 4} \\ -5 \\ \hline 3\ 4 \\ -3\ 0 \\ \hline 4 \end{array}$$

Subtract 5×6

Check $4 < 5$

Checking Division

You check division by multiplying and adding the remainder, if there is one. Remember that multiplying by a number is the opposite of dividing by that number.

To check division:	Multiply:	To check division:	Multiply:
$$\begin{array}{r} 3\ 2 \\ 2\overline{)6\ 4} \\ -6 \\ \hline 0\ 4 \\ -\ 4 \\ \hline 0 \end{array}$$	3 2—quotient × 2—divisor ————— 6 4 ✔ There is no remainder to add.	$$\begin{array}{r} 1\ 6\ \text{R4} \\ 5\overline{)8\ 4} \\ -5 \\ \hline 3\ 4 \\ -3\ 0 \\ \hline 4 \end{array}$$	1 6—quotient × 5—divisor ————— 8 0 add + 4—remainder ————— 8 4 ✔

When you check, you should end up with the number you divided into at first. Remember that this number is called the dividend. Check every division problem by multiplying, and then adding the remainder to get the dividend.

Dividing Three-Digit Numbers

Learn how to divide three-digit numbers by one-digit numbers.

First divide the hundreds.

$$\begin{array}{r} 2 \\ 3\overline{)7\ 5\ 8} \\ -6 \\ \hline 1 \end{array}$$

Subtract 3×2

$1 < 3$

Then divide the tens.

$$\begin{array}{r} 2\ 5 \\ 3\overline{)7\ 5\ 8} \\ -\ 6 \\ \hline 1\ 5 \\ -1\ 5 \\ \hline 0 \end{array}$$

Subtract 3×5

$0 < 3$

Then divide the ones.

$$
\begin{array}{r}
2\ 5\ 2\ \text{R2} \\
3\overline{)\ 7\ 5\ 8} \\
-6 \\
\hline
1\ 5 \\
-1\ 5 \\
\hline
8 \\
-6 \\
\hline
2
\end{array}
$$

Subtract 3×2

$2 < 3$

Check. Multiply and add.

$$
\begin{array}{rl}
2\ 5\ 2 & \text{Quotient} \\
\times\ \ \ \ 3 & \text{Divisor} \\
\hline
7\ 5\ 6 & \\
+\ \ \ \ \ 2 & \text{Remainder} \\
\hline
7\ 5\ 8 \ \checkmark &
\end{array}
$$

Sometimes there are not enough hundreds to begin by dividing hundreds. Then you need to think of the hundreds as tens, and divide the tens.

In the following example divide the tens, since you cannot divide 6 hundreds by 8.

Think of 6 hundreds 2 tens as 62 tens.

Divide the tens

$$
\begin{array}{r}
7 \\
8\overline{)\ 6\ 2\ 7} \\
-5\ 6 \\
\hline
6
\end{array}
$$

Subtract 8×7

$6 < 8$

Divide the ones.

$$
\begin{array}{r}
7\ 8\ \text{R3} \\
8\overline{)\ 6\ 2\ 7} \\
-5\ 6 \\
\hline
6\ 7 \\
-6\ 4 \\
\hline
3
\end{array}
$$

Subtract 8×8

$3 < 8$

Learning long division takes lots of careful practice. Each time you divide and subtract, make sure the remainder is less than the divisor. When you are all done, multiply and add the remainder to check.

Fractions

Numerator and Denominator

A fraction is a part of one thing, or a part of a group. The bottom number of a fraction tells how many equal parts there are. The bottom number is called the denominator. The top number tells how many of the equal parts you are talking about. The top number is called the numerator.

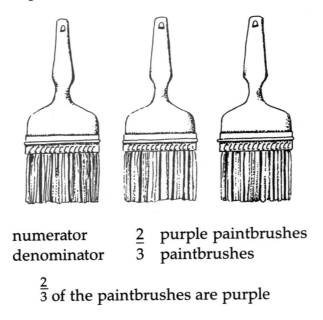

numerator $\underline{2}$ purple paintbrushes
denominator   3   paintbrushes

$\frac{2}{3}$ of the paintbrushes are purple

In the fraction $\frac{4}{8}$, 4 is the numerator and 8 is the denominator. In the fraction $\frac{9}{10}$, what is the numerator?

Equivalent Fractions

Sometimes fractions with different numerators and denominators name the same amount. Fractions that name the same amount are called equivalent fractions.

$$\frac{1}{2} = \frac{3}{6}$$

$\frac{1}{2}$ and $\frac{3}{6}$ are equivalent fractions: they name the same fraction of the circle.

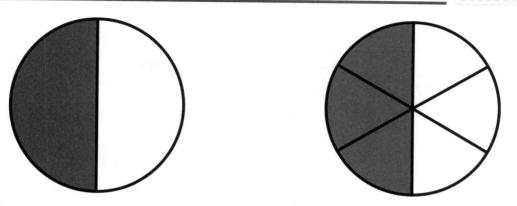

Learn to recognize equivalent fractions. For example, from the picture you should know that $\frac{2}{4} = \frac{4}{8}$

Comparing Fractions

Learn to compare fractions that have the same denominator using the signs $>$, $<$, and $=$.

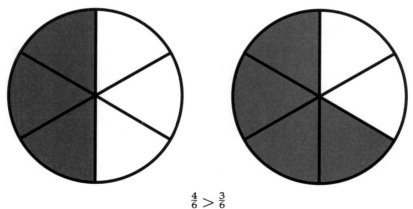

$$\frac{4}{6} > \frac{3}{6}$$

$\frac{4}{6}$ is greater than $\frac{3}{6}$. In $\frac{4}{6}$, there are 6 equal parts and you are talking about 4. In $\frac{3}{6}$, there are 6 equal parts and you are only talking about 3.

Rule: When two fractions have the same denominator, the one with the greater numerator is the greater fraction.

Without using a picture, you should know that $\frac{5}{9} > \frac{3}{9}$; $\frac{2}{7} < \frac{3}{7}$; $\frac{1}{6} = \frac{1}{6}$.

Mixed Numbers and Whole Numbers

The numbers 0, 1, 2, 3, 4 . . . are called the whole numbers. By calling them "whole numbers," we mean that they are not fractions; they name a whole.

A number like $1\frac{1}{2}$ is called a mixed number. It has a part that is a whole number and a part that is a fraction. You read $1\frac{1}{2}$ as "one and one half." When you read a mixed number, you always put an "and" between its whole number part and its fractional part. Here are some more mixed numbers: $2\frac{1}{4}$, $6\frac{1}{8}$, $5\frac{7}{9}$, $3\frac{3}{4}$.

On a number line, $1\frac{1}{2}$ is between 1 and 2. It is 1 *plus* $\frac{1}{2}$ more. In the same way, $5\frac{1}{4}$ is between 5 and 6. It is 5 plus $\frac{1}{4}$ more. $5\frac{1}{4}$ is more than 5, but less than 6.

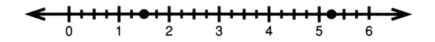

You often use mixed numbers when you measure in inches. Practice measuring to the nearest $\frac{1}{2}$ inch or $\frac{1}{4}$ inch using a ruler divided into $\frac{1}{4}$ inches. For example, draw a line segment $5\frac{3}{4}$ inches long.

Word Problems

In word problems, the important step is deciding what the mathematical problem is that you are being asked. Once you can write the problem in numbers, then you can solve it.

You have already done problems that ask you to add, subtract, multiply, or divide. Sometimes you have to do two different operations in the same problem. These are called two-step problems.

A Two-Step Word Problem

Lisa has $28.50 saved up. For a party, she buys 8 party favors. Each favor costs her $2.39. How much money does she have left after buying the favors?

First, you have to multiply, to find out how much the party favors cost her in all.

You multiply amounts of money the same way you multiply other numbers. Label the cents' point and the dollar sign in the product when you are done.

$$
\begin{array}{r}
3 \quad 7 \quad\quad \\
\$2.39 \\
\times \quad\quad 8 \\
\hline
\$19.12
\end{array}
$$

Then, you have to subtract, to find out how much money she has left.

$$
\begin{array}{r}
1 \ \ 18 \ \ 4 \ \ 10 \\
\$ \ 2 \ 8 \ . \ 3 \ 0 \\
- \quad 1 \ 9 \ . \ 1 \ 2 \\
\hline
\$9. \ 3 \ 8
\end{array}
$$

$28.50 --- how much money she began with
19.12 --- the cost of the favors
$9.38   She has $9.38 left.

An Estimation Problem

Sometimes you do not need to know an exact answer for a word problem. You can estimate. Here is an example.

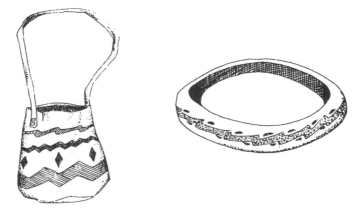

Kim has $20.00. She wants to buy a purse for $13.49 and a bracelet for $8.98. Does she have enough money?

Estimate: $8.98 is about $9.00 $ 9. 0 0
              $13.49 is about $13.00   + 1 3. 0 0
                                    $ 2 2. 0 0

The purse and the bracelet cost about $22.00. So Kim does not have quite enough money.

If your answer is close when you estimate, you need to figure the problem out exactly. For example, if the cost of the purse and the bracelet had come to about $19.00 or $20.00, you would have had to add up exactly how much they cost to answer the problem.

A Problem Where You Need to Guess

Black mollies cost 85¢ and goldfish cost 99¢. Lewis buys some black mollies and some goldfish, five in all. He pays $4.53. How many of each kind of fish does he buy?

You must make a guess to start. Guess that he buys two black mollies. Then he must buy three goldfish. How much will these cost?

$$(2 \times 85¢) + (3 \times 99¢) = 170¢ + 297¢ = 467¢ \text{ or } \$4.67$$

$4.67 is too much. Try another guess. Lewis buys three black mollies and two goldfish.

$$(3 \times 85¢) + (2 \times 99¢) = 255¢ + 198¢ = 453¢ \text{ or } \$4.53$$

The second guess is correct. Lewis buys three black mollies and two goldfish.

V.

NATURAL SCIENCES

Introduction to Life Sciences

FOR PARENTS AND TEACHERS

In this book, children are introduced to the balance of nature, the food chain, environmental pollution, the fascinating lives of social insects, the human nervous system and other topics in human health.

A child's knowledge of the natural world must be gained from observation and experience, not only from books. Here, for example, we suggest that a child observe how a miniature ecosystem works with mosses in a fishbowl. To understand the plant and animal worlds, a child must observe plants and animals, preferably in natural settings, or at second best, in museums and school laboratories.

But book learning does have tremendous importance in bringing system and coherence to a young child's knowledge of nature. Only through systematic presentation of topics can a child make steady and secure progress in scientific learning. The child's development of scientific knowledge and understanding is in some ways a very disorderly and complex process, different for each child. But a systematic approach to the topics of life sciences can at least provide essential building blocks for deeper understanding at a later time. Such a systematic approach ensures that huge gaps in knowledge will not hinder later understanding.

The rationale for our selection of topics bears repeating. In making this selection of topics for beginning life sciences, our committees were guided both by their wide experience in teaching young children, as well as by the careful sequences that have been developed in nations that have had outstanding results in teaching elementary science: Sweden, West Germany, France, and Japan. In addition, our committee members consulted reports by the American Association for the Advancement of Science, and had discussions with the staff of the National Science Foundation. There is no one best sequence for the systematic development of knowledge about life sciences, but we are certain that the one chosen here is a good one that has proved itself to be effective.

That said, please remember that no sequence alone can be truly effective without direct, hands-on experience, or without observation of the natural world. Children also need imaginative help from parents and teachers in stimulating their natural curiosity and interest in the living world around them.

Life Sciences

What Is Nature?

Close your eyes and imagine what nature is like. What do you see? White clouds in a blue sky, or tall grass in a field, or a bird drinking water from a puddle? We use the word "nature" to mean all the things in the universe that were not made by humans, things like trees, mountains, birds, and rivers. The word nature comes from the Latin *natura,* which means "things born." Things that were *not* created by humans are called *natur*-al. Human-made things are called *"art*-i-ficial," because they were made by human art or skill. Have you ever seen an artificial Christmas tree? It is very different from a natural tree that was born from a seed and grew in the ground.

Is a garden part of nature? Well, yes and no. Yes, it is natural because people did not make the plants that are growing there. But no, a garden is not natural; it is artificial because people planned and tended the garden. They did not leave everything to nature. A garden is a good example of people and nature working together.

Are human beings part of nature? Yes, except for the clothes they wear. After all, your clothes were made by human art. The world of nature—all the things that were not made by people—is huge. Nature includes the stars in the heavens, the sun, and the earth; it includes things that are as big as the sky and so tiny that they can be seen only with a microscope.

The Balance of Nature

Did you ever lose your balance and fall down? If you have ever tried to walk on the narrow edge of a board, or have learned to ride a bicycle, you know it's sometimes not easy to keep your balance. If you start falling one way, you have to shift your weight another way. You have to make little movements of your arms or legs to keep from falling down. And if you are pedaling slowly on a bicycle, you sometimes have to pedal faster.

In order to stay healthy, nature has to stay in balance. Nature would be very unhealthy if only one kind of creature lived in it. For example, if suddenly there were only animals in the world and no plants, the plant-eating animals would start to die because they would have nothing to eat. Soon those animals that would normally eat the plant-eating animals would have nothing to eat and they would die too. There would quickly be no living creatures at all. For nature to stay healthy, no one part can be allowed to disappear and make nature lose its balance.

But nature is always changing. So how does it keep in balance? The balance in nature depends upon three groups of creatures that form a circular chain that goes around and around like the chain on a bicycle. One group is called producers; another is called consumers; and the third is called decomposers. The producers (plants) make the food. The consumers (animals) eat it. When

The ecosystem is made up of three basic groups: producers, consumers, and decomposers. Can you find examples of each in this illustration?

plants and animals die, the decomposers (bacteria and fungi) turn the dead matter into material that will be used by the producers. Then the cycle begins again. This food chain cycles over and over again and keeps nature in balance.

Here's what happens. Plants are producers. They capture energy from sunlight, and they use this energy to take in chemicals from the air and soil to make food. The food they produce from chemicals and light lets them grow.

But animals do not produce their own food from light and chemicals. They have to eat either plants or other animals that have already eaten plants. Then the energy and chemicals from the plants pass on to the animals. Because animals eat or consume living things, we call them consumers.

When plants and animals die, they provide food for another group, bacteria and fungi. Bacteria and fungi are called decomposers because they decompose (break up) the dead animal or plant matter and turn it back into the chemicals that plants will use. When the chemicals go back into the soil and the air, the plants start the cycle again.

How does the food chain keep nature in balance? Remember how *you* managed to stay in balance when you were standing on a narrow edge or learning to ride a bicycle? You had to move a little one way, and then another way. If you didn't adjust your weight at all—you would topple over. You can think of the balance of nature as a constant moving and adjusting back and forth. If one group of creatures starts taking over, then nature adjusts itself so they won't take over completely. Plants do not take over the world, because animals eat them. But animals do not take over the world, because if they did, they would have no plants to eat. Of course, the decomposers do not take over the world, because if new plants and animals didn't keep dying, the decomposers would have no food and they would all die too. If any link in the food chain disappears, nature can't function, just as your bicycle won't function if its chain loses a link.

✳️ How the Wolf Broke the Chain

Scientists have seen clear examples of how taking one link out of the food chain hurts nature. One example occurred in Arizona with deer and wolves. Scientists were afraid the deer were dying off too quickly because there were too many wolves killing and eating them. They solved this problem by killing the wolves. In less than twenty years, there were too many deer. They ate all the green plants they could find. They even ate very young trees, which destroyed the forest. Soon, there was no more food for the deer. They began to starve to death. Scientists now know that wolves are a necessary link in the food chain. Wolves control the number of deer, which in turn controls the number of plants that are eaten. Scientists are now working to bring wolves back to places, like the one in Arizona, where wolves are important links in the food chain.

The Invisible Web

Think back on what you've read about in this section. You've read about the food chain and the balance of nature. You've read about producers, consumers, and decomposers. You've read about the relationship between wolves and deer, and you learned that living creatures affect their environment and are affected by it.

In doing all that reading, you were learning about ecology. Ecology is the study of the relations between living things and their environment (the world around them). A scientist who studies the <u>relations between living things and their environment is called an ecologist.</u> An ecologist might focus her or his attention upon one particular ecosystem. An ecosystem is a specific community of living creatures and their environment. If you follow the suggestions below for making a woodland or desert terrarium, you will create an ecosystem, a little world of living creatures that affect each other and their environment, and are in turn affected by their environment.

Nature Under Glass

There's a way you can see for yourself how nature stays in balance. Here are two ways to create and observe a small piece of nature under glass.

I. Woodland Terrarium
Materials: large glass container
            small pebbles
            charcoal chips (the type
               used in potting plants)
            peat moss
            sand
            potting soil
            plants (dwarf ivy, ferns, lichens, mosses, seed plants)
            plant mister
            animals (optional—snails, earthworms, pill bugs, salamanders)

Wash and rinse your container and place a one-inch layer of small pebbles in the bottom. Place about a half-inch of charcoal chips on top of the pebbles. Mix together equal parts of peat moss, sand, and potting soil, and place a three-inch layer of this mixture on top of the charcoal chips. Arrange the woodland plants you have chosen in the soil. Make sure to leave plenty of space for each plant to grow. Spray the soil with a plant mister until it is fully moist. If you wish to add animals to your terrarium, they must be fed. Snails will eat lettuce, salamanders require live insects or mealworms, pill bugs will eat wood chips. Earthworms can get their nutrients from the soil, although you may want to feed them corn meal. Cover your terrarium by sealing it *with a piece of glass or plastic, and place it near a window where it will get daylight but not direct sun.*

II. Desert Terrarium
Materials: same as for woodland terrarium except for types of plants and animals (substitute cacti or succulent plants and, if possible, small animals collected from the desert)

Follow the same directions for preparing the woodland terrarium, except mix together equal parts of peat moss and potting soil with twice as much sand. Place a three-inch layer of this soil mixture on top of the charcoal chips. After the soil is prepared, plant cacti and succulent plants in the terrarium, allowing enough room for growth. Mist the plants lightly after they have been planted. The desert terrarium does not need a cover, but the plants should be misted occasionally. Place the desert terrarium in direct sunlight.

If the temperature in the room is not too warm, the plants in your terrarium should stay alive for a long, long time. Even some little creatures that may have been living on the plants will stay healthy and grow. This little system might stay healthy year after year.

Why does it stay healthy? Because it stays in balance. Water from the plants will go into the air. It will form water drops on the sides and top of the bowl, and these drops will fall back on the plants. This is just like rain in nature. The light, the drops of water, and the food that is in the soil will make the plants grow.

As some of the plants grow old and die, little invisible fungi and bacteria will eat the dead plants and change them back into chemicals in the soil. The chemicals will feed the younger plants. Also, little insects will eat the plants, and when they die, they will be decomposed and make more food for the plants, which are in turn food for the young insects.

But if the insects eat too many plants, what will happen? Nature will go out of balance. The new insects will have too little to eat, and many of them will die. When the insects die, fewer creatures will eat the plants, so they will grow again. Plants, insects, and fungi—producers, consumers, and decomposers—will once more come into balance.

You might think of an ecosystem as a delicate, invisible web that holds life together for a group of living things and changes whenever anything new comes into the web or anything old leaves it. What happens if you break a strand or two of the web? It may continue to hold together. But if you break too many strands, it may fall apart.

For example, think of the web of life in a swamp in Florida. What if a company wants to drain part of a swamp and then build houses on the new dry land? The plants in what used to be swampland would be killed, and the animals would have to move to another part of the swamp. There would then be more animals and less swamp. Do you think there would still be enough food for all the animals?

Remember what happened in the Arizona ecosystem you read about when people tried to get rid of wolves? The people didn't realize that there was an important invisible strand connecting the wolves and the deer. By figuring out how ecosystems work, ecologists can help us see these strands and recognize which are most important to holding together a web of life.

People can be part of an ecosystem too. People are affected by their environment, and they can affect it, sometimes in good ways, and sometimes in bad ways. Let's take a look at some of the bad things people are responsible for, and at what we can do to correct them.

Hold Your Breath!

Have you ever smelled the exhaust that comes out of a car or truck or school bus? Have you ever seen thick smoke pouring out of a chimney on a house or out of a factory smokestack?

All this exhaust and smoke contains unhealthy chemicals that pollute the air. "To pollute" means to make something dirty or impure or unsafe. Polluted air contains a lot of human-made material, including dust and chemicals that are bad for plants and animals to breathe. Besides being unhealthy for plants and animals, air pollution upsets the balance of nature.

Can you think of some of the causes of air pollution? Major sources are factories and cars. Big cities have a serious problem because there are so many people driving so many cars, trucks, and buses. The emissions from these vehicles contain unhealthy chemicals (emissions are what cars and other

Look at what this paper mill is doing to the air.

vehicles put in the air as a result of burning fuel in their engines). On some days, these emissions can turn the air dark and cloudy. This dark, cloudy air is called smog. Smog can be annoying, and it can even be dangerous. If people breathe in too much smog, they can get lung disease.

We can all do our share to reduce air pollution. We can, when possible, ride a bike or walk instead of using a car. We can turn off the lights when we don't need them.

How does turning off the lights help? Lights use electricity, and electricity is often made by burning fuels. Since burning fuels causes air pollution, we can cause less to be burned by switching off the lights.

Water Pollution

Every living thing needs water in order to survive. Keeping water safe and preventing water pollution are important concerns for everyone.

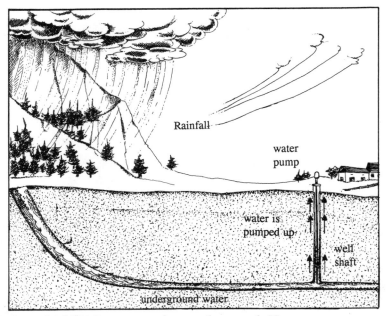

Some drinking water comes from underground. Here, a pump inside the well draws the water upward.

Let's think about how we get the water we need. People get most of their water from lakes, rivers, and underground layers of water. Do you know where the water in your town comes from? If you live in the country, your water may come from an underground well. That water is often very clear and pure, because it has passed through sand and soil and rocks that filter out the particles. Even some cities get their water from underground wells.

Other cities get their water from rivers or lakes. City engineers pass the water through

This is Quabbin Reservoir in western Massachusetts. Its water supplies the city of Boston.

This picture shows only a part of Boston. From it you can get an idea of how many people rely on Quabbin Reservoir.

filters to make it clean, and add tiny amounts of substances that kill germs. Then the water is safe to drink.

Before there were so many people on our planet and so many farms and industries, the water in nature was pure. But nowadays, the world's water supplies are beginning to be polluted with unhealthy chemicals, because so many people are now on the earth, and they are doing so much farming and manufacturing.

How does pure water become polluted? People put particles and chemicals into water much faster than nature does. When factories dump chemicals and waste into rivers and lakes, that causes water pollution. Everything we put into nature has to go somewhere, and many pollutants eventually wash into our water supply. Another source of water pollution is farming, which often causes the dug-up soil to wash into our water supply, along with chemicals from artificial fertilizers and insect killers. The rain washes these materials into rivers, lakes, and underground water.

The effects of water pollution are not good. Particles of dirt from farming and manufacturing reduce the numbers of fish in a river or ocean by smothering their eggs. And certain chemicals cause harmful plants to grow that suffocate fish and other plants. These chemicals can also be harmful for people and other creatures to drink.

Some farmers are trying to help prevent water pollution by keeping soil and fertilizer from running off into the water supply. Some factories are purifying the water they use before sending it back to rivers and lakes.

Sometimes ships carrying oil accidentally pollute the water if their cargo spills. These men are trying to clean the water after an oil spill.

Conserving and Recycling

You can help too. One way is by conserving, which means using something carefully and not wasting it. Conserving means more than making sure you don't leave the bathroom faucet dripping, though. It means understanding that we have to be careful about how we use *all* of the resources that nature offers us.

For a long time in this country, not much thought was given to conserving natural resources. People acted as though they would never run out of anything in nature; there would always be more than enough oil and trees and clean water and good land. But now we've started to understand that we *can* run out of natural resources unless we use them carefully.

Are you doing anything at your home or school to conserve natural resources? Perhaps your school is saving energy by using a little less heat in the winter. Find out if your school or town has a recycling program. When you recycle something, instead of throwing it away it can be used again. If you drink juice or soda from an aluminum can, you could throw the can away, which would be a waste, or you could recycle it. The aluminum will be cleaned, combined with other recycled cans, and re-formed into new cans. Does your school have a special container to collect aluminum cans so they can be taken to a recycling center?

Lots of stuff can be recycled: aluminum cans, glass bottles, newspapers, grocery bags, cardboard, even some kinds of plastic. Recycling conserves natural resources. It helps keep the balance of nature by making sure we don't use up too much of what nature has to offer.

Recycling can even help reduce air and water pollution. If you recycle glass and aluminum containers, then factories won't have to burn as much fuel to make new containers. If a factory burns less fuel, then it will put fewer unhealthy chemicals in the air and water.

Through waste and carelessness, people have upset the balance of nature. But through conserving and recycling and thinking about how humans fit into the balance of nature, people are helping to restore it. Let's hope we succeed.

Animals That Work Together

Can you think of some animals that act in social groups as well as by themselves? You certainly know one kind of social animal—human beings. We humans cooperate with each other in order to get something done. We are able to cooperate because we use language to communicate with one another. Our language enables us to work together on very complicated tasks like getting food to the supermarket or putting a person on the moon.

Some of the most fascinating animals that work in social groups are insects such as ants and honeybees. They live together in large colonies. But can they talk to each other? We'll see.

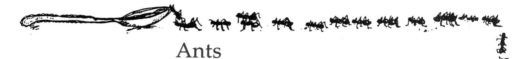

Ants

When you see some ants, you can do an experiment to watch how they work together. Put a drop of syrup near the ants, and then sit back and wait. You may have to wait a whole hour or a day, but after a while, you will see a whole parade of ants moving to the drop in a single file, like soldiers marching in a row. And another line of ant soldiers will be heading away from the drop, back to the ant nest, each of them carrying a tiny droplet to take to the nest.

Since ants don't have a very big brain, how are they able to march in a row, and how can they tell each other where the syrup is? They don't use language like ours, but they do use a kind of language—a chemical language. When one ant discovered the syrup, it got very excited, and laid down a tiny chemical trail to the food. (It probably didn't *know* it was laying down a trail; ants are just born with that ability.) Other ants then found the trail by picking up the chemical signal, and they started moving toward the food. After they gathered a tiny drop of food, they followed a trail back to the nest. (Ant nests are usually built underground and are made up of chambers or small rooms connected by tiny tunnels.)

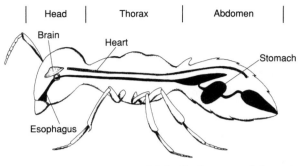

Major body parts of the ant.

There are many different types of ants, large and small. And some have developed special ways to feed themselves. Some ants stroke small insects called aphids so they can drink the "honeydew" that the aphids pass out of their bodies. Another type of ant feeds sweet liquid to some of its workers until they become big sacks filled with honey. These special ants serve as living storage containers for food.

Scientists all over the world are still discovering new kinds of ants. There are so many interesting kinds that some scientists spend their whole lives just studying what ants do. In this book we will tell you about one kind of ant—Atta ants, the fungus growers.

Ants That Grow Their Own Food

One day a boy in Louisiana woke up to find that all the leaves on a tree in his backyard had disappeared; only a few threads of the leaves were left. He knew what had happened. A new colony of Atta ants had come to his neighborhood.

A farmer in Texas said that a heavy sack of crushed seeds for his chickens was emptied by a single colony of Atta ants in one night.

Atta ants aren't very big, but they can carry heavy loads, and there are many thousands of them, sometimes millions, in a colony. In one night, they

These Atta ants are taking leaf parts back to their nest.

can make the leaves of a tree or the plants in a garden disappear. With their scissor-like jaws, they spend hours cutting off pieces of leaf to carry back to their nests. They don't eat these leaves, so *why* do they carry pieces of leaf many times their own weight far away to their nests?

It's because they eat only one kind of food—a special fungus that they grow on the leaves. They are the only creatures who can make this special fungus grow properly. You already know that a fungus is a decomposer. It grows on dead leaves and other dead matter. Did you know that some funguses are good to eat? If you have ever eaten a mushroom from the grocery, you have eaten a piece of fungus. Did you like the taste? Beware of eating any of the mushrooms you see growing in the woods, because many are poisonous to humans!

This picture shows you the chambers, or rooms, in the underground nest of Atta ants.

The Atta ants take their leaves to a cave they have dug deep underground. Some of their caves are as deep as twenty feet! There in their nests they have their fungus farms. On each piece of leaf in their nest they carefully place a tiny bit of the fungus, which starts to grow on the leaf. In a few days, the leaf will be covered with white fungus. After a while the fungus makes little knobs of delicious food that the ants eat.

To grow their crop, the Atta ants must work hard to keep the conditions just right for their special fungus. The air must not be too dry or too damp. If it is too dry, the ants close the opening to the nest. If the air is too damp, they open up holes to let the air circulate. They must also keep the crop perfectly clean by taking away any foreign fungus that might start infecting the food. Hundreds of Atta ants spend all of their time just cleaning the fungus farm, like farmers removing weeds, so only the right kind of crop will grow there.

The Atta ants are just one of the fascinating members of the ant family. Others, like the carpenter ants and the honeydew ants, are just as interesting. If you want to find out more about ants, ask for good books about them in the library.

Bees

Bees are also social insects that live in colonies, but they fly instead of marching in a line like ants. The food for some bees is honey. Have you ever eaten honey? Do you know where it comes from? We humans get it from bees' nests! Where do the bees get the honey? They make it from the sweet nectar that they find in hundreds and hundreds of flowers.

How do the bees tell each other where the flowers are to be found? Like ants, they communicate with each other by giving off a chemical scent. But honeybees also have another way of giving each other information. If a bee finds some flowers that are a very good source of nectar, she returns to the hive and performs what is called a "waggle dance." This dance, which provides directions to other bees about how to find flowers, is actually an imitation of how the bee first flew to the flowers. As she turns from side to side, flapping her wings and buzzing, her "waggle dance" is understood by the other workers in the hive, and they fly off toward the flowers. Their path is so straight that a straight line is known as a beeline. Have you heard anyone say, "I made a beeline for it"—meaning they went absolutely straight for it?

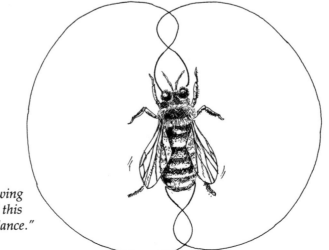

The lines in this drawing show you the path of this honeybee's "waggle dance."

Bees are helped to fly straight by their amazing eyes. They have five eyes, two big ones on the sides of the head, and three little ones on top. The big eyes are not like ours. Each one is made up of six thousand eyes working together. The two big eyes and three small ones enable a bee to see in all directions at the same time—front, back, up, down, and side to side.

Workers, Drones, and Queens

In a honeybee colony, there are different kinds of bees. One kind are the female worker bees, who gather nectar and make honey from the nectar inside their bodies. Only these workers have the special "honey stomach," where honey is produced. These workers also make the wax for building the house (called the hive) where the bees live, and for making the cells where the honey will be stored.

Male bees are called drones. They do not do any work. Their only job is to mate with the queen bee to make more bees.

The queen has only one job. It's to be the mother of all the bees in the hive. She mates with a male or drone and lays eggs in containers made of wax. Some eggs become drones, and some become workers.

Sometimes the bee colony will make a new queen, so a new colony can be started. Where does the new queen come from? The worker bees choose a special baby bee, and feed it a special food that we call "royal jelly." This food that makes a young bee grow into a

WORKER   QUEEN   DRONE

queen is a mixture of pollen, honey, and saliva. (Do you know why we call it "royal"? It's because a human king or queen is called royalty.) The new queen bee goes off to start a new colony in a place where more flowers can be found.

Bee Stings

Human beings can get their honey by encouraging colonies of bees to start living in their backyards or farms in special small houses. The beekeepers wear netting over their heads, and gloves on their hands, so they will not be stung.

Have you ever been stung by a bee? Despite the way it seems, bees are not out to sting people. Bees will sting animals and people only in self-defense; that is, they will sting you if they think you are trying to harm them. In fact, when a bee stings you, it dies soon afterward, because it leaves its stinger and part of its body behind.

THE HUMAN BODY AND HEALTH

In Book One of this series we read about the five senses—sight, smell, hearing, touch, and taste. Now we're going to read about how the human nervous system understands the information it receives from the senses— especially the senses of sight and hearing.

The Nervous System

The nervous system consists of our brain, spinal cord, and nerves. It takes in all the information coming from the senses, and arranges it for us. It is like a busy airport. Information is constantly coming into and out of the control tower (the brain), over the main runway (the spinal cord), through many other runways (the nerves).

The brain itself has three main parts. They are the brain stem or medulla, the cerebellum, and the cerebrum. They each have different jobs to do.

The medulla keeps your heartbeat and your breathing regular.

When you need to balance yourself on a bicycle or skates, your cerebellum is in charge. It coordinates all your muscles so that your body can move as you want it to. The medulla and cerebellum are working all the time, even when we don't know it.

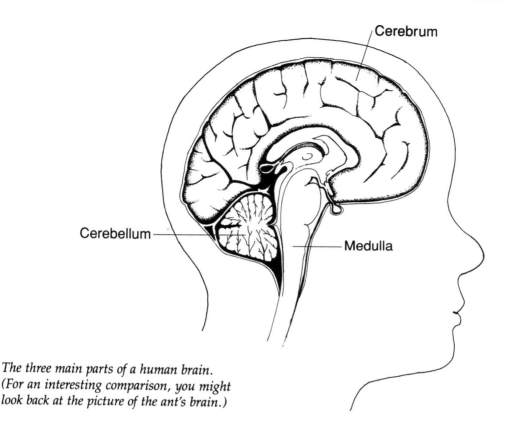

Cerebrum

Cerebellum ———————

————— Medulla

The three main parts of a human brain.
(For an interesting comparison, you might
look back at the picture of the ant's brain.)

When you read a book or play a game, another part of your brain comes
into action. It's the cerebrum, or more precisely, the cerebral cortex, the outer
coiled, gray matter that makes up most of the cerebrum. The cerebral cortex
controls thinking, sensing, and moving. It is in control when we are aware of
the world, and when we are trying to do something like pay attention in class,
or play a game, or read a book. Your cerebral cortex is helping you understand
these words right now!

The spinal cord is a long piece of nerve tissue that runs from the brain
down through the backbone. It connects the brain to the body's nerves. (Can
you feel the hard knobs of your backbone?)

Nerves are tiny fibers found in the spinal cord and throughout the body.
They pick up information and send it up the spinal cord to the brain. Special
nerves tell us when we are seeing, feeling, hearing, smelling, or touching
something. Other nerves act as lines of communication that pass information
on.

Reflexes

There are certain nerves in your spine and brain that tell parts of your body to act really fast—in a split second—whenever you have to dodge a ball, or protect yourself.

Have you ever touched something really hot, like a hot iron? Bam! You jerked your hand away even before you knew what happened. The nerves in your fingers picked up the message that you were touching something hot. That message quickly traveled to your spinal cord. There it was sent to a nerve that sent a message to your arm muscles. It said "Pull your hand away quickly." This all happened in a split second, and saved your hand from getting burned too badly.

When your body must act extremely fast in order to avoid injury, the message from your sensory nerves doesn't go all the way to the brain before you take action. Instead, the message travels from the sensory nerve to your spinal cord. There it is sent back to a muscle right away, causing an action. This quick action is so fast that we can't even think about it. It is called a reflex. A reflex is an action we take even before our brains know about it.

Has a doctor ever tested your reflexes? Try this. Sit in a chair and cross one leg over the other. Let your top leg hang loosely over the bottom one. Give yourself (or have someone else give you) a *gentle* "karate chop" just below the kneecap. Did your leg kick out automatically? That was a reflex.

Reflexes act without our having to think about them. That leaves us free to think about the things we want to do.

Sight

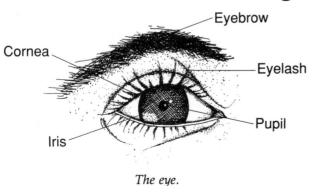

The eye.

Have you ever wondered how your eyes allow you to see the things around you? In the middle of your eyes there is a dark round spot called the pupil. Each pupil gets bigger when you are in the dark, and smaller when you turn on a light. Why do you think the pupil acts that

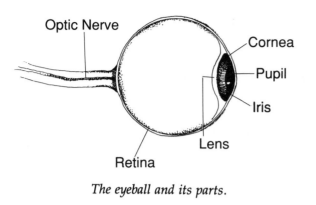

The eyeball and its parts.

way? Let's look at a picture that will help you understand how the eye works.

Light passes first through your cornea, a transparent or see-through covering on the outside of your eye, and then through your pupil, which is really an opening in the eye. Finally it passes through the elastic or bendable lens that sits behind the pupil. Light is put in focus by your lens.

The lens in your eye acts just the way the lens in a camera does. It makes a picture of the outside world. A magnifying glass is a simple lens, and if you have one in your school or house you can see that it does make a picture. Sometime when it's daylight you can try this. Take a piece of white paper and hold it against your chest. Turn yourself toward a bright window. Now move a magnifying glass back and forth near the piece of paper. When the lens is at just the right spot, you will see an upside-down picture of the window on the sheet of paper.

That is a simple version of the way your eye works. The lens of your eye focuses a picture on a special surface at the back of the eye. It is called the

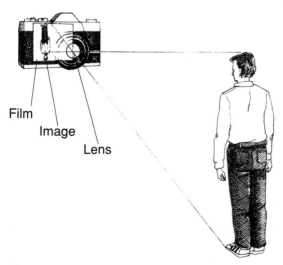

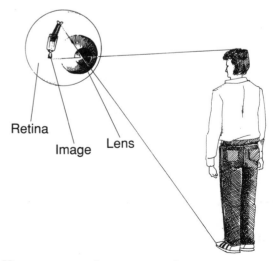

Here you can see how the lens of a camera produces an image inside the camera.

Here you can see how the lens of your eye focuses an image on the retina.

retina. Once the light passes through your lens, it forms an upside-down image on the retina. Muscles attached to the lens help it to get thicker or thinner and bend light from near or far objects to focus on the retina. These muscles serve the same purpose as your hand moving a magnifying glass closer and farther away from a picture to get it in focus.

Your retina sends images to the optic nerve, which sends them to the brain, where they are flipped right-side up. This all happens very quickly, so you don't notice any delay between the time you look at an object and the time your brain receives the image.

Why does your pupil get bigger when the light is dim, and smaller when the light is bright? It's because light that is too bright keeps us from seeing well, and can even injure the eye. Making the opening of your pupil smaller cuts down the amount of light that hits the retina. But if the light is too dim, we can't see very well, so the pupil gets very big and lets in more light when we try to see in the dark.

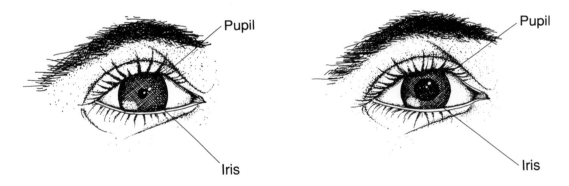

Here you can see the difference between the size of the pupil and the iris. Which eye is exposed to brighter light?

The part of your eye that adjusts the size of your pupil is the circle right around it. It's called the iris. It's the part of your eye that gives it color, and determines whether you are brown-eyed, or blue-eyed, or green-eyed, or whatever special color your eyes have. The Greeks had a goddess called Iris. She was the goddess of the rainbow. Can you guess why the colored part of the eye was named the iris?

Sometimes, the eyes can't work as they should and people need glasses. Some people are farsighted, which means that they can see things far from them, but have trouble seeing things close up. Other people are nearsighted. What do you think that means? Nearsighted people can see things close up, but have trouble seeing things far away.

It is important to have your vision checked by a doctor, so any problems can be caught early. Do you already wear glasses? Many people do. The lenses of glasses are shaped in such a way that they help your eyes do their job properly.

Hearing

How does the ear let us hear sounds? To understand how the ear works, let's find out what sound is.

The next time you hear a radio or TV playing, touch the box near where the sound is coming out. Do you feel some tingling? Now, try another experiment. Close your lips and say, "hmmmmmm." While you are humming, feel your throat under the chin. You *do* feel tingling now! That tingling is called vibration. It is caused by something that moves back and forth rather fast. The loudspeaker in the radio is moving back and forth. So is the voice box in your throat. These vibrations cause sound. Let's see how.

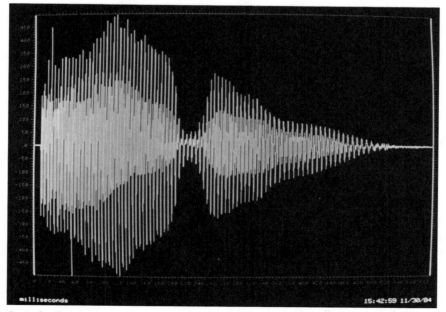

Sound vibrations can be recorded by special machines called speech analyzers.
This picture shows you the pattern made by the sounds in the word "baby."

First, the vibrating speaker or sound box moves the nearby air back and forth, making the air vibrate too. If you have a special radio that plays under water, you can hear it making the water vibrate. Usually we are out in the air, though. The vibrating air, or sound waves, reaches our ears, travels down the ear canal, and makes our eardrums vibrate too. (The eardrum is a thin skin that stretches across the inner end of the ear canal.) But that's just the beginning.

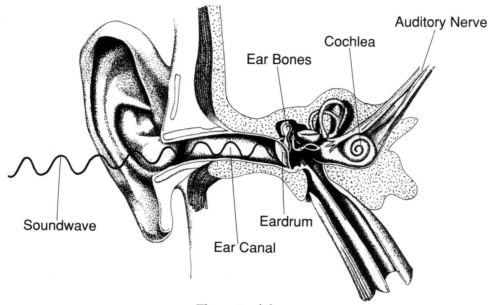

The parts of the ear.

Next, the vibrations of the eardrum cause vibrations in the bones of the inner ear. These bones vibrate a spiral-shaped organ called the cochlea, which is filled with liquid. The vibrations of the liquid then make vibrations in tiny hairs that are inside the cochlea. Each hair has a different length, and picks up a special range of vibrations. Each hair has its own connection with a nerve that goes to the larger auditory (hearing) nerve. Then the auditory nerve sends a signal to the brain.

Just think how different it would be for you to live without your sense of hearing. At first you wouldn't be able to understand what was happening on a TV program, or a movie. You wouldn't be able to listen to your favorite music. But you could still manage quite well. You could learn to read lips, and you could learn sign language, as deaf people do to talk to one another and to hearing people. Your hearing is another sense that should be tested regularly by a doctor so that any problems you might have can be discovered early.

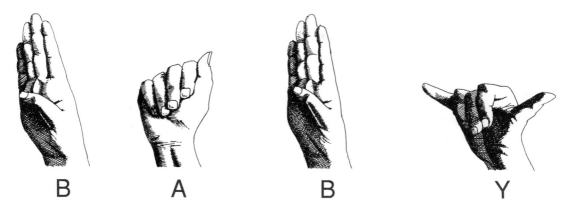

B   A   B   Y

You've already seen the pattern "baby" makes on a speech analyzer. Here are the hand signs for b-a-b-y in sign language.

Listen to some music from the radio or TV, and cup your hands around your ears. Does the sound seem to get louder? Take your hands away and the sound becomes softer again. This is because the curved surfaces of your hands deflect a greater number of sound waves into your ears. The more sound waves the ears receive, the louder the sound is.

You can actually see the vibrations that cause sound waves. Stretch a piece of plastic wrap over the surface of a bowl and fasten it with a rubber band. Sprinkle a few grains of sugar on the plastic. Now take a big pan, hold it near the bowl, and strike it with a spoon a few times. The grains of sugar will jump every time the pan gives out a sound. This is because the pan's vibrations make sound waves. When the sound waves hit the plastic, the surface vibrates and makes the grains of sugar jump.

Introduction to Physical Sciences

FOR PARENTS AND TEACHERS

The physical science topics in this book cover electricity, vacuums and volumes, density, metals and nonmetals, gravity, and the solar system.

Just as in life sciences, the main teacher of the young child is experience. There is a famous experiment by the Swiss psychologist Piaget that shows that very young children think a tall, narrow glass holds more water than a squat, thick one, when in fact the glasses hold the same amount. Older children do not make this mistake. How have children learned a truer understanding of the physical world? Not from books and science teachers, but from actual experience. Knowledge of physical science must first be "proved upon our pulses," by getting our hands wet and dirty with the size and heft of things, by noticing that a rock tossed into the air falls back down, by remembering that thunder comes after lightning.

Unfortunately, not all children come to school with equal amounts of experience and knowledge of the physical world. One of the main tasks of science teaching in the early grades is to fill in the important gaps for all children. This must be done systematically in a planned sequence, even if it means going over ground already familiar to some children. We have tried to make the familiar interesting, too. We hope there will be something new and intriguing for every child.

As in the previous books in this series we have tried to encourage hands-on observation and experimentation.

Physical Sciences

Static Electricity

Twenty-six hundred years ago, a Greek named Thales noticed something peculiar about the yellow glassy beads many people wore. He noticed that when someone rubbed the beads with a piece of cloth, nearby bits of straw would jump to the beads and cling to them for a while before dropping off. (Later we'll tell you how to make this happen.) The beads were made of hardened yellow pine sap that the Greeks called *elektron*. Today we call the material "amber." Why, wondered Thales, did *elektron* attract straw when it was rubbed? No one could give the answer.

Many centuries later, around the year 1600, an English scientist named William Gilbert found that many pairs of substances behave like amber and cloth when rubbed together. This effect, which Gilbert called "electric," is known today as static electricity.

You may have observed static electricity if you have ever tried to separate clothes when they come out of a hot dryer. The clothes cling together and crackle when peeled apart. You can see static electricity another way. The next time you are

The Grecian Thales (THAY leez) was a person of many accomplishments. An engineer, philosopher, and statesman, he is said to have introduced geometry into Greece from Egypt.

combing your hair in front of the bathroom mirror, try this: run a tiny stream of water from the faucet; comb your hair (which must be dry) several times;

This is the kind of activity you should see when you place a comb you've run through your hair near some paper bits.

then bring the comb near the water. You should see the stream of water bend. Or, if you have a comb handy right now, you can try another experiment. Place a small pile of paper bits on a table, then run the comb through your hair ten times really fast. Bring the comb near the pieces of paper and watch them fly up and stick to the comb.

Here is another experiment you can do with static electricity. For the first one, you will need a long piece of string and two blown-up balloons. Attach each end of the string to a balloon. "Electrify" the balloons by rubbing them with a clean, dry cloth or on your clothes, and pick up the string in the middle. What happens to the balloons? Now place a piece of paper in between the balloons and see what happens. What happens when you pull the paper out?

Explanation: The "electrified" balloons both have a negative charge, which is what forces them apart. When a paper is put between them, the electric fields around the balloons give the paper a positive charge, which attracts the balloons. Removing the paper takes away the positive charge, so the balloons move apart again.

Why the Paper Sticks to the Comb

To understand why rubbing things together makes static electricity, we need to know that everything is made of tiny things called atoms. Each atom contains three different kinds of even smaller particles. These particles, which are much too small to be seen, are called protons, neutrons, and electrons. Remember the word "electron"? It comes from the Greek word for amber!

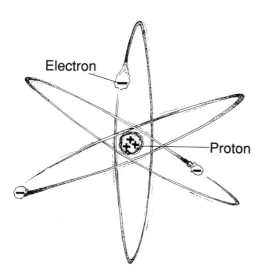

This picture of an atom shows the charges of the protons and electrons.

The heavy protons and neutrons stay in the center of the atom, and the light electrons move rapidly around them. Protons and electrons both have a property we call charge. The charge on the proton is plus one unit, and that on the electron is minus one unit. In other words, protons and electrons have opposite charges of equal size. We call the plus units "positive" and the minus units "negative." The neutrons have no charge. They are neutral, as their name reminds us.

It is a fundamental law of nature that similar charges repel each other—that means push each other away. But opposite charges attract each other. So two electrons brought close together will repel each other, and so will two protons. But an electron and a proton will attract each other. Now let's see what all this has to do with static electricity.

Usually, atoms have equal numbers of electrons and protons. But when you comb your hair, some electrons are transferred from the atoms of your hair to the surface of the comb. Now your comb has more electrons than protons. That is, it has more negative than positive charges. What happens when the comb is

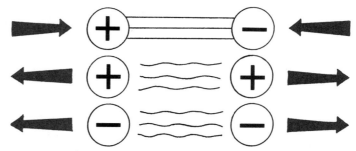

This chart can remind you how charges react to each other. Opposite charges attract each other while similar charges repel each other.

moved close to one corner of a scrap of paper? Like charges repel each other. The extra electrons on the comb's surface push the electrons of the paper to its far corner. Now the corner of the paper near the comb has more positive than negative charges. The attraction between the positive charge of the paper's near corner and the negative charge on the surface of the comb is so strong that paper and comb stick together.

When a sock sticks to a tee shirt fresh from the clothes dryer, the two pieces are held together by the same sort of attraction between charges on the surface of each. Static electricity refers to charged particles that build up in objects; the electrons in static electricity do not flow in a current. Electrons that flow in a current make a different kind of electricity, one that we will learn about next.

You can make an electricity detector to find out more about electric charges. Suspend a plastic ballpoint pen from a piece of string or thread. Gather a variety of objects made of plastic, glass, wood, and metal and different materials like cotton, wool, silk, and a piece of carpet. Rub each object with one of the materials and bring it close to the pen to see if it is "electrified." An object with a charge will make the pen swing around toward it. Which combinations of objects and materials produce the strongest charges?

Electric Circuits

Because electrons had not been discovered in earlier times, physicists in those days didn't understand much about static electricity. Static electricity isn't very useful, anyway, because rubbing doesn't separate positive and negative charges for long periods of time and doesn't make those charges flow in a current. You've noticed that things attached by static electricity soon come apart. The sock will drop off the tee shirt if you just wait awhile.

But in the year 1800, the Italian scientist Alessandro Volta built a device that made a kind of electricity that was different from static electricity. When Volta attached a wire to the two ends of his device, electricity flowed continuously through the wire. Volta had made the first battery! Have you ever used a 9-volt battery to run a toy or a radio? The word "volt" comes from Alessandro Volta's name.

Volta didn't understand electricity. Ninety-seven years would pass before the discovery of the electron. But he realized that electricity that flows through wires from a battery is more valuable than static electricity.

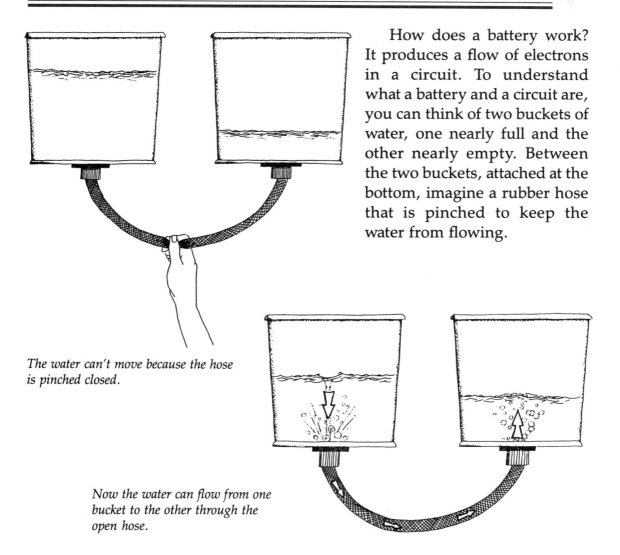

How does a battery work? It produces a flow of electrons in a circuit. To understand what a battery and a circuit are, you can think of two buckets of water, one nearly full and the other nearly empty. Between the two buckets, attached at the bottom, imagine a rubber hose that is pinched to keep the water from flowing.

The water can't move because the hose is pinched closed.

Now the water can flow from one bucket to the other through the open hose.

When you unpinch the hose, what happens? The water flows from the nearly full bucket to the other one. It will keep flowing until the water is at the same height in each bucket. The two buckets are like two parts of a battery, and the rubber hose is like an electric circuit, a path that lets electrons flow from one part of the battery to another. (This comparison will give you an idea of how a battery works, but remember that electrons in a wire don't act exactly the way water in a hose does. For one thing, the water will keep flowing until it is the same height in both buckets. But in a battery the electrons will flow until there is a balance of charges on both poles of the battery.)

A Simple Circuit

Let's look at a simple electric circuit consisting of the following four parts: (1) a battery, (2) a wire, (3) a light bulb, (4) a switch.

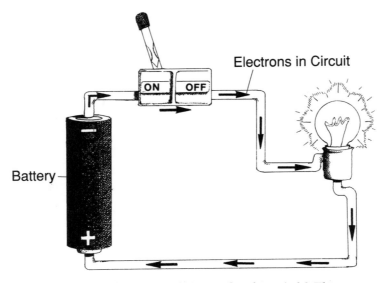

This electric circuit is on. See the switch? The arrows indicate the flow of electrons—electricity— through the wire.

The battery pushes electrons from the negative terminal, where there are many electrons, through the switch, the light bulb, and the wire into the positive terminal where there are not many electrons. The wire is an electron pipe through which the electrons flow. The wire is like a hose that takes the electrons to the light bulb, and then back to the positive terminal of the battery. The light bulb is, of course, the reason for building our circuit. Inside the bulb is a special kind of wire called a filament. As electrons pass through the filament, the bulb lights. When a light bulb burns out with a pop and a flash, the filament has broken, interrupting the flow of electrons.

Now suppose we want to cut the light off. If we wait for the battery to get so old that it stops pumping electrons, the light will go out. But if we want the light off right now, we must interrupt the circuit. By opening the switch, we make a gap in the circuit, and the electrons no longer have a closed path to

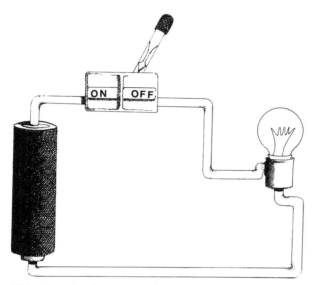

This electric circuit is off. There are no electrons flowing through the wire. What has happened to the light?

travel through the filament. The light goes out. If we close the switch, we complete the circuit, and once again the light comes on.

The wire used in electric circuits is usually made of copper metal. Most metals are good conductors of electricity, which means that electrons flow through them very easily. Silver metal is a slightly better conductor than copper, but it is much too expensive to be used in most circuits.

Other materials, such as plastic, rubber, and glass, are good insulators. This means that they permit almost no electrons to flow through them. Good insulators are poor conductors of electricity, and are used to cover the wires in electric circuits.

While batteries provide the energy for small items such as flashlights and transistor radios, the electric current that flows through refrigerators and stereos is produced in a different way, usually at an electric power plant miles away. But no matter where the electricity comes from, the energy used to freeze ice cubes and play music and light lamps is all produced in the same way—by electrons flowing through a circuit.

This is New York City at night. Think about how much electricity it uses and how many power plants it must have!

More Chemistry

Chemistry is the study of matter and energy. Chemists try to answer questions like, "How much vitamin C do people need to stay healthy?" and, "What gases make up the atmosphere of Jupiter?" All scientists learn about things by doing experiments and making measurements. As we learn more about matter and energy, we will come back to some of these ideas.

Remember, everything you can see or touch, smell or taste, is made up of matter. Mass is the amount of matter in an object, and is often measured in grams. You can usually think of the mass of a thing as its weight. The more mass it has, the more it will weigh.

Volume is the amount of space that a thing fills. Volume may be measured in gallons, liters, or milliliters, just to name a few. An elephant has greater mass than a mouse because it contains more matter. Because it takes up more room than the mouse, it also has a greater volume.

A place that contains no matter at all is empty space, and is called a vacuum.

You may remember that we can

Which animal has more volume? Which has more mass?

The balance shows you which object has more mass.

use a ruler to measure the length of an object. A balance is an instrument used to measure the mass of an object. How do we measure the volume of something? You already know one way to measure volume if you remember the story of Archimedes and King Hiero. The King wanted to know if his new crown was pure gold, and asked his friend Archimedes to find the answer. Archimedes knew that the crown was truly made of gold only if it had the same volume as an equal mass of pure gold. He used a balance to find a mass of gold equal to the mass of the crown.

Do you remember how he found the volume of the crown? He placed it in a bucket of water filled to the very top, and then measured the amount of water that spilled over the sides. The volume of spilled water was equal to the volume of the crown. He then refilled the bucket and measured the volume of the equal mass of gold in the very same way—by measuring the water that spilled over the sides. The crown and the gold had the same mass—that is, the same amount of matter—but different volumes. In other words, the crown and the gold weighed the same but took up different amounts of space. Archimedes concluded that the crown was not pure gold.

The density of an object is a measure of how much matter is packed into the space that the object fills. Some things don't contain much matter at all considering the amount of space they fill. Think about the air in a balloon. It has a greater volume (takes up more room) than a brick, but is much lighter than the brick. The brick is heavier than the air in the balloon, yet it is smaller. And so the brick has a greater density than the air in the balloon.

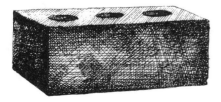

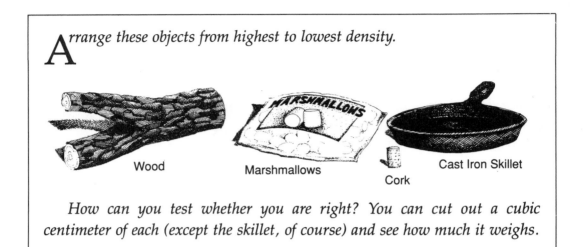

*A*rrange these objects from highest to lowest density.

Wood

Marshmallows

Cork

Cast Iron Skillet

How can you test whether you are right? You can cut out a cubic centimeter of each (except the skillet, of course) and see how much it weighs.

Kinds of Matter: Metals and Nonmetals

A shovel, a dollar bill, and a waterfall are very different things, yet all are made of matter. How many basic kinds of matter are there? Scientists have discovered about a hundred basic kinds, which they call elements.

Some elements you have probably heard of, such as carbon, oxygen, and iron. But some other elements are not so familiar. You probably haven't heard of molybdenum or curium! Most of the one hundred different elements can be put in just two categories: metals and nonmetals.

What Are Metals Like?

Most of the elements found on earth are metals. Some important metals are aluminum, iron, gold, and silver.

Metals are usually shiny and bright. Think of a new aluminum frying pan.

Metals are also usually ductile. This means that at certain temperatures they can be stretched or pulled through a small hole to make a wire. At the factory, the metal in your frying plan could have been made into aluminum wire.

Metals are often malleable. This means that they can be pressed or pounded into thin sheets. At the factory, the metal in your aluminum frying

pan could have been pressed into many thin sheets
of aluminum foil that could be used
in a kitchen to wrap food.

Metals are good conductors of
electricity. That is why electric wires
are made of metal. And metals are
good conductors of heat. Have you ever put your hand on the hood of a car
sitting in the bright sun?

You've just read that typical metals can be shiny, ductile, and malleable,
that they can conduct electricity and heat. Which of these characteristics, or
properties, make metals good materials for frying pans and cooking pots?

Atomic Vocabulary

Matter—*Everything around you that takes up space is matter: a chair, a
piece of chalk, the water in a fish tank, the air inside an "empty" can.
There are three kinds of matter: solid, liquid, and gas. But to talk in any detail
about matter, we need to describe the small parts that make up matter.*

Atom—*Matter is made of units called atoms, which are so small you
can't see them. And atoms are made up of even smaller particles called
electrons, protons, and neutrons. Electrons and protons have electric charges,
but neutrons do not.*

Element—*Scientists have discovered that there are about a hundred basic
kinds of matter. Each of these is called an element. There are many kinds of
atoms, which combine together to make different things, but an element is
made of only one kind of atom. Some things that you're familiar with are
elements—like gold, or carbon—but most things are made up of combinations
of different elements. Water, for instance, is made up of the elements hydrogen
and oxygen. But how are elements combined to make the things around us?*

Molecule—*Atoms combine to form larger units called molecules. Molecules can be made up of just one element or they can be combinations of two or
more elements. A water molecule is always made of two hydrogen atoms
linked to one oxygen molecule.*

A Very Important Metal: Iron

Iron is a very important metal. It is the main ingredient in steel, and steel is the most important material in modern civilization. Without iron there would be no steel to make such things as bridges, automobiles, or skyscrapers.

But iron is not usually found in its pure form. Like many other metals, it is found in the earth mixed with other metals and nonmetals in a mixture called ore. How do we get iron from ore? Usually we have to heat the ore so hot that the iron melts and runs out of it.

Not all mines are underground. This is a picture of a surface or open-pit mine for iron ore.

This picture was taken inside a steel mill. What do you think it is like inside this big room?

Other Metals

Two of the most highly prized metals are gold and silver. Both have been used for thousands of years to make coins and jewelry. In recent years, both gold and silver have become important in the electronics industry because they conduct electricity so well.

Mercury is a metal that is a liquid at room temperature. You probably remember that mercury is the shiny liquid used in some thermometers. In fact, mercury is the *only* metal that is not a solid at normal temperatures.

Do you see where the mercury has stopped in this thermometer? Can you read the temperature in degrees Centigrade? In degrees Fahrenheit?

Alloys

When two or more metals are mixed together, we call the mixture an alloy. We mix the metals together to make a material that is more useful than either metal by itself.

Take aluminum, for instance. It is light in weight, so it should be useful for making airplanes. But pure aluminum breaks too easily to make a safe airplane. So airplane designers mix aluminum with other metals to make an alloy that is stronger than aluminum by itself.

Pure gold is far too soft to be used in making rings and necklaces and bracelets. But gold and copper can be mixed to produce an alloy hard enough to make jewelry.

Bronze is a reddish-brown alloy of the metals tin and copper. Yet it is harder and tougher than either metal alone, so it was used to make tools and weapons thousands of years ago.

French horns like this one are made of brass.

Brass is a shiny yellow alloy of copper and zinc. It is used to make wind instruments like the trumpet and the French horn. That's why we call these wind instruments "brasses."

If you are interested in metals, how they are separated from their ores, and how they are changed into useful forms, then you should read a book on the science of metals—metallurgy. It is one of the oldest of all the sciences.

Nonmetals in the Air

The air that we breathe is made of gases that are nonmetals. The main gases that make up air are nitrogen and oxygen.

You probably know that our bodies need oxygen every minute of every day. But did you know that oxygen is also used in making steel? Oxygen is being used whenever there's a fire, like a candle flame or a bonfire.

The other main gas in the air, nitrogen, is a key ingredient in the cells of plants and animals. This important gas is used to make things as various as fertilizers, explosives, and rocket fuels.

A Remarkable Nonmetal: Carbon

Carbon is another nonmetal found in every living thing. One fact about carbon is so amazing that it is hard to believe. Did you know that the charcoal in a grill, the "lead" in pencil, and the diamond in a ring are all made of carbon? It's true! How can something as crumbly and black as charcoal and something as

hard and bright as a diamond both be made of carbon? It all has to do with the way the carbon atoms are linked together. You see, groups of atoms join to make larger particles called molecules. Molecules can take different shapes, depending on the way the atoms are linked. In graphite and diamond, the carbon atoms join together in different ways. The atoms in pencil "lead," or carbon graphite, link together in a chain-like structure, while the atoms in a diamond link in a diamond-shaped structure.

Chlorine

Chlorine is a nonmetal used in making laundry bleach, purifying drinking water, and disinfecting swimming pools. Fluorine, its chemical cousin, can be combined with carbon to make Teflon, the coating on nonstick frying pans.

What Element Is the Most Plentiful?

If you look at a list of metals and nonmetals, you will discover that there are more metals than nonmetals. You can say that metals are more *numerous* than nonmetals. But two particular nonmetals are very *plentiful*. In fact, hydrogen is by far the most abundant element in the universe. There is much more hydrogen than anything else. (Can you understand the difference we mean here between numerous and plentiful?)

The next most plentiful element in the universe is helium. In the sun and other stars, hydrogen atoms join together to form helium. This process produces enormous amounts of heat and light necessary for life.

A *chart called the periodic table lists all the elements. Some dictionaries contain periodic charts, too. You can also find a periodic table in the library if you ask your teacher or a librarian for help. Then you can see the names of the elements and their abbreviations. For example, the abbreviation for iron is Fe, Carbon is C, Hydrogen is H and Oxygen is O. The periodic table also divides the elements into metals and nonmetals.*

Other Things in the World

Now what about things like water, and glass, and wood? Are these metallic or nonmetallic elements? The answer is, they are not elements at all, but rather *combinations* of elements. Remember that elements are matter that is composed of only one type of atom. But things like water or wood contain atoms of several different elements.

Many things you see every day, like water, glass, and wood, are combinations of elements.

Water, for example, is a combination of two nonmetal elements, the gases hydrogen and oxygen. It's amazing that two gases can come together to produce a liquid that we drink or a solid that we can use to make a drink cold. A molecule of water is made of one oxygen atom and two hydrogen atoms. Abbreviating the elements, you can picture a water molecule like this:

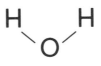

This diagram shows you the structure of a water molecule.

Since this is the structure of a molecule of water, you will sometimes see water written H_2O.

The atoms of all the different elements combine in thousands of ways to produce all the things in the world.

Suppose you place a stainless-steel spoon and a pencil in a cup of very hot water, so that one end of each is sticking out. After five minutes, which would be hotter, the pencil top or the spoon handle? (Hint: Wood is made of nonmetallic elements. Steel is made mostly of iron.) Try it!

Gravity

You know that you slide down the playground slide, not up it. No matter how high you throw a ball, it always comes back to the ground. It seems as if the earth pulls things toward its surface, and, in fact, it does. If it were not for this pull, called gravity, nothing could stay on our planet. Everything would float into the sky.

In our world, people use lots of energy to fight against gravity. If you have ever flown in an airplane, you remember the whine of the engine and the whirl of the propellers just before takeoff. Or perhaps you have watched fire shoot out the tail of a rocket when it is launched. The red-hot flames and the engine's roar mean that energy is being used to lift the rocket and plane off the ground. Every time we lift our feet to step, we use energy too.

Discovery lift-off, October 6, 1990.

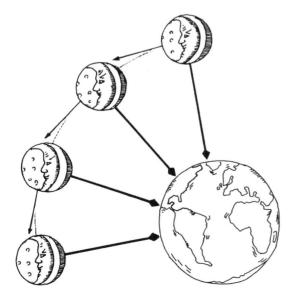

The black arrows show the pull of the earth's gravity on the moon. The purple arrows show the momentum or force of the moon's movement. The dotted line shows the path the moon takes as a result of the effect of these two forces.

The earth is not the only place where gravity is found. The sun, moon, and stars also have gravity. In fact, all things containing matter tend to attract one another. All matter attracts all other matter. The attraction between the earth and the moon holds the moon in its path around our planet. Can you guess what makes the earth stay in its orbit around the sun? It's gravity again—the attraction between earth and the sun. That's the pull that keeps the earth from flying out into space.

How powerful is the pull of gravity between objects? It depends on two things—how far apart they are and how much matter they contain. Objects close together and with lots of matter attract each other strongly. Things far apart and with small masses have very little attraction for one another.

Perhaps you have seen films of the astronauts walking on the moon. If so, you probably noticed that they could leap great distances into the air, much higher than we can jump here on earth. Why do you suppose this is so? Think about the size of the moon. It is smaller than the earth. The moon contains much, much less matter than the earth. Indeed, the moon's mass is so much smaller than the earth's that there is little attraction between the moon and a visitor. An explorer there can jump very high and walk very far without getting tired.

This astronaut, tied by two lines to the Gemini 4 *spacecraft, doesn't feel the effects of gravity at all. He is floating in space.*

Most astronomers believe there are places in the universe where gravity is so strong that it captures everything that comes near. These places are called black holes. They are supposed to be very, very, very dense. Astronomers think that the density of a black hole is so great and its gravity so powerful that not even light can escape from it!

S*ir Isaac Newton discovered gravity. You can read about him in Book Two of this series.*

The Solar System

The word "solar" refers to the sun; the solar system is that part of the universe that includes the sun and all the heavenly bodies that go around it. The most important of these revolving objects are the nine planets and their moons, but comets, asteroids, and meteoroids are part of the system as well. Let's take a mental trip through the solar system, starting with the sun itself.

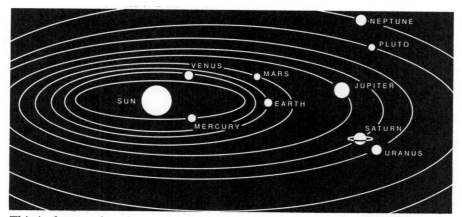

This is the way the solar system will look for most of the 1990's. Neptune's orbit is outside Pluto's until later in this decade.

The Sun

The sun is a star, like those we see sprinkled across the night sky. The sun looks much bigger than those stars only because it is the one closest to us. Though it is huge compared with the Earth, the sun is really rather small, as stars go. The sun is made of two gases called hydrogen and helium. You read about these elements earlier, remember? A process called thermonuclear fusion changes the hydrogen into helium, producing the energy that provides heat and light to the solar system. (Can you take the word thermonuclear apart to figure out what it means? Where have you seen "thermo" before, or "nuclear"?) The sun is *hot*—its temperature can reach 27 million degrees Fahrenheit. It was born about 4.5 billion years ago, and will live about 5 billion more.

The Terrestrial Planets—Mercury, Venus, Earth, and Mars

The word "planet" has its roots in an old Greek word meaning "wanderer," but the planets do not really ramble aimlessly here and there about the solar system. They travel in fixed paths about the sun. Of the nine planets in the solar system, the four closest to the sun are sometimes called the terrestrial planets. The word "terrestrial" comes from the Latin word *terra*, which means "earth." (You may know some other words—like "territory" and "terrace"—that come from the same Latin root.) Although Mercury, Venus, and Mars lack the trees, grass, and flowers that decorate the surface of our planet, they are Earth-like in the sense that they have a solid, earthy surface.

Do you remember reading about mosaics in the Fine Arts section? This picture of Mercury is a "photo mosaic": it is made of many smaller photographs of the planet put together.

The planet closest to the sun is tiny Mercury. In 1974 and 1975 the United States space probe *Mariner 10* photographed this planet and sent pictures back to earth that show a surface marked with craters and wrinkles. Mercury has neither air nor water. Its days are much hotter and its nights much colder than any place on Earth. If Mercury is the sun's nearest neighbor, why are its nights so cold? Here's the reason. On Earth, a blanket of gases—called the atmosphere—traps heat from the sun during the daytime. As the Earth rotates, its "daytime" side becomes its "nighttime" side. Although this side of the Earth is now pointed away from the light and warmth of the sun, it is warmed by the heat trapped in the atmosphere. Unlike the Earth, Mercury has no blanket of gases above its surface.

Venus is the planet between Mercury and Earth. Like the other planets, it reflects the sun's light but has none of its own. Except for the moon, it is the brightest body in the night sky. Though Venus appears beautiful to viewers on Earth, its environment is hostile to life. It is the hottest planet, and pools of liquid metal may dot its surface. Clouds on Venus are made of acid, not water, and are heavy enough to crush a person. Lightning storms are common on Venus, and it may have erupting volcanoes. In ages past, Venus probably had oceans.

Light Show

Have you ever seen a star fall through the night sky? Shooting stars, as they're often called, are not really stars at all. They are meteors, or meteoroids, particles of matter from space that enter our atmosphere at such high speeds that they burn as they fall. Some meteors you can't see. Others burn so brightly they're called "fireballs."

Scientists estimate that several hundred million meteors enter our atmosphere every day! So why don't you have to run for cover? Because on their way down, most meteors burn up and never reach the earth. And if you watch for them, you will only see an average of five to ten an hour.

A meteor that reaches the earth's atmosphere is called a meteorite. Meteorites, which come in all shapes and sizes, are most commonly made of iron or stone. By the time they hit the earth, meteorites are usually not moving very fast, but sometimes a big meteorite is hard enough to dig a crater. Whenever possible, scientists collect and analyze meteorites. Why do you think these space rocks are so interesting to them?

Third from the sun is our home, the planet Earth. Counting out from the sun, it is the first planet with a moon, and the only planet—so far as we know—that supports life.

No planet has inspired more wonder and curiosity than Mars, planet number four. Nicknamed "the Red Planet," Mars can be seen at night from Earth without a telescope. Not so long ago, some people guessed that the streaks and traces seen on its surface were irrigation ditches, and that Mars was home to living creatures. But two *Viking* space probes, launched by the United States, were parachuted to the Martian surface and found no life there. It is almost certain, however, that Mars once had rivers. It is likely that a manned mission to Mars will occur in the early part of the next century. The explorers will search for fossils and other evidence of past Martian life. Mars has two moons—Deimos and Phobos—which may once have been asteroids. What are asteroids? Read on!

The Asteroids

Asteroids are thousands of chunks of rock and metal that orbit the sun, mostly between Mars and Jupiter. They are smaller than any of the planets—some are as small as a basketball. Maybe, one day, space miners will remove minerals from the asteroids for use on Earth or for building space colonies. Where did the asteroids come from? Astronomers disagree, but some think they may be the remains of a planet that was smashed to bits in a space collision.

The Gas Giants—Jupiter, Saturn, Uranus, and Neptune

Traveling away from Mars, and toward the outer boundaries of the solar system, we enter the territory of the gas giants. We call them gas giants because they are made of little or no solid material. The first gas giant, and the largest planet of the nine, is Jupiter (planet number five). You can see Jupiter without a telescope; from Earth it looks like a star. Jupiter is so big that, if it were hollow, 1,300 Earths could fit inside. It is made mostly of hydrogen gas on its surface, and liquid hydrogen inside. There is a violent storm of swirling gases in Jupiter's atmosphere called the Great Red Spot. Jupiter is blessed

Earth

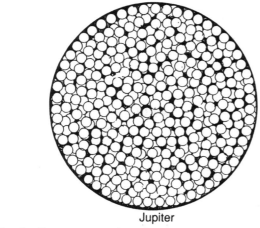

Jupiter

This sketch allows you to relate the sizes of Earth and Jupiter. The artist who drew it filled Jupiter with 1,300 tiny Earth-sized spheres.

with moons—at least sixteen of them. In 1979, the *Voyager 1* spacecraft spotted erupting volcanoes on the surface of one of Jupiter's moons, Io. On Earth, volcanoes spit molten metal and rock called lava, but a type of sulfur snow comes out of the volcanoes on Io!

The "ringed planet," spectacular Saturn, is sixth from the sun. Its rings are made of ice and ice-covered dust and rocks, but astronomers aren't sure where they came from. They may be fragments of an ancient moon

Saturn, the "ringed planet."

that shattered. Saturn has even more moons than Jupiter, twenty-three by the latest count. The atmosphere of one of these moons, Titan, was examined by *Voyager 2*. Though no life was discovered on Titan, the chemical makings of life were detected there. A space mission is being planned to study Titan.

In 1986, *Voyager 2* flew by Uranus, the third gas giant and seventh planet from the sun. Uranus is an unusual planet, because it is tilted on its side, one pole pointed toward the sun and the other aimed toward the rest of the universe. For this reason, the rings of Uranus look almost vertical when viewed from the earth. A day on Uranus—that is, one spin or one rotation of the planet—lasts about 13½ hours. Uranus appears to have a faint green color when sighted through a telescope. On a dark night, it can sometimes be spotted without a telescope.

Neptune, the last of the gas giants, is usually the eighth planet from the sun. Right now, however, and until the year 1999, Neptune is the most distant planet in the solar system; it is further away than the ninth planet, Pluto. Neptune was not discovered by accident. Astronomers had noticed that Uranus wobbled sometimes in its trip round the sun, as if something were pulling it toward the outer edge of the solar system. They speculated the existence of an eighth planet, searched, and found Neptune in 1846. *Voyager 2* photographed Neptune in 1989, sending back pictures of its rings and moons and

---

Revolve and Rotate

All of the planets revolve around, or orbit, the sun. This means that the sun is a central point around which the planets swing in a generally circular or elliptical pattern. Think of a tetherball swinging very slowly around its pole. The planets also rotate, or spin, as they revolve. This means that they turn around a line, or axis, that runs through the center of the planet. Think of how a basketball player twirls the ball on the tip of his finger, or how a top spins on the floor. Our Earth rotates once every 24 hours and it takes 365¼ days to orbit the sun. But all the planets move at different speeds. For example, Jupiter rotates thirty times faster than the Earth. And it takes Uranus eighty-four earth years and Pluto two hundred forty-eight earth years to orbit the sun.

analyzing its atmosphere. *Voyager* revealed Neptune to be a frozen and stormy world, bluish in color. Viewed from Earth, Neptune appears greenish, and can be seen only with a telescope.

The ninth planet, Pluto, is the tiniest of them all. Because it is so distant from the sun, Pluto takes 248 Earth-years to make one complete orbit. Since 1983, Pluto has been traveling inside the orbit of Neptune, but before the year 2000 it will once again take its lonely place as the outermost planet. Some say that Pluto was once a moon of Neptune, but no one really knows for sure.

Out Beyond Pluto

Although some astronomers suspect there may be a tenth planet in our solar system, Pluto is the last planet we know of. But it is not the outermost object in our solar system. Millions of comets also orbit the sun. Comets are sometimes called "dirty snowballs" because they are made of dust, rock, and ice. When a comet passes near the sun, the ice melts and evaporates. Then a huge glowing head of gas appears to viewers on Earth. Trailing the head for millions of miles is a tail made of gas or dust. Halley's Comet passed by Earth in 1986, but, since it reappears every seventy-six years, you can look forward to watching it again some day.

This picture of Halley's Comet was taken in 1986.

Beyond Our Solar System

From end to end, our solar system measures trillions of miles. How far is a trillion miles? Well, it's a distance so enormous that there's hardly any way to describe it. Yet, vast as it is, our solar system occupies only the tiniest fraction of the universe. What wondrous things fill the universe beyond our own little corner?

You may have looked into the sky at night and tried to count the stars. How many did you see? Fifty? One thousand? On a clear, black night, if you didn't lose track, you might count several thousand. None of these stars belongs to our solar system. Now, how about the stars that we can't see? There are so many that you couldn't possibly guess the number.

The universe seems to be organized into galaxies, which are collections of stars, planets, and space dust. Our galaxy is named the Milky Way, because, when viewed from Earth, its billions of stars look like a fuzzy white band smeared across the sky. A close neighbor of the Milky Way is the galaxy Andromeda. But there are billions of others.

The galaxy Andromeda.

One of the most amazing discoveries about the universe is that all of its galaxies seem to be hurtling outward and away from one another. This observation is an important piece of evidence for a theory of how the universe began, called the Big Bang.

Many astronomers believe that about fifteen billion years ago all the matter in the universe was packed into one super-dense sphere. No one knows for sure the size of the sphere, but some say it was no bigger than a bowling ball. Something caused the ball to explode in a big bang, and bits of matter flew apart, eventually becoming galaxies of stars, and dust, and planets. As the galaxies continue to separate today, the universe grows bigger.

How big is the universe right now? Will it keep expanding forever? Or will it collapse back onto itself? Astronomers love to argue about and discuss these kinds of questions, questions so big and exciting that once you start thinking about them you can hardly stop. Now here's something else to ponder. If the Big Bang theory is correct, it means that every bit of matter inside your body came from that super-dense sphere. We are made of the stuff of the stars!

Constellations

Long ago, ancient peoples looked into the night sky and saw shapes in the stars. In various groups of stars they saw maidens, beasts, and mighty hunters. They gave imaginative names to these star groups or constellations. Most of the names now used for constellations came from long ago, names like Draco (the Dragon), Leo (the Lion), Taurus (the Bull), and Orion (a mighty archer).

There are eighty-eight constellations. Most of them are shown on a star chart, which is like a road map of the heavens. Find a star chart and a willing friend, and, on some cloudless night, try to identify a few of the constellations. But don't get discouraged! It takes a lot of imagination to see what people saw long ago. One of the easiest star patterns to make out is the Big Dipper. The Big Dipper isn't itself a constellation, only part of one. It forms the back and tail of the constellation called Ursa Major, the Great Bear.

Once you've found the Big Dipper, you can find the North Star, also called Polaris, and the set of stars called the Little Dipper. Here's how. Find the two stars that form the front of the Big Dipper's cup. Let your eyes follow an

Can you find the Big Dipper in the constellation Ursa Major?

imaginary line starting at the bottom star, going through the top one, and moving off into space. The first bright star you see then will be the North Star, which is also the first star in the handle of the Little Dipper. The North Star is so close to true north that people have used it at night to guide their way for hundreds of years. Once you know how to find it, you can find north, and from north, south, east, and west.

Constellations don't really tell us anything about the history of the universe. Unlike the galaxies, which are natural collections of stars, the constellations are fanciful products of people's imaginations. When you spy Orion the Mighty Hunter or Leo the Lion, you share an experience with shepherdesses and sailors who gazed into the heavens on nights thousands of years ago.

Stories of Scientists

Charles Babbage and Ada Lovelace

People have probably been using numbers since before history began, ever since they started to count on their fingers. Our hands were the first counting machines. We still use the ten-digit system of numbers, because that's how many fingers we have.

Later on, humans invented mechanical counting machines. For instance, centuries ago, the Chinese invented a counting device called the abacus, which keeps track of numbers with colored beads. With it, the Chinese were able to add, subtract, multiply, and divide very fast. In the 1600's, Europeans also invented a machine that could add, subtract, multiply, and divide. But all of these early inventions had one limitation: they were mainly devices for counting, not for computing.

This Chinese merchant uses an abacus to check his calculations of sales.

A true computer is a device that can store, retrieve, and handle numbers according to instructions from a program. The first person to invent a true computer was Charles Babbage, an English mathematician. He lived in the 1800's.

Educated at Cambridge University (where he found he knew more about mathematics than his professors), Babbage went on to study mathematics on his own. He was fascinated by lighthouses, stage lighting, optical instruments, and the history of climate as recorded in tree rings. He also invented the speedometer. He was a man who was always thinking.

Charles Babbage.

One problem bothered him more than any other. He was concerned about the human errors that he found in the mathematical tables that people used for navigation, insurance, and surveying. It worried and annoyed him every time he found an error in one of these tables. These mistakes could cost people money or their very lives.

He dreamed of making a machine that could make long calculations time after time without making any errors. So he developed the "difference engine." It was a complicated arrangement of gears and wheels that could make lengthy calculations without error and print them out.

That first machine wasn't bold enough for Babbage. He next designed a machine that contained all of the essentials of a modern computer:

1. a logic center for manipulating numbers

2. a memory center for storing numbers

3. a control center to tell the logic center what to do with the numbers

4. a way to send different instruction programs to the control center

5. a way to get numbers in and out of the machine

This is part of Babbage's "difference engine." You can tell how big it is by comparing it with the white twelve-inch ruler attached to the table below it.

He called it the Analytical Engine. Because this Analytical Engine could be programmed, a user could send different instructions to the control center to guide the machine's work. In that way, the machine could solve any kind of mathematical problem in any field. It would even be able to play chess, as modern computers do.

Babbage's plan called for a machine that could deal with numbers that were fifty digits long! His design required thousands of wheels, levers, and belts, all working together. The huge machine was to be run with steam. If it had been built, the machine would have taken up an area the size of a football field.

The theory of the machine was so much ahead of its time that most people paid no attention to it. But Ada Lovelace did. When she met Babbage in 1833, it was the start of a lifelong friendship and partnership. Her father was the poet Byron, and her mother was interested in mathematics. From her mother she gained a fine appreciation of mathematics, from her father a fine imagination.

In those days, the study of mathematics was not supposed to be healthy for women. Women were thought to be less intelligent in that subject than men. But Ada Lovelace ignored those ideas. She followed her own interests and tal-

Ada Lovelace.

ents. She found an Italian article on Babbage's Analytical Engine and translated it into English. Her explanations of the machine were even longer than the Italian article itself, and her comments helped people begin to see how exciting the possibilities of the machine really were.

Lack of funds prevented Charles Babbage from ever constructing his machine. If he had, his invention would have been very similar to the first computers that were built a century later. It was Ada Lovelace who explained Babbage's wonderful ideas. She helped people begin to realize the possibilities of the computer.

John Muir

John Muir loved wild places. He devoted years of his life to wandering around the untamed American wilderness and documenting its splendor in his writings. He is remembered as one of the foremost defenders of our natural heritage.

With his family, Muir immigrated to the United States from Scotland in 1849, settling on a Wisconsin homestead farm. Muir had always loved to tinker with tools and inventions, so he enrolled in the state university to pursue mechanical engineering. He soon felt called to "study the inventions of God"; after four years he left college without a degree to devote himself to the appreciation of nature. He set out on foot with only a compass, a small bag of clothes, and a wood press for collecting flower specimens. For his first adventure, he walked from the Midwest to the Gulf of Mexico.

"I drifted about from rock to rock, from stream to stream, from grove to grove. Where night found me, there I camped. When I discovered a new plant, I sat down beside it for a minute or a day, to make its acquaintance and hear what it had to tell." Muir arrived in California's Yosemite Valley in 1868. He spent six years there studying, writing, making sketches, and absorbing the valley's grandeur. Legend has it that he once climbed a hundred-foot pine tree in a windstorm and clung there, swaying in the gale and listening to the whispering needles.

John Muir was an observer of details. He measured California's giant sequoia trees, one of which he estimated was four thousand years old. Noticing deep scratches on sheer rock walls, he formed a hypothesis that the Sierra Mountains and valleys had been formed by the grinding advance of glaciers— slow-moving rivers of ice. His subsequent discovery of sixty-five icefields in the Sierra region supported this theory. When he finally left the Yosemite Valley, Muir went on to explore Nevada, Utah, the Northwest, and Alaska. Throughout his travels, he recorded scientific and personal observations in journals that formed the foundation for numerous articles and books.

While on his wanderings, John Muir began to ask himself, "Why couldn't we set aside large, beautiful natural areas for all Americans to enjoy?" He firmly believed that in years to come, people would need the solitude and spiritual refreshment provided by large, natural areas. This conviction was very radical at the time; most of Muir's contemporaries viewed nature as a wild thing that needed to be subdued.

When he was forty-two, Muir became a successful fruit farmer, but he reserved four months out of each year to retreat into the wilderness. He became alarmed at the degradation of woodlands and valleys by logging, farming, and other economic activities. He wrote and lectured about what he saw and began to urge the federal government to set aside our finest forests and scenic places, and shelter them from harmful human activity. He became a powerful advocate for the preservation of wilderness. (An advocate is someone who supports or defends a cause.) Because of his eloquence and tireless work, Yellowstone, Yosemite, and Sequoia National Parks are some of the areas now protected for all to appreciate. If you ever go to one of these places, you can be grateful to John Muir.

A tireless defender of nature and natural resources and the father of our national park system, Muir was also the founder of an important conservation group, the Sierra Club. He considered the outdoors his classroom. He never forgot the lessons of awe and inspiration that he learned from high mountain meadows, glittering icefields, and cool, dark forests.

John Muir (on the right) is pictured with President "Teddy" Roosevelt in Yosemite Park. Muir's ideas about preserving our forests impressed President Roosevelt very much, and the President became a powerful advocate for preserving our forests.

Jane Goodall

Are human beings the only creatures in the world that feel emotions like anger and love? Are they the only beings that use tools, the only ones that fight wars against each other? Until recently, many people thought humans were the only creatures who did and felt these things.

Jane Goodall decided to find out. Ever since she was a girl, she had been fascinated by "Dr. Doolittle," a man in a storybook who could talk with animals. She decided to go to Africa to study the creature whose body chemistry is nearest to our own—a type of monkey called the chimpanzee. For forty years, she did research on chimpanzees at a game reserve in Tanzania, Africa. What she found out changed our ideas.

Jane Goodall was determined to be accepted by the chimpanzees in their own environment. She found a hill where she could sit and watch the monkeys. Each day, she would move just a little bit closer to them. It took a long time for the chimpanzees to get used to the "peculiar, white-skinned ape" that had come among them. But Jane Goodall was patient. Over time, Goodall came to know the personality of each chimpanzee. Gradually she found out that chimpanzees were more like human beings than people had thought.

She found that, like humans, they feel emotions. "They show emotions similar to our own—pleasure, sadness, curiosity, alarm, and rage," she wrote. She witnessed scenes of great tenderness and love among the chimpanzees, and described their strong family ties between grandparents, parents, children, brothers, and sisters. She watched chimps kiss, hold

Jane Goodall and friend.

hands, hug, and pat each other gently. She watched the mothers carry and hold their babies constantly, and even tickle them!

She also found that chimpanzees go to war. In 1960 she saw a gang of chimps team up to hunt and kill a young baboon. Over a period of several years, she watched several males kill all of the members of a neighboring chimpanzee group.

She found that they, like humans, use handmade tools. The chimpanzees would take long pieces of grass and dip them into the holes of termite houses. Then the chimps would fish them out and nibble the delicious bugs that clung to the grass.

When Jane Goodall went to Africa she was scared. Wouldn't you be afraid to go off into the jungle all by yourself? But she knew that a close study of chimpanzees in the wild would be the only way to find out the truth about these creatures. Her work has made people change their ideas about the class of animals we call primates, which include monkeys like the chimpanzees.

Edward Jenner

In the late eighteenth century, epidemics of a disease called smallpox killed two hundred thousand people in Europe every year. An epidemic is an outbreak of disease that is caught by a large part of the population. Those victims of smallpox who didn't die were often left blind or sickly, with ugly scars on their skin.

But if they survived, they never caught the disease again. This gave doctors an idea. Some doctors attempted to prevent future epidemics by injecting live smallpox into people who were not sick. The injection might make people very, very sick, and sometimes might kill them, but if they survived it, they would be protected from an epidemic. The idea was that you were better off getting the disease on purpose, when you were strong and doctors could take care of you. During an epidemic, doctors were too busy to take care of everyone, so the chance was greater that you would die. One problem with this idea was that patients who received an injection of smallpox often spread the disease to those around them by accident. This way of preventing epidemics was risky and not very effective.

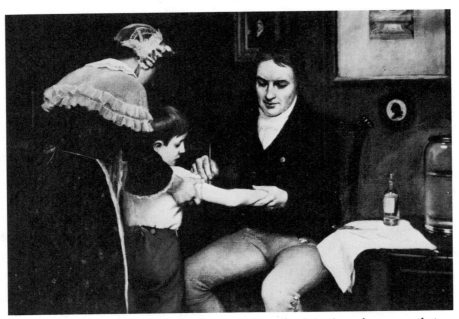

Edward Jenner is depicted giving James Phipps the injection of cowpox that proved to be so effective against smallpox.

This was the state of affairs when Edward Jenner became a doctor. Orphaned at an early age, he was raised by his eldest brother. He served as a doctor's apprentice for nine years, then went to London to study medicine. When he began to practice medicine in Berkeley, England, in the 1780's, he was often asked to perform smallpox inoculations (injections).

Like many great scientists, he noticed something that other scientists had seen but had not been curious about. Jenner became curious when he noticed that some of the people he injected with smallpox did not come down with the disease. When he looked into their histories, he noticed that many of them were dairymaids who milked cows and had gotten sick from doing so. People who milked cows often got a disease called cowpox. It was similar to smallpox, but much milder, and it never killed or seriously injured people.

On May 14, 1796, Edward Jenner tried a daring experiment. He scraped the cowpox blister of a milkmaid and inserted the infected matter into the arm of eight-year-old James Phipps. As expected, Phipps came down with cowpox fever, headache, and pustules, but he was soon well again. Then, on July 1, Jenner infected Phipps with fluid he had taken from a deadly smallpox sore. But the boy remained perfectly healthy!

Jenner published a seventy-five-page book that contained stories of cow-pox victims who had become immune to smallpox. He introduced the idea of vaccination with a mild substance to protect against a serious disease. Edward Jenner soon discovered that cowpox fluid could be dried and kept for as long as three months, enabling it to be shipped to distant places.

Vaccines spread quickly to British colonies such as India. In America, Thomas Jefferson supported vaccination, as did chiefs of several American Indian tribes. And although France and England were at war, Napoleon Bonaparte made all French soldiers get vaccinated against smallpox and gave Edward Jenner a special medal. Despite his success, Jenner was forced to spend the rest of his life defending his discovery against superstition and ignorance. Some people spread rumors that cowpox injections caused people to sprout cow-like growths.

Have you been vaccinated against polio, diphtheria, tetanus, measles, or mumps? You are lucky to be protected from those diseases by the method that Jenner started. In fact, the word vaccination is taken from the Latin word *vacca*, which means cow. So, when you were vaccinated, you were "cowed," and the word reminds us that Jenner, some milkmaids, a brave little boy named James Phipps, and some cows started it all! You are one of hundreds of millions of people who have benefited from Jenner's keen eye and courage to try something new.

Elijah McCoy

"*It's the real McCoy!*" Have you ever heard this expression used to describe something that is genuine? It's like saying, "It's the *real* thing." This expression is a tribute to an inventor named Elijah McCoy, who was born in Canada on May 2, 1844.

Elijah McCoy's parents were ex-slaves who had escaped to Canada through the Underground Railroad. Do you remember learning about Harriet Tubman and the Underground Railroad? When Elijah was a small boy, the McCoy family returned to the United States to buy a farm in Michigan. On the farm, his parents noticed that their son was interested in engines and how they worked. They decided that he should get an education. At age fifteen, Elijah McCoy went to Scotland to study engineering.

Elijah McCoy.

When he returned to the United States, Elijah McCoy was an expert. His desire was to be a train engineer in charge of a powerful locomotive. But some people looked at his dark skin and thought he was not qualified. The only job he could get was feeding wood into a train furnace, and oiling the engine, wheels, and train parts. Elijah McCoy loved trains, so he decided to make the most of any opportunity he could get to work with them.

Machines have to be oiled to keep the moving parts from rubbing against each other. In the mid-1800's most machines had to be stopped whenever they needed oiling, which was done by hand. The frequent stops wasted a lot of time and money. And if a person used too much oil by mistake, the machine would stall. Elijah McCoy decided to find a way to feed a continuous flow of oil to a machine while it was still operating.

After two years of experiments, Elijah McCoy perfected his first locomotive lubricator on June 23, 1872. His invention was simple: a small cup with a valve that slowly dripped oil onto the surface of moving parts. McCoy taught railroad engineers how to use the cups, which he installed himself. Within just a few years, McCoy's cups were used in trains, factories, and huge ships that crossed the oceans. When a worker saw a new piece of machinery, he would often ask, "Is it the real McCoy?" The phrase caught on and soon everyone was using it.

But McCoy was not satisfied with one success. He founded the Elijah McCoy Manufacturing Company and continued to tackle mechanical problems. Over time he received fifty-seven patents for different inventions. Elijah McCoy did not believe that he was special in any way. Until his death, McCoy encouraged young people in his home city of Detroit to apply all of their imagination and energy to whatever they wanted to do. "If you do this," he would tell them, "you can accomplish anything."

Illustration and Photo Credits

Courtesy of the Freer Gallery of Art (04.241). Japanese painting; Edo period; Ukoyoe school; by Hokusai; *Tuning the Samisen;* ink on paper, 24.8 × 21.0 cm. (9¾ × 8¼): 172(a)

Jonathan Fuqua: 203, 204, 207, 208, 235(a, b), 239(a, b, c), 240, 255, 260, 263, 264, 265, 272, 278(a), 282(a, b), 283, 287, 288, 289(a,b,c), 290, 292, 293, 296, 297(a, b), 299(a, b), 300, 301(a), 302(b), 303(a, b), 304, 305, 308(b, c), 310, 319(a), 324

The Granger Collection, New York: 78(c), 79(a), 93(b), 95(b), 97, 98, 104(b), 105(a), 132(c), 134, 135(b), 136, 139, 145(b), 155, 191, 314, 334

Haags Gemeentemuseum/© 1938 M. C. Escher Foundation, Baarn, Holland: 177

Julie C. Grant: 36, 38, 281, 284(a, b, c), 285(a, b), 302(a)

Phillip Jones: 190

Gail McIntosh: 27, 28, 33, 128(a, b), 130, 307(a)

Edward Hicks, *A Peaceable Kingdom,* 1840–45, oil on canvas, 17.5 × 23.5 in., Maier Museum of Art, Randolph-Macon Women's College, Lynchburg, Virginia: 179

Mary Evans Picture Library: 108

Jack Swedberg/Massachusetts Division of Fisheries and Wildlife: 278

The Metropolitan Museum of Art, Gift of Henry G. Marquand, 1889. (89.15.21): 171

National Aeronautics and Space Administration: 311(a)

Jefferys, Charles Wilson/National Archives of Canada/C-069767: 125(b)

New York State Historical Association, Cooperstown, N.Y.: 77

Ohio Historical Society: 306(b)

© Michel Follorou/Photo Researchers, Inc.: 280

© Hank Morgan/Photo Researchers, Inc.: 291

© Judy Poe/Photo Researchers, Inc.: 306(a)

© NASA/Photo Researchers, Inc.: 316

Photo by Bob Schwalkwijk. Mural by Diego Rivera: *The History of Medicine in Mexico—The People's Demand for Better Health,* Hospital de la Raza, Mexico City, 1953: 187

Shelburne Museum, Shelburne, Vermont: 175, 176

Joel Smith: 127, 135

Smithsonian Institution, Department of Anthropology: 161

Index

About the Author

E. D. Hirsch, Jr., a professor at the University of Virginia, is the author or editor of ten books, including *Cultural Literacy, The Dictionary of Cultural Literacy,* and *A First Dictionary of Cultural Literacy.* He and his wife Polly live in Charlottesville, where they raised their three children.

*"The best year of teaching I ever had. This year has
been so much fun: fun to learn, fun to teach."*

Joanne Anderson, Teacher,
Three Oaks Elementary School
Fort Myers, Florida

COLLECT THE ENTIRE CORE KNOWLEDGE SERIES

ISBN	TITLE	PRICE
41115-4	What Your 1st Grader Needs To Know	$22.50/$28.00Can
41116-2	What Your 2nd Grader Needs To Know	$22.50/$28.00Can
41117-0	What Your 3rd Grader Needs To Know	$22.50/$28.50Can
41118-9	What Your 4th Grader Needs To Know	$22.50/$28.00Can
41119-7	What Your 5th Grader Needs To Know	$22.50/$28.00Can
41120-0	What Your 6th Grader Needs To Know	$22.50/$28.00Can

READERS:

The titles listed above are available in your local bookstore. If you are interested in mail ordering any of the Core Knowledge books listed above, please send a check or money order only to the address below (no C.O.D.s or cash) and indicate the title and ISBN book number with your order. Make check payable to Doubleday Consumer Services (include $2.50 for postage and handling). Allow 4–6 weeks for delivery. Prices and availability subject to change without notice.

Please mail your order and check to:

Doubleday Consumer Services, Dept. CK
2451 South Wolf Road
Des Plaines, IL 60018

EDUCATORS AND LIBRARIANS:

For bulk sales or course adoptions, contact the Bantam Doubleday Dell Education and Library Department. Outside New York State call toll-free 1-800-223-6834 ext. 9238. In New York State call 212-492-9238.

FOR MORE INFORMATION ABOUT CORE KNOWLEDGE:

Call the Core Knowledge Foundation at 1-800-238-3233.